The Control
of the
Middle East
Arms Race

Geoffrey Kemp
with the assistance of Shelley A. Stahl

CARNEGIE ENDOWMENT FOR INTERNATIONAL PEACE

ISBN Number: 0-87003-046-9

Library of Congress Catalog Card Number: 91-061775

Price: $11.95

Contents

Figures and Maps

Appendix I

Appendix IV

Foreword

This book was prepared under the auspices of the Carnegie Endowment's Middle East Arms Project. The project has received additional funding and conference support from the John D. and Catherine T. MacArthur Foundation, the United States Institute of Peace, the Rockefeller Foundation, and the Ford Foundation.

We believe the book's publication is very timely in view of the Gulf crisis and the new attention being given to regional arms competition. The Middle East is still a dangerous region. Most countries face multiple threats to their security; many international boundaries are in dispute; and some of the conflicts are thousands of years old. The Gulf war has altered the regional strategic balance but the hope for a more stable environment remains elusive. Each of the key countries has reason to be nervous about its security, and in the last resort, none feels it can rely on the international community, or a new world order, for protection. Hence, the continued demand for arms and the requests by many for direct American military assistance.

While this study is supportive of new arms control initiatives, including those proposed by President Bush, its basic message is that far-reaching arms control agreements among the Middle East countries will depend on progress in resolving regional conflicts. This does not rule out confidence-building measures and limited arms control initiatives prior to negotiations on conflict resolution. Indeed, if the Arab-Israeli conflict is to be resolved, arms control will be a crucial component of a final settlement. However, the elimination of major classes of weapons and production capabilities must wait until regional peace has weathered the test of time.

Geoffrey Kemp, the author of the study, is a Senior Associate at the Endowment. He has served on the National Security Council Staff in the White House, in the Department of Defense, and as a consultant to the Committee on Foreign Relations, United States Senate. In each appointment his work has focused on Middle East issues. He has also pursued an academic career and has written extensively on political-military affairs. He received assistance for this book from his colleague on the Carnegie Middle East Arms Project, Research Associate Shelley A Stahl, who has a background in proliferation issues and has served as legislative assistant in the U.S. House of Representatives.

As always, Endowment sponsorship of this report implies a belief only in the importance of the subject and the credentials of the author. The views expressed are his. Comments or inquires are welcome and may be addressed to the Carnegie Endowment for International Peace, 2400 N Street, N.W., Washington, D.C. 20037-1153.

Morton Abramowitz
President
Carnegie Endowment for
International Peace

Thomas L. Hughes
President Emeritus
Carnegie Endowment for
International Peace

August 1991

Preface

This book began as a study to examine the Middle East and South Asian arms races in the broader perspective of regional conflict and the motivations for weapons proliferation. A first draft was prepared for review in July 1990, literally days before Saddam Hussein invaded Kuwait. The subsequent Gulf crisis required major revisions of the manuscript to take into account the war and the new agenda created by its aftermath.

As a result, two substantive changes in approach were made. First, it was decided to focus most attention on countries in the Middle East. While there are still numerous references in this book to the arms race in South Asia, in part because of the increasing linkage between the strategic problems of the Gulf and South Asia, the sections on India and Pakistan do not pretend to be comprehensive and should be read in conjunction with the pioneering work on South Asian arms control led by Stephen Philip Cohen of the University of Illinois.[1] Second, there has been a great deal of material published in the past year for public consumption on the statistics of the Middle East arms race, including orders of battle, weapons performance characteristics, arms transfer patterns, and defense procurement trends. There have also been several studies by specialists, in and out of government, on the detailed components of specific arms control initiatives such as the proposed chemical weapons convention. For these reasons, this study is more concerned with geopolitical and strategic issues and the political problems of applying arms control concepts to the Middle East. It is designed to provide an overview of the arms control agenda and how its fits into the complicated labyrinths of Middle East politics.

The completion of this study coincided with the failed Soviet coup against Mikhail Gorbachev in the last days of August 1991. Several minor

---

[1] See Stephen Philip Cohen, editor, *Nuclear Proliferation in South Asia: The Prospects for Arms Control* (Boulder, Colorado: Westview Press, 1990).

changes were made to the text to take into account uncertainty about future U.S.-Soviet cooperation on regional conflict and arms control. However, its basic thesis remains unchanged: supplier agreements to impose arms control regimes on the Middle East can only work in the long run if they are supported by key regional countries and are ultimately part of a broader agenda on conflict resolution.

I am especially grateful to Thomas L. Hughes, President Emeritus of the Endowment, and Larry Fabian, the Endowment's Secretary, for their unfailing support for this project and their sound judgment at all stages of its progress. My closest collaborator in preparing this book has been Shelley A. Stahl, who works with me on Carnegie's Middle East Arms Control Project. Her substantive contributions to the research and writing of the chapters, and her indefatigable skills as an editor and coordinator, have been invaluable. We have both been ably assisted by four secretaries over the duration of this study: Kathleen Defty, Andrea Brown, Farhana Khera, and Maria Alunan. We also owe special thanks to Jennifer Reingold who served as a full-time Carnegie intern and, later, as our secretary for two months. Other invaluable support came from full-time interns: Alvaro Tafur, Laura Klivans, Ross Agre, and Robin First. Three volunteer interns, Roula Najjar, Linda Pitcher, and Nawaf al Sabah, did excellent work for us over the course of two summers.

Several colleagues read all or part of the manuscript. I owe them a great debt for incisive criticism at the right time. I am especially grateful to W. Seth Carus, Larry Fabian, Leonard S. Spector, Jenonne Walker, and Tamara Weisberg. I have benefited greatly from advice and support from Anthony Cordesman, Shai Feldman, Marvin Feuerwerger, Robert Harkavy, Mary King, Stephanie Neuman, Janne Nolan, and Brad Roberts.

To William Quandt of the Brookings Institution, and Martin Indyk, Director of the Washington Institute for Near East Policy, I owe special thanks for including me as a participant in their respective projects on Middle East policy and making it possible for me to travel with them for meetings with regional officials and specialists. Lewis Dunn, Lise Hartman, Judith Kipper, Gilbert Kulick, Samuel Lewis, Joseph Nye, William Perry, and Robert Shuey all provided prestigious fora for me to sound out some of the ideas in the book. And Christopher Van Hollen, editor of the *Middle East Journal*, published an article drawing on this study in the Journal's Summer 1991 edition.[2]

---

[2] Geoffrey Kemp, "The Middle East Arms Race: Can it be Controlled?," *Middle East Journal*, Vol. 45, No. 3, Summer 1991.

Our three dimensional map specialist, Professor Po Chin Lai of The Ohio State University, has our deep gratitude for pioneering work in this field. Other thanks go to: Rick Clark and Janet Stoeke for additional maps and illustrations; Tyler Whitmore for her work on the book's charts and tables; and Lisa Tepper who did a great job on the index. Finally, to Michael O'Hare, the Endowment's Director of Administration and Finance, Jane Lowenthal, Jennifer Little, Betsy Hamilton, and the truly professional staff at Carnegie, I owe a million thanks.

Geoffrey Kemp
Carnegie Endowment, August 1991

CHAPTER ONE

A New Arms Race
or Arms Control?

An accelerated arms race in the Middle East will continue unless political initiatives are taken to stop it. The past record on regional arms control is not good, but new circumstances in the international environment provide a unique opportunity to explore more far-reaching policies. The realistic goals and limitations of arms control must be examined against a backdrop of competing policy priorities and a long history of regional conflict.

Introduction

The Persian Gulf war has raised the dangers of the Middle East arms race to the top of the American policy agenda. In an effort to limit these dangers, arms control -- along with security arrangements, economic development, and the peace process -- has been designated as one of the four pillars of President Bush's post-war strategy for the region. On May 29, 1991, the president unveiled his Middle East arms control policy in a speech at the U.S. Air Force Academy in Colorado. The key elements of the plan include: a proposal to freeze and eventually ban the purchase, production, and testing of surface-to-surface missiles (SSMs); a global ban on chemical and biological weapons; an effort by the key suppliers to identify the most dangerous conventional weapons in the region and to curb their sales (suppliers would also inform each other of major sales); and a verifiable ban on the production and acquisition of weapons-usable enriched uranium and plutonium.[1] In response to Bush's arms control plan, the five permanent members of the UN Security Council -- also the five principal weapons suppliers -- met in Paris in July 1991 to discuss mutual restraints on conventional arms sales to the Middle East.

These policies fall short of the more severe measures sought on Capitol Hill and elsewhere. Proposals for highly restrictive legislation on arms and technology transfers to the region have been considered by several congressional committees.[2] These efforts are paralleled by strong voices in the media supporting arms control, and by increased activity among

1

research institutions and private foundations to explore such possibilities. The generally shared view in the United States, Europe, and the Soviet Union is that unless the Gulf victory is quickly exploited to make diplomatic progress on the agenda items, the arms race will continue, and perhaps intensify.

While the immediate objective of Middle East arms control must be to assure that Iraq never again assembles such a large and dangerous arsenal, there are other dimensions of the regional arms race that give cause for concern. These include: massive rearmament planning in Saudi Arabia; military upgrading and modernization in Egypt, Israel, Turkey, and Syria; the continuing chemical weapons programs of Syria and Libya; the sophisticated nuclear weapons and missile programs in Israel, and in neighboring India and Pakistan, as well as the nuclear ambitions of Iran and Libya; Iran's potential military renaissance; and the expectation that large quantities of military equipment made surplus as a result of conventional arms reductions in Europe will find their way to the Middle East.

The Gulf war, and the conflicts that preceded it, including the Iran-Iraq war and the war in Afghanistan, have drawn attention to the growing sophistication of modern weapons and their ability to project power over far greater distances than in the past. Iraq's ability to target Tel Aviv and Haifa with Scud missiles during the Gulf war is the most obvious, although not the most significant example of these capabilities. Saudi Arabia and Israel have SSMs with much longer ranges in their inventories. Over the next decade, India is likely to deploy its own indigenously-produced long-range missile, thereby extending its reach far beyond South Asia. Equally significant from a strategic perspective, is the increased sophistication of combat aircraft in the region, with greater capacity to project power over long distances using in-flight refueling and long-range stand-off weapons.

Another development concerns new, long-range artillery and rocket systems that can reach targets up to 100 kilometers away. This has particular relevance to the security relationship between Israel, Syria, and Jordan. All three countries are subjected to what can be termed the 'sixty kilometer rule.' Jerusalem, Tel Aviv, Haifa, Amman, and Damascus are all within 60 kilometers of the Israeli-Syrian-Jordanian borders. Modern multiple rocket launch systems (MRLS) have ranges in excess of 60 kilometers, and these are increasing. They are highly mobile, cheap, and can be fired in large numbers over a very short time period. Saturation bombardment of rear echelon regions and population centers without the use of aircraft is now possible. In the future, new generations of cruise missiles will be able to hit targets perhaps over 1000 kilometers away.

2

Further blurring the strategic landscape are changes in the geopolitical map of the region that could have a major impact on both the geographical definition of the Middle East and on which countries impact on its dynamics. The Persian Gulf straddles the Middle East and South Asia, serving as a conduit for influence and interest between the two regions. The Gulf war highlighted the growing role of Turkey, not only as a military and political ally of the United States and the moderate Arabs, but also as a key player in the increasingly important area of regional water management. Indeed, access to water may become such an important strategic issue in the coming decade that Egypt may find itself increasingly embroiled with its southern neighbors, Sudan and Ethiopia, while access to Lebanon's abundant water supplies may propel Israel, Syria, and Jordan toward some dialogue, or, alternatively, conflict over this resource.

Another geostrategic change concerns the crisis in the Soviet Union, its possible breakup, and the reemergence of more independent Muslim republics. The so-called 'Turkic swath', which traverses a West-East axis from Turkey, through Azerbaijan, Turkmenistan, Uzbekistan, Tajikstan, to Kirghizia and the Chinese border, is certain to have an impact on, and be influenced by the politics of the Islamic states to its South. How this will affect the overall dimensions of Middle East politics is difficult to predict, but there is already concern among Hindu nationalists in India, for example, who fear encirclement by militant Islamic countries. This fear has strengthened the support in India for a nuclear weapons program, and the need for vigilance with regard to the security of the subcontinent and its surrounding neighbors.

Effective constraints on this wider arms race, including the weaponry acquired by the countries most immediately involved in the Arab-Israeli conflict, will be difficult to achieve, and will require the cooperation of the regional powers themselves.

Previous Efforts at Middle East Arms Control

Controlling the Middle East arms race will be neither easy nor cost-free, and the efforts of the past 40 years to do so are not encouraging. After World War II, arms supplies from both legal and illegal sources to the newly-founded State of Israel played a central role in Israel's victory during the 1948-49 War of Independence. The Arab countries, meanwhile, had access to huge stocks of allied weaponry left behind after the war and were able to buy more on the open market. In order to limit regional

3

rearmament after the 1949 armistice was signed, Britain, France, and the United States signed the Tripartite Declaration in 1950, and imposed an arms rationing scheme for conventional weapons on Israel and the Arabs, administered by the Near East Arms Coordinating Committee (NEACC). It was effective until France supplied Israel with greater numbers of advanced aircraft than was permitted by the NEACC and, most dramatically, the Soviet Union entered the region by concluding massive arms deals with Syria and Egypt in 1955.[3] Equally important, it would turn out, was France's decision in 1956 to sell a nuclear reactor to Israel without requiring a safeguard agreement against non-peaceful use.[4]

By the early 1960s, in keeping with the administration's even-handed policy toward the Arab-Israeli conflict, President Kennedy decided to seek an arms limitation agreement between Israel and Egypt. In June 1963, Kennedy sent his coordinator for disarmament activities, John J. McCloy, on a mission to Egypt and Israel to obtain assurances that Egypt "would not acquire sophisticated weapons such as West German 'ground-to-ground missiles'," and that Israel would not "initiate 'cross-border military action' nor develop nuclear weapons." McCloy's arguments to President Nasser about the dangers of proliferation had an ironic, if predictable, effect. Nasser, listening carefully to McCloy, became convinced that missiles indeed had great political importance. McCloy came home empty-handed and never went to Israel on this trip.[5]

During the 1970s, the combination of rising oil prices and Britain's decision to leave the Persian Gulf resulted in a massive infusion of western arms to both Iran and the oil-rich Arabs. This created concern in the U.S. Congress about the extent of U.S. military programs in the region, particularly in Iran, and led to efforts to reduce the extent of the Middle East arms race through legislation.[6] There was throughout this period a concerted effort to limit nuclear proliferation through the establishment of the Nuclear Non-Proliferation Treaty (NPT) in 1968. The NPT was successful in capping nuclear proliferation in Europe and other industrialized nations, but its record in the Middle East and South Asia was dismal. Both Israel and India acquired the bomb during this period, while the nuclear programs of Pakistan and Iraq progressed.[7]

The Carter Administration made several attempts to limit conventional arms sales to areas of regional conflict. In its early days, the administration announced a far-reaching global policy on arms transfers. The president had concluded "that the United States will henceforth view arms transfers as an exceptional foreign policy implement to be used only in instances where it can be clearly demonstrated that the transfer contributed to our national security interests."[8]

4

To implement a policy of arms restraint, the Carter Administration established a set of controls applicable to all arms transfers, except those to countries with which the U.S. had major defense treaties (NATO, Japan, Australia, and New Zealand). However, Carter stated that: "We will remain faithful to our treaty obligations and will honor our historical responsibilities to assure the security of the State of Israel."[9] The administration soon discovered that exceptions also had to be made for Saudi Arabia and Iran, the two key U.S. allies in the Gulf. In fact, only Pakistan's military aid was cut off during this period, primarily for nuclear proliferation reasons. By 1980, the total amount of military aid and sales granted by the Carter Administration to the Middle East approached the levels of the previous administration.

The Carter Administration also embarked on a series of talks with the Soviet Union about conventional arms transfers. These ended in disharmony, however, when it became clear that both sides sought to tailor the agenda to serve their respective strategic interests; the Soviet Union wanted to focus on U.S. arms transfers to Iran, while the U.S. preferred to focus on Soviet transfers to Latin America. All hope of mutual limits on Middle East arms transfers ended with the Soviet invasion of Afghanistan in the closing days of 1979.

During the Reagan Administration, U.S. policy toward the Middle East and South Asia was not overly concerned with questions of arms control. The primary emphasis was on military cooperation, military assistance, and arms sales to friendly countries. There was no major effort made to talk to the Soviet Union about conventional arms transfer controls, and while there was continued concern about nuclear proliferation, there were no serious efforts made by the administration to stop nuclear activity in Israel, Pakistan, or India. Other strategic questions considered more pressing at the time, such as the Iran-Iraq war and the war in Afghanistan, took precedence over conventional arms control and nuclear non-proliferation policy. In this vein, then, one of the first decisions of the Reagan Administration in 1981 was to dramatically increase the amount of military assistance offered to Pakistan.[10]

The Reagan Administration expressed some concern about the global spread of chemical weapons and ballistic missiles, and made efforts to move the international community forward on these issues. Vice-President Bush offered the administration's initiative at the UN Conference on Disarmament in Geneva in 1984, to impose a world-wide ban on chemical weapons. In 1987, the U.S. and six other industrialized nations formed the Missile Technology Control Regime (MTCR) to halt the spread of nuclear-capable ballistic missiles. And in his address to the UN in September 1988, following Iraqi chemical attacks on Kurds after the cease fire with Iran, and reports of Libya's growing chemical capability, President Reagan called for an international meeting on chemical weapons that was held in January 1989.

Prior to the Gulf Crisis, the Bush Administration's regional arms control policy focused on the problems posed by chemical weapons and SSMs. However, it was not until Saddam Hussein threatened, in April 1990, to use chemical weapons against Israel if it attacked Iraq's growing military arsenal, and the Gulf crisis began in earnest with the invasion of Kuwait in August 1990, that broader questions of regional arms control were taken seriously.

New Expectations

Despite a rather gloomy track record on arms control, there are some indications that the environment may now be more conducive to new initiatives, provided they are integrated within the context of regional stability and security needs. The end of the Cold War has signaled a depolarization of superpower involvement in the region. For the first time, the United States and the Soviet Union have joined forces to work toward mutual goals. In the wake of every previous Middle East war, the arms race intensified, in part because the two superpowers were on opposing sides and were subsequently played off against one another by regional countries. Until August 19, 1991, they were working together to put arms control on a post-Gulf war agenda and to resolve the Arab-Israeli conflict.

No matter who controls the Kremlin, the Soviets are increasingly concerned with the arms race in the region. Soviet statements before and after Iraq's invasion of Kuwait suggest shared concern with political and military developments in the Middle East. In a major foreign policy address in Cairo on February 23, 1989, then-Soviet Foreign Minister Eduard Shevardnadze stated that the Middle East "is threatened by an arms race which, sooner or later, may grow into a nuclear catastrophe," and argued against Israel and the Arabs "repeating the path along which East-West nuclear rivalry developed."[11] He stated that the arms race in the Middle East is now transcending its traditional boundaries and that the deployment of ballistic missiles in the region "represent[s] a threat both to the Soviet Union and to the countries of Europe, and to the interests of the United States."[12]

The Control of the Middle East Arms Race

Prior to the May 1990 U.S.-Soviet Summit, the Soviet Union made public its support for restrictions on exports of ballistic missile technology. In a statement to the Soviet News Agency, Tass, the Chief of the Soviet Foreign Ministry's International Organizations Department, Andrey Kozyrev, said: "Measures to restrict the arms trade must assume an important place on the world community's disarmament agenda....Several countries are making alarming attempts to acquire missile technology, identical to that subject to elimination under the Soviet-American INF Treaty." He added, "It is high time to resume bilateral Soviet-American negotiations to restrict the sale and deliveries of conventional armaments and to draw arms suppliers and receivers into an international dialogue on this subject."[13]

In the wake of the Gulf war, Soviet officials continued to call for restraint in the Middle East.[14] Sergey Vladimir, chief of the Gulf Section at the Soviet Foreign Ministry, stated that "Moscow believes in the need to guarantee the region's security primarily by peaceful and political means." He added, "Experience has shown the need to keep armament within the limits and boundaries of defensive considerations."[15] Vladimir called on all states within the region to join the NPT and to sign a treaty banning chemical weapons.

Soviet policy also appears to be responding to the enhanced diplomatic and military status of the United States in the Middle East, and the perceived shortcomings of Soviet weapons used by Iraq in the war. Expecting a shift by many Arab countries from Soviet to American weapons, and a corresponding decrease of Soviet influence in the region, Soviet officials may continue to pursue a multilateral arms control policy. Foreign Minister Alexander Bessmertnykh expressed the Soviet desire to link the arms embargo against Iraq with a new attempt to limit arms sales to the region as a whole. He stated that new initiatives should be based on "a collective decision on limiting arms supplies to that explosive region" rather than on a "unilateral and individual" basis.[16]

The principal West European supplier countries -- Britain, France, and Germany -- are now more supportive of multilateral arms control efforts. European arms transfer policies have come under sharp review in the wake of the Gulf war. European leaders, especially in France and Germany, have had to accept a good deal of the responsibility for the transfer of high technology and conventional arms to Iraq.

In comparison to the new attitudes of the Soviet Union and the Europeans, Chinese policy remains something of an enigma. Appearing to follow France's lead, China announced in June 1991 that it was considering signing the NPT. Under pressure from Washington, China also announced that it may join the MTCR, and it attended the U.S.-sponsored Paris meeting of major arms suppliers in July 1991. Previously, China's Foreign Minister, Qian Qichen, stated China's hope that "countries which are major weapons exporters will take effective measures to restrain arms sales. China itself...takes a serious and responsible position and sells only a strictly limited number of armaments."[17] However, its continued pursuit of missile sales in the Middle East and South Asia remains a matter for concern.

A second set of reasons for optimism about arms control concerns developments in the region. Egypt and Israel, two of the countries central to progress, have shown more willingness to discuss arms control than in the past, even though each has a different approach to specific issues such as nuclear proliferation. One reason for their concern is an acknowledgement that an open-ended arms race will literally bankrupt them; high technology, while very effective, is extremely expensive and the days of unconditional aid may be numbered.

Relations between the United States and certain key Arab countries are very close as a result of the Gulf conflict. American presence on Saudi soil, and the forgiveness of billions of dollars of Egyptian debt are the most practical manifestations of this improved relationship. Even Syria has become a friend of the West, having cooperated with the coalition during the war. Syrian compliance stemmed largely from the Soviet decision to cut off access to its open-ended arms supplies, leaving Syria nowhere to turn but to the Arab world, and forced to strengthen its ties with the West.

Relations between the United States and Israel remain strong, despite bickering over the peace process. The deployment of American military personnel to man Patriot air defense systems that defended Israel's major cities during the war was of great symbolic importance. Israel, for the first time, placed the direct, physical protection of its citizens in the hands of another country. At the same time, Israel showed great restraint by not retaliating for Iraqi Scud missile attacks. In this way, Israel has demonstrated that it can cooperate and compromise long-standing security doctrines to achieve a broader regional goal.

In the international arena, the United Nations has risen to a new level of legitimacy and may be seen as a key actor in resolving regional conflict in an emerging new world order. Never before have so many countries acted together under UN auspices to confront a single problem. The Gulf war has created an international awareness of the dangers of the arms race and the need for new forms of control on the transfer of arms and the technology required to build them. These trends point toward a more determined effort at regional arms control.

And finally, with Iraq isolated and financially crippled by the Gulf war, and Iran weakened by the Iran-Iraq war, the number of potentially hostile and powerful states is lower than at any time in the recent past.

The Limitations of Arms Control

The Gulf war may have sensitized the international community to the far-reaching, and potentially disastrous consequences of an open-ended arms race, but the causes for this phenomenon go far beyond Iraq's military buildup and the belligerence of Saddam Hussein. The reality is that the arms race in the Middle East and South Asia has multiple sources and, in its current guise, has been underway for over four decades.

Arms races do not emerge out of thin air. The first requirement is the existence of conflict between countries or political or tribal groups. In the Middle East and neighboring South Asia, conflicts have been fueled by historical and contemporary animosities, as well as by external factors, including the competitive policies of the great powers. These interactive pressures, in turn, spur competitive regional arms procurement policies, funded and supported from both local and external resources. For example, prior to the oil boom of the 1970s, most of the resources fueling the Mideast arms race came in the form of military assistance from the superpowers and the former colonial powers. But with the massive rise of oil revenues in the 1970s, the oil-rich countries were able to fund their own military programs and did so with alacrity. This, in turn, led to the provision of compensatory aid to non-oil-producing countries, with the United States and the Soviet Union competing to provide weapons to their respective friends and allies.

In sum, the Middle East arms race derives from many different causes, some of which are linked to one another, and some of which are very distinct and separate. As in the case of other arms races, until the fundamental political disputes that lead countries to arm against one another have been addressed, there is little hope for far-reaching arms control agreements that include either significant force reductions or the elimination of classes of weapons and technologies such as nuclear and chemical weapons.

Nevertheless, with more attention focused on the issue, it may be possible to develop an embryonic arms control architecture in the Middle East that can contribute to a more stable regional balance of power, thereby reducing the risks of preemptive strategies and confrontation by miscalculation. While such goals may fall far short of the revolutionary new agreements between NATO and the Warsaw Pact countries, codified in the Treaty on Conventional Armed Forces in Europe (CFE), they are the most realistic as long as the political problems remain unresolved.

Priorities for U.S. Arms Control Policy

For most laymen, the term arms control, when applied to the Middle East, is synonymous with arms limitations, the purpose of which is to slow down or stop the sale of advanced weapons and to put an end to the production of weapons of mass destruction. Yet, according to the classical definition of arms control, its primary objective should be to reduce the risks of war. Therefore, this does not automatically mean arms limitations, although if reductions are part and parcel of arms control, so much the better. For instance, a case can be made that in order to prevent a new Gulf war, or Arab-Israeli war, key American allies in the region need sufficient strength to deter aggression from radical states. This may mean providing additional weapons to friendly countries rather than seeking ways to restrict their inventories. In these cases, restricting arms supplies to Iraq, Syria, Iran, Libya, and Yemen -- the most radical states in the region -- may be the preferred objective of U.S. arms control policy, however one-sided it appears to be.

Over time, it may be in American interests to pursue global objectives, including the total elimination of weapons of mass destruction and accepted limits on major weapons systems, especially long-range weapons delivery systems. However, such goals will inevitably be contingent on parallel improvements in political relationships. In the meantime, the focus must be on practical steps that secure U.S. interests while, at the same time, reducing the risks of a new Middle East war. This requires an arms control agenda tailored to the political realities of the region, and one that is deliberately discriminatory; that is to say, in balancing the pros and cons of various short-term arms control proposals, the United States must assure that friends are not penalized along with adversaries.

In the wake of the Gulf war, and subsequent demands to put a cap on the arms race, it is frequently suggested that the misguided policies of the supplier nations were largely responsible for Iraq's huge arsenal that gave Saddam Hussein the ability to threaten his neighbors. This is often linked to a criticism of overall U.S. policy on Middle East arms transfers.

10

While there were many mistakes in past U.S. policies, it is worth stating some blunt facts. First, Iraq had no American arms; U.S. policy denying arms to Iraq was consistent and correct. Second, Egypt, Saudi Arabia, and Turkey, the three regional countries most important to the allied war effort, were friends of the United States and primary recipients of American arms. Third, the facilities and logistical support available to the U.S. forces in Saudi Arabia did not magically appear overnight; they were the result of a carefully scripted policy of providing military capabilities to Saudi Arabia, while upgrading Saudi capabilities for an American military deployment *in extremis.*

The American policy of arming the Gulf states has had bipartisan support for many years, and one could argue that the Gulf war proved it to have been a success. Unless the United States wants to keep its own military forces in the region indefinitely, it is in American interests to see that its friends are strong and capable of providing for their own security and for the stability of the region.

If this relationship is to continue, the vulnerabilities of these states must be taken into account. This is particularly true since the eruption of the Kurdish crisis following the allied victory. Washington's reluctance to involve American military forces in the Iraqi civil war has not only given a new lease on life to Saddam Hussein, but it has also made his neighbors more nervous in the wake of a major U.S. withdrawal. This anxiety will invariably translate into more requests for U.S. military assistance, i.e., arms sales.

These facts conflict with the argument that now is the time to freeze further arms sales and to limit the regional arms race. In this regard, there are some serious criticisms of American Middle East arms policy during the 1980s. First, it was accused of being too passive concerning the arms supply policies of other states. Washington also appeared to turn a blind eye to nuclear proliferation in Israel and Pakistan -- in the latter case waiving legislation designed specifically to target Pakistan's nuclear program. The U.S. did nothing when Iraq used chemical weapons against Iran and against its own Kurds. It wavered when Saudi Arabia bought Chinese intermediate-range ballistic missiles. Finally, Washington failed to establish working guidelines with its European allies concerning common Middle East security goals.

How to reconcile security assistance to friends in need, while at the same time advocating a policy of arms restraint is a major dilemma for the United States and other supplier countries. The basic thesis advanced in

11

this study is that these two goals are not incompatible, provided that arms control initiatives are carefully crafted for the unique security environment of the region. This first requires a thorough understanding of the sources of regional conflict and their impact on the security perceptions of the local countries.

Focus and Framework of Study

The focus of this study is on the broader political-military dimensions of the Middle East arms race and efforts to bring it under control. Because of the unique and rapidly changing landscape in the Persian Gulf, and because of the international arms control regime imposed on Iraq, more space is devoted to the Arab-Israeli conflict than to the Iran-Iraq or other Gulf conflicts. To the degree that the Indo-Pakistani conflict contributes to the overall risk of war in the Middle East, South Asia will be considered as well.

The conceptual framework assumes that while there are examples of a particular arms race itself taking on a special dynamic and, for a time, becoming a direct cause of conflict, in most cases arms acquisitions follow conflicts rather than precede them. This analysis of the arms race begins by examining the sources of regional conflict and, where relevant, the role of the external powers in stimulating them. It is then followed by an analysis of what sorts of arms control measures are most likely to work in the Middle East.

Notes

1. See the Fact Sheet on Middle East Arms Control Initiative, May 29, 1991, White House Office of the Press Secretary.

2. Examples of proposed legislation to deal with weapons proliferation pending before Congress in summer 1991 are: Section 242 of H.R. 2508, the Foreign Assistance Authorization Bill for FY 1992, calling for an immediate and indefinite moratorium on arms sales to the Middle East and Persian Gulf; H.R. 2315 and S. 1046 calling for the establishment of an international arms suppliers regime to limit arms sales to the Middle East; and S. 309, which seeks to control arms transfers to countries that threaten world peace, and would establish sanctions against foreign countries and companies engaging in proscribed arms sales. For details of

legislation on weapons proliferation see *Weapons Nonproliferation Policy and Legislation* (Washington, D.C.: Congressional Research Service, 1991).

3. For more details on this period see Paul Jabber, *Not by War Alone: Security and Arms Control in the Middle East* (Berkeley: University of California Press, 1981); J.C. Hurewitz, *Middle East Politics: The Military Dimension* (New York: Frederick A. Praeger, 1969); and Yair Evron, *The Role of Arms Control in the Middle East*, Adelphi Paper #138 (London: International Institute for Strategic Studies, 1977).

4. For details of the early days of Israel's nuclear program, see the section on Israel in Leonard S. Spector, *Nuclear Proliferation Today* (New York: Vintage Books, 1984), pp. 117-148.

5. Douglas Little, "From Even-Handed to Empty-Handed: Seeking Order in the Middle East," in Thomas G. Paterson, *Kennedy's Quest for Victory* (New York: Oxford University Press, 1989), pp. 52-54.

6. Some of these attempts were: The 1974 Nelson Amendment, intended to oblige the executive branch to give Congress 20 days' advance notice of foreign military sales of over $25 million; a bipartisan letter to Kissinger from 102 members of Congress signed October 31, 1975, deploring the arms escalation; the International Security Assistance and Arms Export Control Act of 1976, seeking to "shift the focus of U.S. arms sales policy from that of selling arms to controlling arms sales and exports." From U.S. Congress, Senate Committee on Foreign Relations Report on S. 3439, 94th Congress, 2nd Session, May 14, 1976, p. 10. Quoted in Andrew J. Pierre, *The Global Politics of Arms Sales* (Princeton: Princeton University Press, 1982), pp. 49-52.

7. See Leonard S. Spector with Jacqueline R. Smith, *Nuclear Ambitions* (Boulder, Colorado: Westview Press, 1990).

8. Statement by President Carter, May 19, 1977, *Department of State Bulletin*, Vol. 76, April-June 1977, pp. 625-627.

9. Ibid.

10. In response to the Soviet invasion of Afghanistan, the Carter Administration offered Pakistani President Zia $400 million in assistance. After being cut off by the same administration in 1977 and 1979, Zia rejected this offer as "peanuts." The Reagan Administration subsequently offered Pakistan a six-year, $3.2 billion package in 1981, which Zia

accepted. See *Nuclear Weapons and South Asian Security* (Washington, D.C.: Carnegie Endowment for International Peace, 1988), pp. 33-35.

11. See "Shevardnadze Cairo Speech on Mideast Conflict," Moscow, Izvestiya, 24 February 1989, translated in *FBIS-SOV*, February 24, 1989, pp. 12-19.

12. Ibid.

13. Quoted in "Kozyrev Calls For Limiting Arms Trade," Moscow, Tass, 1127 GMT, 16 May 1990, in *FBIS-SOV*, May 17, 1990, p. 3.

14. See Patrick E. Tyler, "As the Dust Settles, Attention Turns to New Arms Sales," *New York Times*, March 29, 1991.

15. "Ministry Aide on Saudi Ties, Mideast Policy," 'UKAZ, 29 March 1991, translated in *FBIS-SOV*, April 5, 1991, p. 16.

16. Quoted in Michael Dobbs, "Moscow Urges Creation of Gulf Security System," *Washington Post*, March 1, 1991.

17. "PRC Foreign Minister Holds News Conference," Isvestiya, March 29, 1991, translated in *FBIS-SOV*, April 1, 1991, pp. 11-12.

CHAPTER TWO

A Dangerous Neighborhood: The Dynamics of Middle East Conflicts

The Middle East is a dangerous neighborhood. There are dozens of unresolved conflicts, some dating back thousands of years. Most of the countries face multiple threats to their security; many international boundaries remain in dispute; and improvements in power projection capabilities have made it more difficult to isolate the various conflicts into restricted geographical areas. While the Gulf war has temporarily altered the regional strategic balance, the hope for a more stable environment remains elusive. Each of the key countries has reason to be nervous about its security, and in the last resort none feels it can rely on the international community or a new world order for protection.

Underlying Sources of Conflict

It is impossible to understand the origins of the arms race, much less propose options for reducing its dangers, unless the basic sources of regional conflict are appreciated. Over the past decade and longer, three dominant conflicts -- Arab-Israel, Iran-Iraq, and India-Pakistan -- have been responsible for the influx of high technology weaponry into the region extending from North Africa to South Asia.

An analysis of these conflicts reveals several ingredients: the major adversaries have, in one way or another, been fighting one another for centuries; religion, nationalism, geography, and resources are the dominant issues over which they have fought; and to the extent that the U.S.-Soviet rivalry exacerbated these conflicts, the end of the Cold War has not necessarily made conflict resolution easier.

Before examining the present status of these conflicts, two general explanations concerning the arms race must be emphasized. First, seen from their respective national perspectives, most of the key countries in the region believe they are surrounded by enemies, facing a military threat from virtually every direction, and thus, must arm accordingly. Second, the resultant arms races that have evolved from this perspective interact with one another, in part because of the extended range and lethality of modern weapon systems. Regional conflicts can no longer be isolated and analyzed independent of one another. The Arab-Israeli conflict can no more be treated in isolation from the Persian Gulf conflict than the Indo-Pakistani rivalry can ignore Indian-Chinese competition.

Threats from All Directions

The following figure depicts the threat perceptions of the key countries in the region.

Egypt. Although at peace with its neighbors, Egypt cannot ignore Libyan leader Colonel Qaddafi's military ambitions any more than it can discount the possibility of confrontation with Ethiopia and Sudan over the control of Nile waters. Egypt must also assume that Israel could reemerge as a threat if there were a new Arab-Israeli war.

Israel. Likewise, Israel cannot rule out an Egyptian threat while continuing to regard Iraq, Libya, Syria, Jordan, and Saudi Arabia as its most likely adversaries in the event of new hostilities. Threats from Lebanon must be taken very seriously as well.

Syria. Syria is surrounded on all sides by potential and existing adversaries, including the strongest military powers in the region, Israel, Turkey, and, until recently, Iraq. Threats emanating from Jordan are also relevant.

Jordan. Jordan is a weak power surrounded by more powerful neighbors. While only Israel and Syria are acknowledged as potential adversaries, Jordan is fearful that it could be drawn into a conflict between Israel and either Iraq or Syria and become the killing fields for a new Arab-Israeli war.

Iraq. Beaten and humiliated on the battlefield, Iraq faces a very vulnerable strategic situation. With Iran, Israel, Turkey, and Syria as primary adversaries, it has much to worry about. This is especially true if Iran continues to rearm and embarks on its own strategic weapons program while Iraq's capabilities remain restricted by the UN arms embargo.

Saudi Arabia and Kuwait. Together with the other members of the Gulf Cooperation Council (Bahrain, United Arab Emirates, Qatar, and Oman)

16

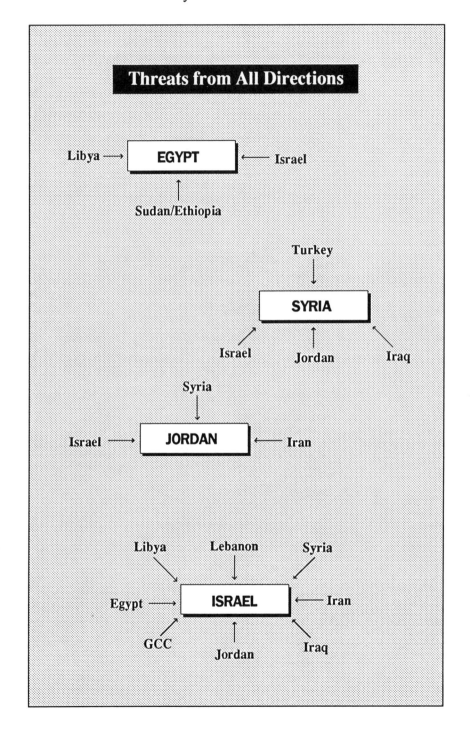

Threats from All Directions

Libya → EGYPT ← Israel

↑ Sudan/Ethiopia

Turkey ↓ SYRIA

Israel ↗ Jordan ↑ Iraq ↖

Syria ↓

Israel → JORDAN ← Iran

Libya ↘ Lebanon ↓ Syria ↙

Egypt → ISRAEL ← Iran

GCC ↗ Jordan ↑ Iraq ↖

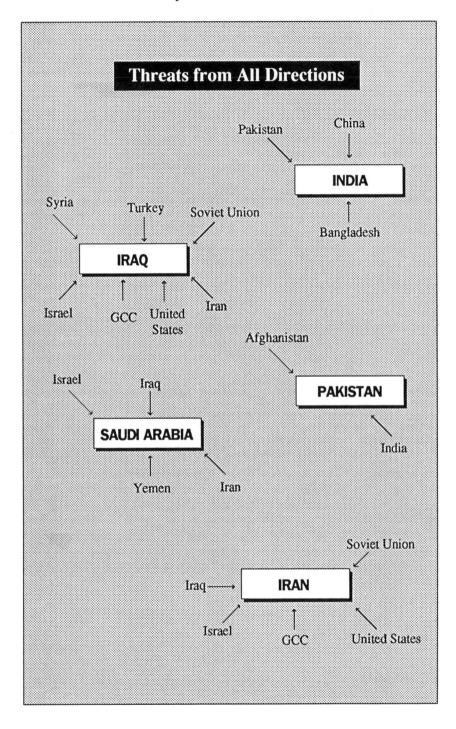

Saudi Arabia and Kuwait are the richest and the most vulnerable of the Arab states, as the Gulf crisis so amply demonstrated. They face multiple threats, including one from a resurgent Iraq. While Saudi Arabia must be concerned with Israeli threats as well as those from Iraq and Iran, Kuwait's primary threats come from Iran and Iraq.

Iran. Iran must deal not only with Iraq's putative military threat, but it also cannot ignore American military power in the region. In addition, the fact that it borders the Soviet Union is a source of continuing concern, especially given the changes taking place in Soviet Central Asia.

Pakistan. Pakistan's main threat comes from India; however, as long as the war in Afghanistan continues, Pakistan is vulnerable to attacks from that border, including missile threats.

India. India faces military problems from both Pakistan and Bangladesh but, most importantly, it views China as its primary strategic rival.

The perception of threats from all directions has strategic implications for the regional arms races that have evolved from these conflicts. For instance, the Arab-Israeli arms race not only has to be examined under different permutations of Arab coalitions against Israel, but its dynamics have been influenced, for example, by the Persian Gulf conflict and the civil war in Ethiopia which has seen Israel and the Arabs cooperate with opposing sides. Likewise, the Indo-Pakistani arms race is influenced by Afghanistan and the strategic rivalry between India and China.

There are two reasons why these interactions are important. First, as modern weapons -- especially missiles, combat aircraft, and warships -- extend the power projection capabilities of the various adversaries, changes in weapons inventories in one regional conflict will have influence on adjacent conflicts. Second, if there are to be serious efforts to put some restrictions on the spread of such weapons, the nature of the conflicts must be fully understood. It is, for instance, highly unlikely that Israel and the Arabs could ever agree to arms limitations if Iran were left out of the equation.

The Key Conflicts: Origins and Issues

To get a better grasp of the complexity of the Middle East and why the major conflicts pre-date, sometimes by thousands of years, the crises of the post-World War II era, a review of their origins, as well as more contemporary events, is necessary.

19

The following chart summarizes the main components of the most important regional conflicts. In each case the sources of antagonism are centuries old and recent wars must be seen against this backdrop of historical animosity. The immediate causes for conflict can be traced to territorial disputes, including access to water, religious rivalry, economic and environmental issues, terrorism, separatism, and the financial and human legacies of recent wars, including desires for revenge to right past wrongs.[1] In each conflict, the superpowers continue to play important, though differing roles, even as they have diffused their own ideological competition and prior insistence on viewing the region as part of a zero-sum game.

The Arab-Israeli Conflict

A History of Suspicion. Jews and Arabs have been fighting in the Levant for thousands of years. In fact, Canaanites and Israelites battled each other over the same land before Arabs and Jews emerged as distinct peoples. Since the creation of the State of Israel in 1948, there have been six interstate wars between Israel and its neighbors. In December 1987, a new Palestinian uprising, the Intifada, began and remained unresolved three and a half years later.

The Jews lay historical and religious claim to the land of Israel from the time of Abraham. The Zionist movement, begun in the late 1800s, was justified as a call to Jews to escape persecution and return to their homeland -- from which they were forcibly expelled -- to rebuild the land of Israel that was their birthright. The Palestinians, in turn, point to their centuries of inhabiting Palestine as their claim to the territory now called Israel. The Palestinians seek a recreated Palestine as a homeland to preserve their national identity.

Ownership of land is fundamental to understanding the Arab-Israeli and Palestinian-Israeli conflicts. Arguments about control of territory on both sides range from the irreconcilable to the wary but negotiable. Within Israel, some extremists argue that all of the territory currently controlled by Israel should be annexed to become part of a greater Israel, closely resembling the biblical land of Israel, or Eretz Israel. As for the Palestinian population, it should be required to resettle in Jordan, which should become the official Palestinian state in the Middle East. On the Arab side, the most extreme argument asserts that the state of Israel has no right to exist in the Middle East and the entire territory currently occupied by the Zionists should be reclaimed for the Palestinians and

Major Sources
of Regional Conflict

HISTORY OF CONFLICT	CURRENT TERRITORIAL DISPUTES	OTHER SOURCES OF CONFLICT
ARAB-ISRAEL		
• Animosity dates back thousands of years • 1948-49 War • 1956 Suez War • 1967 Six Day War • 1968-70 War of Attrition • 1973 October War • 1982 Lebanon war • 1987– Intifada	• Legitimacy of Israel • West Bank • Gaza • Golan Heights • East Jerusalem • South Lebanon	• Water and environment • Immigration and right of return • Religious freedom • Terrorism • Palestinian support of Iraq in Gulf war
IRAQ-IRAN		
• Historical Arab-Persian conflict • 1969-75 conflict over Shatt al-Arab and Kurds • 1980-88 full-scale war	• Shatt al-Arab • Remaining border	• Shi' a-Sunni rivalry • Terrorism • Kurdish question • Reparations • Iraqi aircraft in Iran
IRAQ-KUWAIT		
• Non-recognition of Kuwait by Iraq since independence	• Bubiyan and Warbah islands • Rumaila oil field • Remaining border	• Oil pricing • Debt repayment • Reparations
INDIA-PAKISTAN		
• Historical Hindu-Muslim rivalry • 1947-49 War of Partition • 1965 War over Kashmir • 1971 War over Bangladesh and Kashmir	• Kashmir	• Punjab and separatism • Religion • Terrorism and smuggling

reconstituted as the state of Palestine. Israel is a crusader remnant with no more legitimacy in the land of Palestine than the medieval knights who occupied it in the Middle Ages.

Between these two extremes lies an array of positions, ranging from a willingness to create a Palestinian state in the occupied territories in exchange for peace and security, to arrangements for Palestinian autonomy in the territories under Israeli occupation, to a confederation between a Palestinian entity and the Hashemite Kingdom of Jordan.

Religion plays a central role in the Arab-Israeli conflict, as modern-day Israel was created specifically to be a Jewish homeland. And while there are both secular and religious Jews in Israel, religious extremists play a pivotal role in the shaping of Israeli domestic and foreign policy. At the same time, the Palestinians, who have traditionally been more secular than their Arab brethren in other states, are now paying more attention to Muslim fundamentalists who are challenging the PLO's poor record of progress toward the goal of a Palestinian state.

Arab and Israeli suspicion and animosity about one another's intentions have reinforced each side's nightmare scenario. The following illustrations characterize Israel's and the Arabs' worst-case perceptions of one another's intentions and capabilities.

Israel's nightmare is that of a small, geographically vulnerable state hemmed in on all sides by hostile Arab forces that question its very legitimacy. The peace treaty with Egypt does not rule out eventual Egyptian involvement in a full-scale assault on Israel. If Israel gives back occupied territory, Arab tanks in the Gaza Strip, West Bank, and Golan Heights could once more threaten the tiny state. Lebanon remains a danger for Israel, as indeed do all the Arab air and missile forces, especially in light of the experience of the Scud attacks during the Gulf war. With their backs to the wall, the Israelis fear that chemical weapon attacks, if not worse, will someday occur and that Arab armies may eventually be able to cut the state at its narrowest juncture and to literally push them into the sea.

Israel faces an exceedingly hostile international environment, with the UN invariably siding with the Arabs on all major motions concerning the Mideast, including the infamous UN Resolution equating Zionism with racism.[2] World opinion, while occasionally supportive of Israel, is seen as increasingly hostile due to biased reporting on the Intifada and on Israel's human rights record. On the other hand, world opinion tends to ignore the behavior of Israel's totalitarian neighbors who engage in far more

ISRAEL'S NIGHTMARE

Illustration by Janet Stoeke

THE ARAB NIGHTMARE

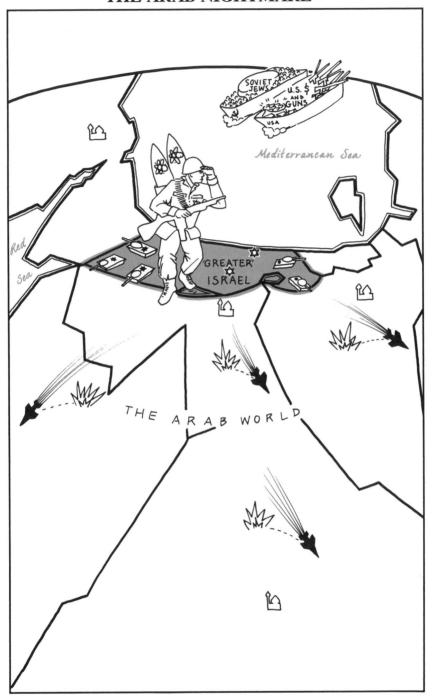

Illustration by Janet Stoeke

heinous abuses of human rights than does Israel.

The reverse image is the Arab nightmare. It is a fear that Israel will never retreat back to its 1967 borders; that Greater Israel is here to stay; and that Israel already has its eyes on further Arab territory to exploit, occupy, or use as a dumping ground for West Bank Palestinians. The Arabs point to Israeli General Ariel Sharon's 'Jordan is Palestine' slogan and couple it with the conviction that Israel wants to annex Lebanon up to the Litani River to assure water supplies.

Israel is seen as a highly organized, militant state far superior to all the Arabs combined, both in terms of its technology and armaments. The Arabs face a strong, ruthless Israel equipped with nuclear weapons and a ubiquitous air force that can fly at will over the Arab world, dropping bombs and flaunting its military prowess to intimidate its neighbors. Furthermore, Israel is supported by two ominous, powerful external forces: a massive pipeline of American money, arms, and political support that assures Israel its qualitative edge and immunity from world opinion; and the Soviet Union, which has approved the mass immigration to Israel of highly-trained and skilled Soviet Jews, whose numbers may surpass one million in the coming decade and add an additional 25 percent to the Jewish population.

In addition to the simplistic, but frequently accepted stereotypes of the conflict reflected in the preceding illustrations, there are important changes occurring in the region that are having a profound impact on the political and strategic environment. These changes help to explain the current preoccupation with the arms race. The following paragraphs examine recent events influencing the strategic perceptions of the key regional countries.[3]

Israel's Strategic Perspective. Israel's strategic perspectives have undergone a dramatic shift in the past four years. The period 1978-88 was a relatively safe decade for Israel, despite the traumas of the war in Lebanon between 1982-84. Israel signed a peace treaty with Egypt, removing it as a military threat. In addition, between 1980 and 1988, Iraq, one of Israel's principal antagonists, was tied down in a brutal war with Iran. During this period, the only strategic challenge to Israel came from Syria. However, despite Israel's concern with the Syrian threat, particularly with regard to the impact of increased Soviet arms supplies following the Israeli invasion of Lebanon in June 1982, Israeli analysts never believed Syria was ready for war. A war through miscalculation would have been a disaster, but Israel, nevertheless, would have won.

Israel's perception of its security environment began to change in December 1987, when the Intifada, or Palestinian uprising, began. At this time Israel received a rude shock: its internal security problems could wrench the country apart unless solutions were found for dealing with the immediate violence and the political sources of Palestinian discontent. In 1988, Israel received further shocks when Iraq took the offensive against Iran. The collapse of the Iranian front took the region by surprise, and left Iraq with the largest standing army in the Middle East -- an army whose confidence had been reinforced by several stunning victories in the closing months of the war, and that employed the widespread use of chemical weapons and surface-to-surface missiles (SSMs).

Until the end of the Gulf war in February 1991, Israel's most important military concern was the emergence of Iraq as a power with which to be reckoned. Israel feared the Arab world would fall under the spell of Saddam Hussein, the first Arab leader since Saladin in 1187 to win a major battle against external powers when his armies defeated the Iranians in 1988. During the spring of 1990, Saddam's rhetoric against Israel found a receptive audience in the streets of Arab capitals. Fears of a military confrontation between Iraq and Israel escalated in the weeks preceding Iraq's invasion of Kuwait in August 1990. While no one expected either side to deliberately initiate hostilities, there was concern that a war might commence accidentally.

The dramatic events of August 1990, and the subsequent crisis and war in the Gulf had a profound impact on Israel. On the one hand, the defeat of Saddam, the destruction of much of his forces and weapons of mass destruction, and the punitive terms of UN Cease Fire Resolution 687 have drastically reduced the Iraqi threat to Israel.[4] On the other hand, Israel's inability to defend itself against Scud bombardment during the war has made it conscious of its own vulnerabilities, particularly to high technology weaponry, including items provided by the U.S. to countries like Saudi Arabia, with which it is still technically in a state of war.

However, Israel has benefited the most from the changes in Soviet policy brought about by the Gorbachev revolution. Under Gorbachev, the Soviet Union reassessed its Middle East policies and, in a series of decisions, has undercut the support it provided in the past to the Arab regimes, especially Syria and Iraq. Gorbachev's announcements to Syrian President Hafez al-Assad in 1988 and 1989, that the Soviets would no longer continue open-ended arms supplies, and that Syria should end all attempts to redress the Arab-Israeli conflict through war were a source of great satisfaction to the Israelis.[5] Furthermore, the ultimate prize, the release of Soviet Jewry from the Soviet Union, opened the prospect of resolving Israel's long-term demographic disadvantages, and bringing to the country many more immigrants than had originally been anticipated.

Yet, while the end of the Cold War and the defeat of Iraq have brought confidence that Israel's immediate security is assured, it continues to worry about the future of the American commitment to its long-term security, particularly in the context of financial assistance and its pre-Gulf war status as a strategic ally of the United States. During the Reagan Administration, there was a deliberate attempt on the part of Israeli decision-makers to focus on the strategic cooperation aspect as a cornerstone of the relationship with the U.S. This was cemented in the 1983 Memorandum of Understanding (MoU) between Israel and the United States, as well as in growing military-to-military cooperation.[6]

Israel now fears that reductions in the U.S. budget will lead to cutbacks in American aid, training, and valuable U.S.-Israeli technical agreements. Also, there is some fear and envy that America's new-found friendships with its Arab military partners will dilute its commitment to maintain Israel's qualitative edge, making it more difficult to campaign against U.S. arms sales to friendly Arab countries.

Viewed from Israel's worst-case perspective, the future strategic environment appears somber. There remains an unresolved internal security problem -- the West Bank and Gaza Palestinians as well as the Israeli Arabs are all increasingly discontented and likely to become more so because of social disruption caused by the vast influx of Soviet Jews. Concerning the future external security environment, Israel worries about the eventual reemergence of Iraq and the creation of a formidable eastern military front. It also worries about the impact that radical Islamic fundamentalism in Egypt will have on its critical relationship with Cairo. If Egypt were to end its peace with Israel and revert once more to an adverserial role while, simultaneously, Iraq and Syria repaired their relationship, it would be a nightmare only mildly ameliorated by the presumed absence of the Soviet Union from the equation. Furthermore, the Soviet withdrawal, while removing some of the immediate threat of a direct superpower confrontation, also eliminates the urgency of intervention to prevent a regional confrontation from becoming a global war. The relationship between internal security, terrorism, and long-term trends in weapons proliferation contributes to this equation of insecurity.

Arab Strategic Perspectives. The Arabs view the new strategic landscape of the region differently than do their Israeli neighbors. The Arab world was bitterly divided over the Gulf war, and it is too early to assess its long-term impact on Arab nationalism and hopes for Arab unity. Each

Arab country has a unique perception of its strategic role in the Mideast and how it has changed as a result of the war. While some common Arab themes persist despite changing inter-Arab relationships, the perspectives from each capital are dictated by the specific issues facing each regime.

Broadly speaking, there is growing concern in Arab capitals that the end of the Cold War and the defeat of Iraq have allowed three non-Arab countries to enhance their power -- Iran, Israel, and Turkey. While few Arab leaders had much respect, let alone affection for the Soviet system, Soviet diplomatic and military activity in the region provided some balance to the United States, with its strong pro-Israeli leanings. For Syria, Moscow was the vital lifeline for its strategic security. Even a country like Egypt, with its close ties to the United States and its dependence on American aid, took some comfort in its good relations with the Soviet Union. Syria's Hafez al-Assad has correctly calculated that the Soviet Union has other priorities and will not become involved in inter-Arab politics if it means a fight with the United States and Israel, no matter who controls Moscow.

The best evidence of new Soviet attitudes toward the region has been the decision to permit open-ended Jewish emigration to Israel. Arabs find it impossible to believe that the Soviets would have permitted such an exodus to take place unless Moscow had deliberately downgraded the importance of its relations with the Arab world in its effort to win approval for its human rights record from the United States. In short, the Arab world feels it is once again becoming the victim of pressure in Europe, North America, and the Soviet Union to deal with anti-semitism, the factor encouraging so many Soviet Jews to emigrate. Furthermore, the Soviet Union is seen to be in league with the United States; Soviet Jews are coming to Israel primarily because they have been denied access to America.

There is also concern in the Arab world, a concern paralleled in Israel, about the impact the new world economic order will have on the future of their respective countries. All Arab states, particularly those bordering the Mediterranean, worry about how they will relate to the European Community as it both strengthens and tightens its economic cohesion in 1992. The emphasis on a rich versus poor syndrome in the Arab world, exploited by Saddam Hussein during the Gulf crisis, will not disappear with the defeat of Iraq and the eventual demise of Saddam. Yet, hope for a new economic order in the Middle East, with greater burden-sharing among the countries, will invariably go nowhere as long as the scars left by the Gulf war remain unhealed. Meanwhile, the desperate economic plight of some Arab states increases the appeal of Islamic fundamentalism, with its demands for radical solutions to current economic problems.

Egypt. Egypt in 1991 is the most important strategic player in the Arab world because of geography, size, its relationship with all the key players in the region and the external world, and the role it played in the alliance against Saddam Hussein. This status represents a sea-change from its position in 1979, when Cairo signed a peace treaty with Israel and was ostracized for almost a decade from Arab councils. While Egyptian-Israeli relations have had their high and low points, their relationship has endured, and there is no evidence that Egypt has any wish to become embroiled in a new military confrontation with Israel. Because Egypt suffered from isolation in the Arab community, it has sought to play an active role in promoting a solution to the Palestinian problem and is the best-placed Middle East country to do so, especially following the defeat of Iraq. Thus, while Egypt will not risk breaking its peace with Israel, it can be expected to stand firmly with the mainstream Arab view that Israel must return land for peace and be more accommodating of Palestinian rights.

In the wake of the Gulf war, Egyptian leaders worry that without an active Arab-Israeli peace process, they will lose credibility. They must be able to demonstrate that close cooperation with the West in an alliance against an Arab state brings rewards. As long as there is some dialogue between Egypt, Israel, and the United States concerning the future of the Palestinians, Egypt can play an important and constructive role, and can serve as an ombudsman for an eventual political settlement. Cairo is likely to remain a preferred locale for Middle East peace talks involving Israelis and Arabs.

The absence of a peace process and a number of seemingly retrograde actions by Israel -- such as the expulsion of West Bank Palestinians and the construction of more settlements in the occupied territories -- will embarrass Egypt and detract from its legitimacy as the most powerful Arab state. Under such circumstances, Egypt's internal cohesion could be threatened and extremist pressures could grow. One of Saddam Hussein's efforts in the spring of 1990 was to compete with Egypt for the heart and soul of the Arab world. He overplayed his hand, but others, such as Assad of Syria, are likely to be much smarter in these efforts and, therefore, more dangerous.

Egypt's strategic posture depends on its continuing good relationship with the United States and on U.S. willingness to act as a broker in the peace process, as well as on its acceptability in the Arab world, and its friendship with the Soviet Union. Because of its domestic problems, Egypt has given up any pretension of achieving military parity with Israel, although it is determined to strengthen its current military posture.

Egypt cannot, in the near term, be seen as a strategic threat to Israel, except in the context of a united eastern front, or in the event that there is a revolution to overthrow the Mubarak regime in which an Islamic fundamentalist regime comes to power. Egypt will continue to play an important role in diplomatic fora, and, possibly, in the pursuit of arms control initiatives. The fact that its peace with Israel has survived many upsets, combined with the durability of the multinational peacekeeping force in the Sinai Desert with its ability to guard against random accidents and events, suggest that the peace treaty is durable. The exception to this durability would be a radical change of regime in Egypt, or some catastrophic event such as a major terrorist act by Jewish fundamentalists against Islamic institutions.[7]

In addition to its focus on the Arab-Israeli conflict and its place in the post-Gulf war Arab world, Egypt must also be concerned with North Africa. While there has been some rapprochement between Egypt and Libya, the sources of conflict between these two states remain unresolved. Egypt also faces unrest to its South where bitter civil wars in the Sudan and Ethiopia pitted Arab and non-Arab, Muslim and non-Muslim populations against one another. Furthermore, in terms of religion, Egypt is fighting its own battle to remain a secular state under pressure from the wave of Islamic fundamentalism that is sweeping much of the Arab world.

Egypt faces daunting economic problems, some of them so structurally endemic that they seem hopeless. It is experiencing a population explosion at a time when potential water problems with its southern neighbors are of great concern. These are the issues, more than the well-publicized concerns about the peace process, that ultimately feed the discontent in the streets of Cairo. While the absence of diplomatic achievements adds to the lack of credibility of the regime, it is the failure to deliver domestic services that is at the crux of Egypt's problems.

Syria. Syria's key, but ambiguous role in the Arab-Israeli conflict cannot be understood without an appreciation of its position within the Arab world. During the 1980s, much attention was focused on the dangerous state of Israeli-Syrian military relations. Due to Israel's military superiority, no one believed that Syria could defeat Israel in any one-on-one confrontation. Nevertheless, the fact that Hafez al-Assad was prepared, despite these odds, to speak out aggressively against Israel gave him some clout in the Arab world as the one strongman prepared to stand up to the Zionists. Unfortunately, Assad's pan-Arabism was offset by his support for

Iran, which was seen as a direct challenge to Iraq and, indirectly, a threat to Arab nationalism.

Israel's invasion of Lebanon in 1982 was met with little resistance by the Arab world, leaving Syrian forces stationed in the area to face the superior Israelis alone, and its air force to suffer a humiliating defeat in the air battle. Decisions by Arab states to reestablish relations with Egypt, following a 1987 Arab League ruling, left Syria even more isolated. Such actions legitimated Egypt's decision to accept Israel's existence in exchange for land captured in the 1967 war, and ignored the fact that Syrian territory in the Golan Heights was still held, and indeed had been annexed by Israel. Furthermore, in July 1988, King Hussein of Jordan renounced all Jordanian claims to the West Bank in favor of the Palestinians, a move that ostensibly removed Jordan from the front line of the political conflict with Israel. And, in December 1988, PLO Chairman Yasser Arafat announced his support for a two-state solution to the Arab-Israeli conflict and accepted the right of Israel to exist.

Then, in 1989, in a move that seemed to cement Syrian isolation, the Soviet Union, long the steadfast supporter and ally of Syria in the Middle East, advised Damascus that it should no longer assume Soviet support for its policy of strategic parity with Israel.[8]

However, Hafez al-Assad is, above all else, a survivor. Syria's principal goal over the past year has been to regain credibility within the Arab and international communities. Unlike Saddam Hussein, who viewed the demise of Soviet power as an opportunity to challenge the United States, Assad drew the opposite conclusion: good relations with the West were now essential. Syria has begun to recover from its isolation. As a result of its support for the allied cause during the Gulf war, and of its support for a peace conference leading to negotiations with Israel, Damascus has endeared itself to many Arab moderates and to the United States.

Like Egypt, Syria has problems it must address in addition to the Arab-Israeli conflict and its long-standing rivalry with Iraq. It remains deeply embroiled in the occupation of Lebanon despite both the 1989 Taif accord between Christian and Muslim legislators on power-sharing and the use of force to oust Maronite leader Michel Aoun.[9] It also remains dependent on economic assistance from Saudi Arabia, although in the long run its oil production could rise and begin to provide much needed hard currency.[10]

Jordan. Jordan is a small state, surrounded on all sides by   stronger potential adversaries. Before the Gulf war, most observers considered it a tribute to King Hussein's wisdom and skill as a statesman that he had survived for so long.   However, Jordan's position during the war, supporting Iraq more openly than any other Arab country aside from Yemen, antagonized its traditional supporters; it will take time for the wounds of this rupture to heal.   Nevertheless, King Hussein and Jordan are too important strategically to be dismissed from the Middle East equation.

The two main military threats to Jordan continue to come from Syria and Israel. Jordan is also concerned about the power of both Iraq and Iran, and their capacities to create strategic difficulties for the Kingdom. Jordan has always had to rely on other powers for protection in the neighborhood. In the past, the United States and Israel -- and Britain in the immediate post-World War II era -- played this role, although over the past two years, Iraq had begun to assume the job. Now that Iraq has been defeated, the U.S. and Israel will likely continue to protect Jordan from overt threats in view of its strategic importance as a buffer state.

King Hussein must also protect himself against domestic strife, which he has done in the past three years by invoking the 'two D's': disengagement and democracy. By severing all official links with the West Bank, Hussein washed his hands of all responsibility for the West Bank Palestinians, knowing full well that Jordan must be included in any future settlement.[11]   It is in this context that Jordan's real estate plays such an important role. Without some security relationship with Jordan, no Israeli government will ever agree to a peace settlement with the Palestinians, let alone an independent Palestinian state.   The Jordanians know this. Disengagement is seen as a temporary measure, allowing the Palestinians to get on with their affairs without blaming Jordan for their lack of success.

Similarly, the King's decision to invoke democracy and limited elections, while resulting in Islamic fundamentalist gains in the Parliament, diffused some of the anger and tension that was building against the Kingdom in the late 1980s.[12]   The extent to which Jordan can overcome its domestic problems depends in part on its economic strength, and in part on the King's ability to defuse the Palestinian situation and the frustration that the Palestinians feel toward the impasse in the peace process. From a domestic perspective, King Hussein's handling of the Gulf crisis was masterly and won him much approval at home from his Palestinian majority population. It clearly diffused what could have been an extremely serious political crisis.

Jordan has no military pretensions other than to protect its own interests; this it can do only with minimal force, given its budgetary limitations. The danger, of course, is that as Jordan's defense preparedness falls below a certain level, it may be forced to seek closer cooperation with radical states, such as Syria or Iraq. This carries major risks, however. For example, Jordan's decision in February 1990, to establish a joint air corp with Iraq, placing Iraqi aircraft directly on Israel's eastern border, was considered a dangerous harbinger by Israeli defense planners.[13]

In the aftermath of the Gulf war, Jordan's worst-case scenario must be that some catastrophic event will occur in the West Bank, leading to a mass expulsion of the Palestinians. This could, in turn, trigger turmoil and anarchy in the Kingdom, threatening the monarchy itself. Jordan must also remain skeptical about Syria's claim to have abandoned its dreams of regional hegemony.

Conflict in the Gulf

Iraq. Iraq is a key Middle East player, both because of its pivotal location, linking the Arab-Israeli arena to the Gulf conflicts, and because of its participation in the two most violent Middle East wars in recent memory. Prior to the outbreak of the Iran-Iraq war in 1980, Iraq was one of the most vocal, if not the most powerful of Israel's Arab enemies. When Egypt made peace with Israel in 1979, Iraq and Syria were left as the two principal military threats to Israel. This scenario only served to fuel their pre-existing rivalry for preeminence in the Arab world. Seeking to cement his bid for supremacy in the region, Iraqi President Saddam Hussein blundered into the Iran-Iraq war, which became an eight-year long struggle for survival. He won the war with Iran, only to lose everything he had gained thirty months later in the Gulf war.

Prior to Iraq's invasion of Kuwait and the war that followed, Iraq's predominant strategic concern was Iran. As with the Arab-Israeli conflict, the Iran-Iraq war was one more battle in a centuries-old struggle. Persians and non-Persians had battled over the land of Mesopotamia long before the birth of Islam. Since the revelations of Islam, the rivalry between Sunni and Shiite sects of the religion has grown, with Iran as the champion of the minority Shiites battling the Sunni Arabs who control the holy Muslim sites in the Arabian desert.

During the Iran-Iraq war, Iraq had numerous allies, including most Arab states and western countries. Saddam Hussein was tolerated because of the shock of events in Iran following the overthrow of the Shah in February 1979. For years the Shah had served as a pillar of stability in the Mideast. The ascension of the Ayatollah Khomeini was unacceptable to a western sense of order in the region and it threatened the conservative Arab regimes. Furthermore, Khomeini's blatant anti-Americanism, and the taking of American hostages on November 4, 1979, made the Ayatollah a devil incarnate to western observers. The impotence of the Carter Administration in dealing with the Khomeini threat was a source of anger and anxiety for most Americans. The failure of the "Desert One" rescue attempt on April 25, 1980, further compounded the sense of weakness.

As a result, there was little international outcry, or even interest, when Saddam Hussein invaded Iran in September 1980. However, Iraq's failure to exploit its military advantages in the early days of the war and Iran's subsequent recovery worried the U.S. administration. By the summer of 1982, when the Israeli invasion of Lebanon was at its height, Iraqi forces were in retreat and Iran was poised to achieve a military breakthrough, possibly capturing the city of Basra. At that point, the West became more active on Iraq's behalf as there was a distinct possibility that Khomeini's army might defeat Saddam Hussein. In such a case, Iran would straddle the road to Kuwait. The fall of Kuwait would have set in motion a series of dominos, including Saudi Arabia, the Emirates, and possibly Jordan. The consequences of Iranian hegemony in the Gulf were considered as dire and unacceptable to the West in 1982 as was the prospect in 1990 that Saddam would control the region.

The strategic importance of containing the Iranian threat led the United States and the Europeans to tilt in favor of Iraq in the war. Formal diplomatic relations between Washington and Baghdad were restored in November 1984, and by November 1987, the United States and its western allies had significant military forces in the Gulf, in effect supporting Iraq's war efforts.[14]

Another reason why most western governments tolerated Saddam Hussein's behavior concerned money. Unlike with most Arab countries, doing business with Iraq was efficient and relatively graft-free. A highly competent technocratic class had emerged in the 1970s and 1980s. With enormous proven oil reserves, Iraq was believed destined to become another Saudi Arabia. Thus, economic interests, as well as strategic goals, allowed governments to ignore the more blatant human rights violations of the Iraqi government. These violations were well-documented every year by the State Department and Amnesty International. The scenes of the Iraqi gas bombings of Kurds at Halabja are one example.

With the end of the Iran-Iraq war, the Iranian threat was effectively rendered insignificant. Perhaps at that time a more determined effort should have been made to contain Saddam Hussein, or at least to give him notice that his human rights behavior was intolerable. This was not done, in part because of continued anger toward Iran; equally important was anger toward Iran's cohorts in the region, Syria and Libya, at the time considered more dangerous to western interests than was Iraq.

It was assumed that Iraq, exhausted from an eight-year war, would want to spend the post-war period reconstructing its damaged economy. Unfortunately, Saddam Hussein had more hegemonic ambitions. These, it is fair to say, were fed by the speed of the victory against Iran in the closing months of the war during the summer of 1988. Had the Iran-Iraq war ground to a halt with the cease fire Iraq had requested for so many years, a more humbled Saddam Hussein might have been less adventuresome.

Iraq justified continued high investment in its military infrastructure after the defeat of Iran in the context of long-term strategic goals. Iraq had little confidence in its truce with Iran and expected the Iranians to eventually rebuild their armed forces and embark on a war of revenge. To counter such activity Iraq needed to develop an Israeli-style defense: a citizen army that could be mobilized at a moment's notice, a high technology infrastructure, and qualitative superiority that would compensate for its inherent strategic disadvantages vis-à-vis Iran in terms of geography and population.[15]

As noted earlier, during the time between the last months of the war with Iran and the crisis in the spring of 1990, the Soviet Union abdicated its traditional Middle East role as counterweight to the West. The Iraqi perception was that one superpower remained in the region, the United States, with its extremely close ties to Israel, a military presence in the Gulf itself, as well as friendships bordering on alliance with Saudi Arabia, Egypt, and the small Gulf countries. To the extent that Saddam Hussein had a coherent strategy for hegemonic power in the Arab world, the United States was now the primary obstacle to this aspiration. It is in this context that the events from February to August 1990 must be viewed.

On February 24, 1990, Saddam delivered a speech in Amman to the Arab Cooperation Council. He discussed waning Soviet influence in the Middle East which he claimed was in sharp contrast to the challenge posed by the United States:

"The USSR turned to tackle its domestic problems after relinquishing the process of continuous conflict and its slogans. The

USSR shifted from the balanced position with the U.S. in a practical manner, although it has not acknowledged it so far.

"It has become clear to everyone that the U.S. has emerged in superior position in international politics. This superiority will be demonstrated in the U.S. readiness to play such a role more than in the predicted guarantees for its continuation.

"One may cite recurrent statements by U.S. officials about their intention to keep their fleets in the Gulf for an unlimited period of time, and their support for an unprecedented exodus of Soviet Jews to Palestinian territory.

"The U.S. may have the famous red lines beyond which it does not tread concerning the interests of other nations that deal peacefully with it, but its policy so far has no red lines warning the concerned sides in the U.S. not to tread beyond them where Arab interests are concerned."[16]

Barely three weeks later, a series of incidents occurred that were to rapidly precipitate a crisis in both American and British relations with Iraq. On March 15, 1990, an Iranian-born journalist working for the *London Observer*, Farzad Bazoft, was hanged in Baghdad for alleged spying, despite public appeals from Britain and others that he be spared. It was said at the time that plans to execute Bazoft were irreversible once Britain had publicly challenged Saddam. The next day Britain recalled its ambassador to Iraq, but avoided a diplomatic break by continuing to offer Iraq trade credits and arms sales. There were equally hesitant responses to this incident from the United States and the United Nations.

A week later, on March 22, Gerald Bull, a Canadian artillery engineer working for Iraq, was assassinated in Brussels. On March 28, 40 nuclear-weapons grade electronic capacitors were seized at London's Heathrow airport on their way from the U.S. to Iraq as part of an American-British sting operation against illegal technology transfers to Iraq. This event created major headlines and was followed by increasingly hostile stories about Iraq's military intentions, and fears of an Israeli preventive strike on Iraq's nuclear facilities. Partly in response to these incidents, and again to show his defiance, on April 2, Saddam delivered his now infamous speech threatening Israel and claiming possession of binary chemical weapons. He stated: "We have the binary chemical. We did not use it against the Iranians.....By God, we will make fire eat up half of Israel, if it tries to do anything against Iraq."[17]

36

On April 9, Iraq expelled an American diplomat in retaliation for the U.S. expulsion of an Iraqi diplomat at the United Nations suspected of involvement in a plot to murder two opponents of the Baghdad government. On April 12, British authorities seized steel tubes bound for Iraq that were presumed to be used to build the 'supergun' Gerald Bull had been masterminding. Other parts of the supergun were seized in Italy, Greece, Turkey, Germany, and Spain.[18] (See Appendix III.)

Despite, or perhaps because of these rapidly escalating events, on April 16, five U.S. Senators met with Saddam and struck a conciliatory pose. The administration, as well as some in Congress, believed that attempts to isolate or confront Iraq might increase regional instability and was, thus, prepared to oppose any attempt by Congress to pass economic sanctions against Iraq.[19]

On July 16, in testimony before Congress, Assistant Secretary of State for the Near East, John Kelley, formally opposed sanctions against Iraq.[20] He expressed the administration's concern that sanctions might damage Washington's important economic relationship with Iraq.[21] A good working relationship with Iraq was also considered a high priority in order to diffuse a potential Iraqi-Israeli confrontation. Throughout the early summer of 1990, the possibility of war erupting between Israel and Iraq was openly discussed. While it was not believed that war was imminent, there was great concern that miscalculations were potential triggers for armed conflict.

Post-War Iraq. Iraq has emerged from the Persian Gulf war with its economy in chaos and its military establishment sufficiently weakened, removing it as a threat to its neighbors for the foreseeable future. However, one of the causes of the Gulf crisis remains unresolved. While a border dispute over a waterway may appear comparatively petty in relation to the level of destruction unleashed by Iraq's two recent wars, it should not be forgotten that the Shatt al-Arab dispute spurred Iraq to start the war with Iran. Baghdad's preoccupation with its limited access to the sea will long outlive Saddam Hussein and the Ba'ath party. For Iraq, control of the Shatt al-Arab means the difference between access to international trade and commercial routes versus economic isolation and stagnation. With the Shatt al-Arab waterway blocked and unusable as a result of war, Iraq is land-locked. Its oil pipelines have also been shut. The pipeline through Syria has been closed since April 1982; the pipelines through both Turkey and Saudi Arabia were closed in August 1990.

Before the Gulf crisis, Iraq was considering the construction of a canal that would connect Basra with the city of Umm Qasr (see the following map of the Shatt al-Arab). This canal would require the permanent diversion of water from the Shatt al-Arab, making the old waterway unfit for navigation and rendering the Iranian ports of Abadan and Korramshahr unusable. While the canal would provide a solution to Iraq's Shatt al-Arab waterway problem, and at a price comparable to what it would cost to clear the waterway, it would also add further obstacles to reconciliation with Kuwait. Iraq's spurious territorial claims over the Islands of Bubiyan and Warbah that occupy strategic position in front of Umm Qasr, combined with a dispute over three miles of the border between Iraq and Kuwait, brought the two countries to the brink of armed conflict in March 1973. These two areas of contention were also mentioned frequently in Saddam's rhetoric to justify the seizure of Kuwait in August 1990.[22]

Finally, Iraq's internal security is threatened by the hostility of both Kurds and Shiites to Saddam Hussein's rule after the Gulf war. Despite their failure, the Kurdish and Shiite revolts in the spring of 1991 raised doubts about the future of Iraq as a unified state, and the possibility of independent provinces, if not states, in the North and South. In addition, Saddam Hussein's ruthless suppression of dissent before, during, and after the Gulf war has led to speculation that even if he is ousted, civil strife may follow, as there are no trained political cadres to replace him or his regime.

Iran. Although Iran emerged from the Gulf war with enhanced prestige and power, its leaders remain an enigma in the current strategic tapestry of the Middle East and South Asia. Following the defeat by Iraq, Iran's military forces were in a shambles, and their rebuilding is still proceeding in a haphazard manner. Nevertheless, there are reports that the Soviet Union has agreed to supply Iran with some advanced weapons, including tanks, air defense missiles, and at least 20 MiG-29 fighters.[23]

However, while Iran is racked with internal dissent, chronic economic problems, and an overwhelming population problem, its strategic importance is as great as ever. This is particularly true in view of the changes occurring in the Soviet Union and the possibility that there will be independent Islamic republics emerging in the coming decade. Iran will be a key player in the politics of the region, which may now have to embrace countries to the North in addition to the Soviet Union. This suggests that its relations with the Soviet Union, or Russia, will remain critical in the years ahead, and that one would anticipate good ties between Moscow and Tehran, if only to manage the Islamic issue and avoid major confrontations.

Bitterness and animosity still remain between Iran and the Arab

Iraq's Border Problems

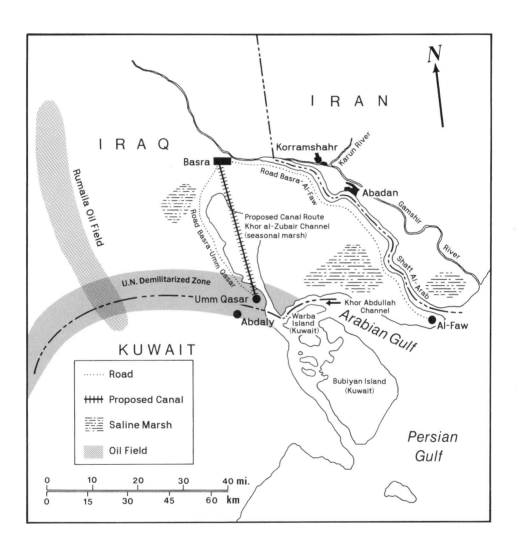

countries, however. Iran is unlikely to forget the humiliation and casualties it suffered at the hands of Saddam Hussein, including the use of gas against unprotected soldiers and missile attacks on cities. Hence, regardless of what peace agreement was reached between Iran and Iraq at the height of the Gulf crisis, lingering suspicions and doubts will almost certainly guarantee that Iran will rebuild its military capabilities.

The GCC Countries. The events of 1990-91 made clear to the world that the Gulf Cooperation Council (GCC) countries -- Saudi Arabia, Kuwait, Bahrain, Qatar, Oman, and the United Arab Emirates (UAE) -- have enormous strategic importance because of their geography and oil production capabilities. Despite the defeat of Iraq, the GCC countries remain nervous about their security.

Like all weak countries, they have sought to accommodate their larger neighbors while simultaneously building and maintaining relations with external powers. The United States has consistently had good relations with most of these countries, particularly Saudi Arabia, Oman, and Bahrain, and in recent years had improved relations significantly with Kuwait and the UAE. While none of the Gulf states has turned primarily to the Soviets for protection against aggression from more powerful neighbors, Kuwait has good relations with the Soviet Union including both a diplomatic and an arms relationship. The UAE also established diplomatic relations with the Soviet Union in 1985.

Saudi Arabia, in particular, has walked a narrow line between actively seeking American military assistance and support for deployment in times of crisis, and a 'hands off' policy toward the permanent stationing of American forces in Saudi Arabia for fear of alienating both the internal population and its neighbors. However, the good relationship between the U.S. armed forces and Saudi Arabia during the Gulf war has, for the time being, lessened this concern. For the foreseeable future, the GCC has no alternative but to rely on American military power for its protection.

The Indo-Pakistani Conflict

Although the focus of this book is on the Middle East rather than South Asia, it is increasingly difficult to avoid mentioning the strategic climate on the subcontinent in view of the overlap in interests and military reach discussed earlier. Thus, some reference to the Indo-Pakistani conflict is both useful and necessary.

The Indo-Pakistani conflict dates from the creation of India and

Pakistan as independent states in 1947. It has its antecedents in centuries of Hindu-Muslim rivalries on the Indian subcontinent. Britain's policy of 'divide and rule' in India encouraged these rivalries and introduced a tradition of political oppression that both Hindus and Muslims directed toward one another when either was in power.

The communal violence that accompanied the partition of formerly British India and the war that followed left millions dead, while deepening the mistrust and suspicion between India and Pakistan. Religious differences continue to plague the Indo-Pakistani relationship as a result of partition along religious lines. While Pakistan was created as a haven for British India's Muslim population, there are more Muslims in India, which is five times Pakistan's size, than in Pakistan. The reason for Pakistan's creation being specifically to be *not India*, Pakistan's foreign policy is understandably Indo-centric. There is a good deal of suspicion in Pakistan that modern India harbors designs on its former western provinces, particularly after New Delhi's key role in the creation of Bangladesh out of Pakistan's former eastern province in 1971.

Meanwhile, India, which prides itself on being a secular democracy, officially rejects the communalism on which Pakistan's creation is based. As one of the world's largest states in geographic size, population, economic potential, and military capability, India also rejects a strictly subcontinental foreign policy. Rather, India aspires to be regarded at the global level on a par with its eastern neighbor China. For example, China achieved great power status -- including a permanent seat and veto power in the UN Security Council -- by acquiring nuclear weapons prior to the cut-off date inscribed in the 1968 Nuclear Non-Proliferation Treaty. India, which has not tested or deployed nuclear weapons since its 1974 test, has received no such status. This adds weight to the notion in India that only by acquiring the currency of global power, nuclear weapons, will it be taken seriously as a great power in its own right. For India's nuclear capability to be equated with that of Pakistan, and for India to be subject to the same superpower reprimands as Pakistan for its high technology achievements only adds insult to the injury of not being taken seriously already.

The different Pakistani and Indian approaches to foreign relations are also reflected in their relations with the superpowers. Pakistan, concerned primarily with the perceived Indian threat, and suffering from an extreme disadvantage in size and capabilities, has traditionally turned to the West, and particularly to the United States, for assistance. India, on the other hand, wants to be considered a great power in its own right and has been loathe to accept the bipolar nature of the international system. Finding the Soviets much more amenable to providing assistance with few strings attached, India signed a treaty of friendship and cooperation with the Soviet Union in 1971. Since 1981, Pakistan has received the bulk of its arms imports from the United States, while Indian arms imports are primarily from the Soviet Union. India also has an extensive defense industry of its own, although it is still dependent on imported western technology for most high technology systems.

India does not see its relationship with the Soviet Union as that of client and patron, and resents any attempt to twin it with Pakistan's relationship with the United States. Thus, when Washington joins Pakistan in pushing for a quid pro quo in concessions on arms control issues, such as nuclear weapons, or political issues, such as the disputed Kashmir region, India only feels more determined to acquire the components of great power status and independence.

The primary bone of contention between the two countries has historically been the status of the disputed state of Jammu and Kashmir, itself partitioned between India and Pakistan by the 1947-48 war. The issue was left unresolved and was the basis for the second Indo-Pakistani war in 1965. The third, and most recent, war between India and Pakistan in 1971, saw the creation of the independent state of Bangladesh out of the former Pakistani province of East Pakistan.

Since the 1971 war, India and Pakistan have been at peace, albeit an armed, mistrustful, and fragile peace. India achieved its primary goals in the 1971 war: the wrenching of East Pakistan from Pakistani control; continued control over its portion of Jammu and Kashmir state; and Pakistan's signature on the Simla agreement, stipulating that future disputes between them would be resolved bilaterally. Pakistan, however, was defeated on virtually every front. The Simla Agreement represented capitulation to New Delhi as it guaranteed that India, now even more powerful than Pakistan in comparison after the loss of East Pakistan, could dictate terms to Pakistan without the latter being able to appeal for outside assistance against its stronger neighbor.

The conflict in Afghanistan has also complicated Indo-Pakistani relations and continues to pose a threat to Pakistan's security. The Soviet invasion of Afghanistan in 1979 brought the U.S. into the region firmly on the side of the anti-Soviet Afghan rebels and their benefactor, Pakistan. The subsequent flow of arms and aid from the U.S. to Pakistan became a cause for alarm in India. In addition to greatly increasing Pakistan's military capabilities against India, the U.S. assistance program inadvertently provided Pakistan with an umbrella under which it could safely complete its program to acquire a nuclear weapons option against India.[24]

The Indian subcontinent was also rocked by the war against Iraq in the neighboring Persian Gulf. Pakistan sent troops to join the coalition forces against Iraq, while at the same time, the head of the Pakistani military publicly praised Saddam Hussein. There was a great deal of appeal for the Pakistani people in Saddam's Islamic rhetoric. Similarly in India, there were a number of public pro-Saddam, anti-U.S. demonstrations among India's Muslims, despite the government's attempt to remain as neutral as possible. Even the small gesture of allowing U.S. military aircraft to refuel in India caused an uproar.

The subcontinent has also suffered its own crises in the last year which have been overshadowed by events in the Gulf. Both India and Pakistan have had a changeover in government: former Pakistani Prime Minister Bhutto is on trial in Pakistan for corruption; India has changed Prime Ministers twice, while Congress-I leader Rajiv Gandhi was assassinated during elections in May 1991.

As elsewhere in the region, religious fundamentalism, separatism, and economic stagnation are increasingly at the heart of each country's internal problems. Pakistan continues to wrestle with its Islamic roots, ethnic violence, and economic corruption, while Indian democracy faces a Hindu fundamentalist threat to its secular status even as it contemplates a future without a leader from the Nehru/Gandhi political dynasty, and a bureaucratic infrastructure that is corrupt and inefficient.[25] In the past, periods of internal instability in India and Pakistan have resulted in inter-state conflict. Any such conflict will now include a nuclear dimension that could, in turn, spill over into the even more volatile Middle East.

Conclusion

The above analysis provides the setting for discussing the more specific impact that the Middle East and South Asian arms races have on the security policies of the regional players. Until these are better understood, the role of arms control cannot be fully explored. However, before either the security or arms control issues will be examined in detail, Chapter 3 will examine the politics and economics of arms sales. Chapter 4 will then examine the principal military acquisition programs underway in the region, and the asymmetries in regional capabilities.

Notes

1. Revenge as a factor in the Arab-Israeli conflict is stressed in a new analysis by Robert Harkavy. He compares Arab-Israeli dislike for one another to the open hatred felt by Americans and Japanese during World War II, and contrasts these with the relatively benign feelings of most Americans toward Soviet citizens during the Cold War years. Robert Harkavy, "The Future of Israeli Nuclear Strategy," *The Washington Quarterly*, Summer 1991, pp. 161-179.

2. General Assembly Resolution 3379 (XXX) Determining that Zionism Is a Form of Racism, November 10, 1975, UN Document A/RES/3379(XXX) (1975), reprinted in John Norton Moore, editor, *The Arab-Israeli Conflict Readings and Documents*, abridged and revised edition (Princeton: Princeton University Press, 1977), pp. 1235-1237.

3. The descriptive material in this chapter draws upon the author's frequent visits to the region and his discussions with senior officials from all the countries mentioned. Of particular importance were: a visit to Iraq in April 1989; several visits to Israel and the Indian subcontinent in 1989 and 1990; two seminars organized by William Quandt of the Brookings Institution with Israeli and Arab participants meeting in France in 1990 and 1991; a study trip to Egypt, Jordan, and Israel led by Martin Indyk, Director of the Washington Institute for Near East Policy, in June 1990; and a conference on the lessons of the Gulf war organized by the International Institute for Strategic Studies, in London in April 1991.

4. UN Security Council Resolution 687 For a Formal Cease Fire in the Gulf War, April 3, 1991, UN Document S/RES/687.

5. See James M. Dorsey, "Syria wary of Soviets, seeks new arms seller," *Washington Times*, July 15, 1988; Caryle Murphy, "Syria Urged to Stress Defense," *Washington Post*, November 11, 1989; and John P. Hannah, "Moscow Puts the Brakes on Syria," *New York Times*, November 28, 1989.

6. The U.S.-Israeli strategic cooperation agreement was announced by President Reagan in November 1983. See "Remarks of the President and Prime Minister Yitzhak Shamir of Israel Following Their Meetings," November 29, 1983, in *Public Papers of the Presidents of the United States: Ronald Reagan 1983*, Book II (Washington, D.C.: United States Government Printing Office, 1985), pp. 1631-1633.

7. An example would be the destruction of the Muslim Dome of the Rock in Jerusalem. In April 1984, members of the Gush Emunin (the block of the faithful) Jewish fundamentalists were arrested for acts of terror against the Palestinian population. At the time of their arrest, it was discovered that they had elaborate plans to blow up the Dome in the hopes of precipitating an Arab-Israeli war. See Ehud Sprinzak, *Fundamentalism, Terrorism and Democracy: the Case of Gush Emunin Underground*, Occasional Paper (Washington, D.C.: The Wilson Center, 1986).

8. See note 5 above.

9. The Taif accord on a new Lebanese constitution, negotiated between Christian and Muslim members of the Lebanese Parliament, was accepted by all factions to the Lebanese civil war except Michel Aoun, the renegade Christian leader, and his supporters. Aoun continued to fight against the accord and its supporters, and to occupy the presidential palace until the Syrians finally forced him out in October 1990. See Youssef M. Ibrahim, "Lebanese Factions Agree On Charter To Resolve Strife," *New York Times*, October 23, 1989; and Nora Boustany, "Syrians Drive Out Lebanon's Aoun," *Washington Post*, October 14, 1990.

10. For details on Syria's oil industry and its prospects, see Naji Abi-Aad, "Steady growth in Syrian exploration and production," *Petroleum Review*, February 1991, pp. 74-77.

11. See Joel Brinkley, "Hussein Reduces Ties To West Bank And Palestinians," *New York Times*, July 31, 1988.

12. See Caryle Murphy, "Jordan Holds Parliamentary Election In New Mood of Political Openness," *Washington Post*, November 9, 1989.

13. See Godfrey Jansen, "Nightmare for Israel," *Middle East International*, 16 March 1990, pp. 8-9.

14. Fear of Iran and the bitter memories of the hostage affair explain the extraordinarily low-keyed response in the United States to the incident on May 17, 1987, when an Iraqi Excocet missile killed 37 U.S. sailors aboard the U.S.S. Stark in a supposedly accidental attack. See John H. Cushman, Jr., "Iraqi Missile Hits U.S. Navy Frigate in Persian Gulf," *New York Times*, May 18, 1987.

15. Personal interviews by the author with senior Iraqi officials in Baghdad, April 1989.

16. "Iraq's Saddam Husayn," Amman Television Service, 1010 GMT, 24 February 1990, translated in *FBIS-NES*, February 27, 1990, pp. 1-5.

17. "President Warns Israel, Criticizes U.S.," Baghdad Domestic Service, 1030 GMT, April 2, 1990, translated in *FBIS-NES*, April 3, 1990, pp. 32-36.

18. See Appendix III on long-range artillery, pp. 197-202.

19. Patrick E. Tyler, "U.S. Working to Lessen Tension with Iraq," *Washington Post*, April 23, 1990.

20. Clifford Krauss, "Bush Aide Opposes Sanctions On Iraq," *New York Times*, June 16, 1990.

21. The United States bought an average of 447,000 barrels of Iraqi oil a day at $2 billion a year. In 1989, the U.S. exported $1 billion in agricultural products to Iraq.

22. For a detailed account of the territorial dispute between Iraq and Kuwait, see Richard Schofield, *Kuwait and Iraq: Historical Claims and Territorial Disputes* (London: Royal Institute of International Affairs, 1991).

23. "Russian Deputy Says Tanks Exported to Iran," Berlin, ADN, 1148 GMT, 30 April 1991, translated in *FBIS-SOV*, May 1, 1991, p. 17. See also Statement of Rear Admiral Thomas Brooks, USN, Director of Naval Intelligence, before the Seapower, Strategic, and Critical Materials Subcommittee of the House Committee on Armed Services, March 7, 1991.

24. For a full account of U.S. assistance to Pakistan, the latter's nuclear weapons program, and its effects on Indo-Pakistani relations, see *Nuclear Weapons and South Asian Security* (Washington, D.C.: Carnegie Endowment for International Peace, 1988).

25. For greater detail on the state of Pakistani politics, see Mahnaz Ispahani, *Pakistan: Dimensions of Insecurity*, Adelphi Paper #246 (London: Brassey's for the International Institute of Strategic Studies, 1990).

CHAPTER THREE

The Geopolitics and Economics of Arms Transfers

The arms race in the region results from the demand for weapons by the local powers and the willingness and ability of external powers to supply weapons and associated technologies. This chapter focuses on the supply side of the equation. Its purpose is to explain why, despite the growing threats to their interests posed by proliferation, the primary suppliers continue to transfer arms and technology. The geopolitical reasons for such arms transfers are first considered, followed by the economic motivations, and the economic restraints on recipients.

Geopolitical Interests of the Supplier Countries

United States Strategic and Political Interests

There are two dominant reasons why the United States has sold or given so much weaponry to Middle East countries over the past four decades. First, successive administrations feared this resource-rich and geographically pivotal region might fall under the control of countries hostile to American and western interests. Second, arms were transferred to assure Israel's security, and to strengthen U.S. ties to friendly Arab regimes. Economic motives for arms sales, while certainly important, have always taken third place to strategic and political considerations in Washington.

Following World War II, the U.S. Department of Defense determined that access to Middle East oil was critical in the event of hostilities with the Soviet Union. It was then assumed that a new world war could last from three to four years. The few atomic weapons in the U.S. arsenal at that time would not have been decisive, and the United States did not have enough reserves to 'oil another war' beyond a year or two. "If the Near and Middle East oil areas are not retained, or retaken in the early phases of the war," it was maintained that "the oil position of the Allies would necessitate subsequent actions to retake it."[1]

The Control of the Middle East Arms Race

The Soviet Union has always been considered the prime threat to the region; since 1978, however, Iran and later Iraq were added to the list. The deployment of American military forces, including intelligence-gathering units, to bases in Pakistan, Turkey, Iran, Morocco, Libya, Saudi Arabia, and Bahrain in the 1950s and 1960s was part of the strategy to contain Soviet influence. The rationale for deploying major U.S. naval forces in the Gulf in 1987 -- the reflagging of Kuwaiti oil tankers -- was based on the fear that if the U.S. did not get involved, the Soviets would. In addition, billions of dollars of U.S. military assistance have been spent on the region to give strategic allies the ability to deter Soviet expansionism, thereby protecting the oil.

The end of the Cold War and the beginning of U.S.-Soviet cooperation during the Gulf war have led to a depolarization of East-West tensions in the Middle East, greatly reducing the threat of a superpower confrontation there. Now, the greatest threat to the stability and security of the Middle East is posed by local radical regimes. The breakdown of the superpower rivalry also removes this conflict as a driving force in arms sales to the region.[2]

The security of Israel has been a key element in U.S. Middle East policy since the creation of the Jewish state in 1948. However, it was not until the aftermath of the 1967 war, when France abandoned its role as Israel's major arms supplier, that the U.S. commitment to promote Israeli security reached the level at which it remains today. U.S.-Israeli relations since that time have grown stronger, reaching a new height during the Gulf war when U.S. personnel were committed to Israeli soil for the first time for the defense of the state. This intimate relationship will continue for the foreseeable future, and will help determine key U.S. policy decisions in its relations with the Arabs, on arms sales, and on strategic planning for the security of the eastern Mediterranean.

In the aftermath of the Gulf war, the goals of American foreign policy are:
- To keep the oil-rich resources of the region from falling into hostile hands and to assure the uninterrupted flow of reasonably-priced oil. Since this must still include military contingencies for intervention, good military relations with key Arab countries are necessary;
- To assure the survival of Israel through the provision of military assistance, while seeking a diplomatic solution to the Arab-Israeli conflict and improving U.S. political and economic relations with all Middle Eastern countries, including Iran;
- To retain and develop close political and economic relations with India and Pakistan, the world's largest and fifth largest democracies

48

respectively;
- To protect American citizens and facilities from attack by terrorist groups operating in the region; and
- To defuse and control the most dangerous components of the arms race.

In pursuing these interests and goals, the United States must balance military policy, diplomatic and economic interests, and the desire to provide security and stability to the region. In order to assure access to oil, preserve Israel's security, support friendly Arab states, and defend against terrorism, U.S. policy will continue to contain a strong military component, including military assistance and military intervention.

The successful prosecution of the Gulf war has highlighted the importance of oil and the need to assure its accessibility. This is a principal reason for keeping American forces in the region. Others include the need to provide for the security of the Gulf states, the desire to protect the Kurds, and to set the groundwork for a long-term security framework for the region. The size and composition of American forces, as well as the time frame of their deployment, will depend on a number of factors, including the perception that Iran and Iraq will not emerge as major military powers for the next few years.

Clearly, one factor influencing security planning will be the degree to which the U.S. can rely on the capabilities of local forces in the early stages of a new crisis, before American reinforcements can arrive. The United States must, therefore, be sensitive to the security requirements of friendly Middle Eastern countries. This means meeting many of their requests for military capabilities and satisfying their desire to work with the U.S. to build credible defense forces.

In anticipating such contingencies, the most important military problems relate to the changing threat environment in the region. Until such time as Iraq and Iran are governed by trustworthy leaders with whom the United States can do business, prudence necessitates that security considerations be given priority over arms reduction proposals if the two goals conflict. This is equally true of Syria, despite its participation in the anti-Iraq coalition. Syrian support for, and Iranian non-opposition to the Gulf war reflected their on-going disputes with Iraq rather than a new-found commitment to the rule of law, or to peace in the region.[3]

It is also of great importance to Washington that the dynamics of the Arab-Israeli military balance not change to a point where a new war is more likely, or to a point where this balance adversely affects the peace process between Israel and its neighbors. The United States must balance its policy of maintaining Israel's qualitative edge through high technology arms sales against the Arab fear that Israel's qualitative superiority makes it less likely to compromise in a political settlement. In the past, American administrations have dealt with this problem by supporting high levels of military assistance, grants, and sales to both Israel and moderate Arab states. While this policy has had its detractors in Congress, Israel, and the Arab world, it remains a practical one, unlikely to be changed in the absence of regional arms control arrangements.

Terrorism remains a key factor in determining American policy toward the region. Those countries suspected of, or clearly guilty of aiding and abetting terrorist acts against American citizens and facilities will continue to be regarded as pariahs. The same will likely hold true for any state seeking to export radical, anti-western Islamic fundamentalism. In Iran these two factors overlap. Such states will, therefore, be unable to purchase American arms until hostages are released and acts of terrorism cease. In practical terms, this means that a rapprochement between the United States and Libya, Iraq, and Iran will not take place until they denounce terrorism and sever their ties with known terrorist organizations. Iraq is now in a special situation in that it must meet many other requirements, specifically those outlined by Resolution 687, before its relations with the United States and the West can improve.

Syria poses a rather different problem. There is strong circumstantial evidence that Syria was involved in the terrorist bombing of Pan Am flight 103, and that it serves as a base for a number of Middle Eastern terrorist groups. However, policy imperatives before and during the Gulf war, combined with a more moderate Syrian stance toward terrorism, dictated a heightening of diplomatic activity with Damascus. Syrian President Assad made the American decision to include Syria in the coalition easier by helping to ease the terrorist threat created by Iraq.[4] And despite Syria's willingness to participate in a regional peace conference, its long-term intentions are still difficult to gauge. The U.S. will continue to be wary of Syrian activities as long as its terrorist links remain intact.

Soviet Geopolitical Interests

Like the United States, the Soviet Union has strong strategic and political motives to provide arms to Middle Eastern and South Asian countries. It is also placing increased emphasis on the economic benefits of such sales. Now that the U.S. is no longer seen as an enemy in the region, the Soviet Union must find a way to balance its traditional regional interests so that they do not lead to confrontation with the United States. These interests derive from its geography, the political turmoil in Soviet Central Asia, and the continued war in Afghanistan.

Whatever type of entity the Soviet Union becomes, it is bound to have important relations with the key regional states in both the Middle East and South Asia. It will, therefore, remain sensitive to direct or indirect threats emanating from this region. Like the United States, the Soviet Union will continue to balance the transfer of arms to selected regional countries -- for reasons of influence and economic benefits -- against its security concerns about proliferation. Although the significance of Soviet military power in the eastern Mediterranean has diminished, the Soviet Union will continue to have strategic reasons for wishing to retain access to port facilities, possibly even bases, in Syria and Libya.

Although it is too early to tell how Soviet new thinking on foreign policy will ultimately affect arms transfers, the Soviets have a growing interest in arms control. Political and economic conditions now indicate that the Soviet Union will become increasingly reluctant, and will find it increasingly difficult to subsidize Third World clients that cannot pay their bills. On the other hand, the Soviet demand for hard currency may elevate the importance of the economics of arms sales, and translate into sales to virtually any country that can pay cash.

Soviet arms sales to the Arabs inevitably create problems for Israel. The Soviet Union has strong interests in seeking better relations with Israel, especially in the context of its image in the United States. Soviet-Israeli relations steadily improved during 1990, marked by the opening of the Israeli consulate in Moscow on Jan 31, 1991 -- 24 years after the Soviet Union broke ties -- and by the wave of Soviet Jewish emigration to Israel.[5] At the time of the attempted coup, both countries were moving toward full diplomatic relations, and discussed the Israeli purchase of a Soviet nuclear reactor.[6] While Moscow continues to weigh its ties with Israel against its military ties with Israel's adversaries, Soviet officials have reason to see Israel as a worthy partner through which they hope to establish and maintain a credible political role in the region. This role will, in turn, be shaped by the arms transfer policy they choose to follow.

The arms races in the Middle East pose some clear strategic and political problems for the Soviet Union. The countries that will have the most sophisticated military capabilities in the coming decade -- India, Israel, and Pakistan -- will all, in theory, be able to target the Soviet Union with nuclear weapons. Turkey, Iran, and Afghanistan will all have the capacity, at least in theory, to arm dissident groups within the Soviet

Union. It is no longer unrealistic to envisage scenarios in which terrorists, operating from around the southern Soviet perimeter, participate in operations against military and civilian nuclear facilities in the Soviet Republics, for example.[7]

Both Moscow's close relationship with India, and the proximity of the region to increasingly volatile Soviet Central Asia, make any potentially destabilizing military developments there of great concern to the Soviet Union. In addition, while the Soviet Union and India are currently close allies, India's rising status as a regional great power could eventually threaten Moscow's freedom to maneuver in Asia and the Indian Ocean and could force Moscow to redefine its relationship with New Delhi.[8]

European Geopolitical Interests

In the 1950s and 1960s, Britain and France sold arms to the Middle East for geopolitical reasons. However, for the past 20 years, the primary motivation for arms sales of these and other European states has been economics.

The end of the Cold War has had an enormous impact on Europe. Together with the expected completion of the European Community's (EC) Single Market in 1992, the likely result will be dramatic changes in the politics, economics, demography, and security of Europe in the next decade. These changes are viewed with increasing concern in the Middle East because of the importance of Europe as both an economic market and as a source of political and economic power. Most of the North African states as well as Israel, Syria, Lebanon, and Jordan, have great stakes in their future relations with the European Community and are unsure how these will evolve.

The North African states are bracing themselves for increased restrictions on access to the European market. Israel worries about its own access to this market and fears that a more united Europe will impose political conditions on economic ties with Israeli industries, making them contingent on a settlement of the Palestinian problem. Egypt and Jordan are concerned that the capital-rich Arab countries of the Gulf Cooperation Council (GCC) will invest their money in Europe rather than in the region. Turkey is in an anomalous position -- it is part of both Europe and the Middle East. It has increasing interests in the Middle East and has gained new stature in the region through its contribution during the Gulf war. But Turkey will find it increasingly difficult to keep from being drawn into conflicts with neighbors such as Syria and Iraq over access to water.

For their part, the Europeans are concerned about how they will deal with the vast human drama of integrating Eastern Europe into the western economic system, while also preventing the continent from becoming overrun with immigrants intent on a better life from Africa and the Middle East, as well as from Eastern Europe and the Soviet Union.

The future of European relations with its southern neighbors is uncertain at best, and these relations will continue to change in the post-Cold War and post-Gulf war era. One of the most important determinants of European relations with the Middle East will be the future deployment of the U.S. and Soviet fleets in the Mediterranean. If the United States decides instead to greatly reduce its naval presence in the region, the littoral states will be forced to take greater responsibility for their security. For instance, the United States has been largely responsible for policing the activities of Libya's Colonel Qaddafi in the Mediterranean. Some Europeans have viewed the U.S. preoccupation with Qaddafi as overblown and unnecessary; but there is no doubt that in the absence of the Sixth Fleet, a belligerent Libya could not be ignored by countries such as Italy and France. In this case, the Europeans could find themselves increasingly embroiled with the military dimension of North Africa and the eastern Mediterranean.

In this context, the unchecked proliferation of advanced, long-range delivery systems to North African states would also pose new problems. As a taste of things to come, one must only recall Libya's use of SSMs against the Italian island of Lampedusa following the U.S. bombing raid against Tripoli and Bengazi in April 1986.[9] At the time, the Libyan attack was seen as relatively harmless since it did no damage. However, the fact that Libya could fire missiles against a northern neighbor did not go unnoticed.

The gradual buildup of long-range missile inventories in the Middle East will have an impact on defense planning in Greece, Turkey, Italy, France, Spain, and Portugal, and perhaps further to the North as well. While missiles themselves may not have much impact on regional security, the possibility that they might be armed with chemical, biological, or nuclear warheads is enough reason to expect some form of reaction from the European states most directly concerned. This could take the form of unilateral or multilateral efforts at arms control, increased defense preparedness through anti-missile systems, or both.[10]

The European Community is now considering the development of a common export policy on conventional arms and weapons-related technology. Proponents of this measure argue that the dismantling of intra-European trade barriers could increase Third World access to European arms. If no common policy is established, weapons could be transferred through member nations with less restrictive export controls. Although the development of a common policy will be quite difficult, especially when dealing with dual-use technology, such a multilateral agreement will be necessary if the major European weapons producers hope to control the transfer of their products to the Third World.[11]

Chinese Geopolitical Interests

China also has important geopolitical interests in the Middle East and South Asia. Foremost, the Chinese hope to gain political influence in these areas in response to regional fears of superpower condominium. Since the early 1980s, China has pursued an aggressive export policy, stepping in when ideological or political pressures have constrained the traditional western suppliers. China may now view a reduced Soviet presence in the Middle East as an opportunity to increase its political role, at least in part through weapons transfers.[12] Arms sales to the Middle East and South Asia continue to translate not only into much needed foreign currency, but also into "enhanced domestic power and greater international influence."[13]

China shares a 3380 km border with India against which it fought a war in 1962 over disputed territory. China also shares a border with Pakistan along the boundaries of Pakistan-controlled Kashmir, and maintains a strong security relationship with Islamabad. As long as China has unresolved territorial disputes with its other powerful neighbor and India's primary arms supplier, the Soviet Union, it is bound to continue to regard Pakistan as an important ally. Thus, while Chinese arms sales to the countries of the Middle East and Persian Gulf can best be explained in terms of economic motives, Chinese military cooperation with Pakistan has political overtones motivated by the two states' common perception of the Indian and Soviet geostrategic threats.

Economic Motivations for Arms and Technology Sales

In addition to their geopolitical interests, the outside powers have strong economic interests behind their arms relationships in the region. With the end of the Cold War and the shrinking of NATO and Warsaw Pact country defense budgets, the competition for defense markets in the Third World is likely to intensify. This trend could be exacerbated by the leveling off of arms purchases by states in the Middle East and South Asia that has occurred over the last few years. Arms sales to the Third World peaked in 1982 at $61 billion, fluctuated between $40-48 billion through the middle of the decade, and fell dramatically in 1989 to $29 billion.[14] New purchases of arms following the Gulf war could begin to shift this downward trend. American high technology weapons have become desirable and may be seen as an alternative to a large American military presence in the region. Even Soviet arms, which proved to be inferior to their American counterparts, will remain popular with countries like Syria that have little hope of gaining access to American or European arms in the absence of a breakthrough in the Arab-Israeli peace process.

The Soviet Union and the United States claim the lion's share of the arms market in the Middle East and South Asia. While they are likely to continue to do so, other suppliers, such as Britain, France, China, West Germany, Italy, Argentina, and Brazil, regard the Middle East and South Asia as key markets.[15] Some sense of the relative economic importance of foreign arms sales to the suppliers' economies can be seen in the following table showing arms exports as a percentage of total exports.

U.S. Arms Sales

In the United States, defense budget cuts mean fewer contracts for the defense industry. Before the Gulf war, Defense Secretary Richard Cheney told the U.S. armed services to prepare for defense budget cuts of up to $180 billion for fiscal years 1992-1994. These cuts translate into as much as five percent in real terms.[16] Ultimately, cuts may be deeper as concern about the federal deficit grows and defense is increasingly seen as an unpopular form of spending. The impact of the Gulf war on overall military spending will probably be minimal, although it may result in reapportioning funds within the budget between certain items.[17]

During the military buildup under the Reagan Administration, many defense contractors grew rapidly, incurring large debts in the process. Cuts in the defense budget have left the industry facing excess capacity.[18] Some companies have switched to civil contracts, space technology, and non-defense electronics. Others have turned to foreign sales to help boost domestic production. By 1989, for example, Sikorsky, which produces helicopters, was receiving 25 percent of its revenues from exports, up from six percent in 1984.[19] In addition, the U.S. arms industry is a large employer; Maryland, for example, will lose 187,000 jobs due to defense cuts. At the same time, however, American foreign policy prohibits the administration from pursuing unrestrained arms sales to make up for lost revenues.

Arms Exports
As a Percentage of
Total Exports

COUNTRY	1983	1984	1985	1986	1987	1988
USSR	21.06	21.20	19.95	19.69	19.68	19.30
USA	5.78	4.86	5.20	4.18	5.03	4.40
China	6.74	7.23	2.15	3.83	5.80	6.50
France	4.52	4.20	4.72	3.20	1.75	1.10
UK	1.96	1.81	1.08	1.30	1.59	.50
FRG	1.18	1.63	.47	.25	.61	.10
Brazil	.59	2.31	1.36	1.20	2.28	1.10

Source: United States Arms Control and Disarmament Agency, *World Military Expenditures and Arms Transfers 1989* (Washington, DC: Government Printing Office, June 1990).

Following the Gulf war, the administration expressed a desire to reintroduce Export-Import Bank guarantees for arms sales to Middle Eastern nations. By providing loans and loan guarantees through the Ex-Im Bank, the government could subsidize its arms sales to allies in the region. In 1974, this practice was terminated due to strong opposition in Congress. Congress has been quick to voice criticism of the administration's proposal. Opposition is rooted in the belief that arms sales should be based on strategic and political considerations, not economic concerns. Some congressional leaders point out the hypocritical nature of the administration's arms control policy which seeks to control the transfer of weapons -- especially unconventional and high technology conventional arms -- to the region while, at the same time, attempting to commercialize the sale of American weapons.[20] At the same time, however, most members of Congress support those defense industries located in their district or state.

Soviet Arms Sales

The Soviet Union was the leading exporter of major weapons to the Third World in the period from 1984-1988.[21] However, in early 1989, President Gorbachev announced that the Soviet Union intended to reduce defense expenditures by one-seventh and arms production by one-fifth.[22] Secrecy surrounds most of the arms transfer policies of the Soviet Union. The nature of the Soviet system, to date, is such that arms transfer decisions are made without the cumbersome process of parliamentary approval common in some western states. This puts the Soviets in a better position to take advantage of unforeseen opportunities more quickly.

Some details of Soviet arms transfers have now become public. The Soviet share of the international arms trade in 1989 was 28 percent, with 32 percent of those arms going to Third World countries. Twenty-five percent of the annual output of the Soviet arms industry is believed to be exported.[23] In the period from 1985-89, 54 percent of all Soviet arms transfers to the Third World went to the Middle East and South Asia, albeit often at subsidized rates for economically weak but strategically important allies such as Syria and Afghanistan.[24] Superpower competition in the Third World, the special status of the military industry, the dependence of local regimes on the Soviet Union, and the increasing profitability of arms transfers have all been motivations for Soviet sales.[25]

A growing attraction for Soviet arms sales is hard currency. In March 1990, Soviet arms manufacturers attended an international military show in Kuala Lumpur with the hope of increasing their hard currency sales.[26]

Faced with growing military surpluses from a reduction of commitments in Eastern Europe, the Soviets have even begun negotiations for the sale of military technology to their longtime rival the PRC.[27]

Like the United States, the Soviet Union also faces the dilemma of reconciling its Middle East arms sales policy with its strategic goals in the region. In May 1990, Chief of the Soviet Foreign Ministry's International Organizations Department, Andrey Kozyrev, stated that "understandable commercial interests and the states [sic] legitimate concern about dependable security" are perpetuating the existing arms trade.[28]

West European Arms Sales

Until the Gulf war, each of the three key arms producing West European countries -- France, Britain, and West Germany -- had different attitudes toward arms transfers to the Middle East. The net result was that economic motives played a more important role than in the U.S. case.

France was the third leading exporter of major weapons to the Third World in 1982-1989, after the USSR and the United States.[29] By region, in 1986-1989, France accounted for 8.8 percent of the total value of arms sales to the Middle East and South Asia.[30] Between 1982 and 1985, France had almost 15,000 defense contracts with countries in the region. This number fell to just over 6,000 contracts between 1986 and 1989.[31]

In the mid-1970s, France began supplying arms to Iraq. An initial transfer of helicopters was followed by Mirage F1 aircraft in 1978. France also helped Iraq begin construction of the nuclear research reactor that Israel destroyed in 1981. By this time, Iraq owed France some 15 billion francs, a strong economic incentive for France to continue assisting Iraq in its war with Iran.[32]

France produces most of its own defense systems, including nuclear and conventional weaponry. This is a costly practice, and in order to make up for insufficient domestic demand France maintains a large export market. This explains the pressure within France to increase arms exports in response to the need to reduce the budget deficit.[33] Since the end of the Gulf war, more discriminatory arms sales policies are being established to combat criticism of French sales to Iraq and other aggressor nations.

From 1982 to 1989, Britain was the fourth largest exporter of major weapons to the Third World.[34] In July 1988, Britain announced a major arms agreement with Saudi Arabia to provide it with aircraft, ships, and construction projects. The value of the package was estimated at $29 billion. The agreement followed a 1986 agreement between the two countries in which Britain supplied Saudi Arabia with 72 Tornado aircraft.[35] Like France, Britain's arms transfer policy is based on a number of factors, including employment, balance of payments, and autonomy considerations. Similarly, Britain does not have the domestic demand to maintain competitive unit costs for arms unless domestic sales are supplemented by exports. This is likely to be exacerbated by reductions in the British military establishment as a result of planned conventional force reductions in Europe and the Soviet Union. Along these lines, Britain, France, and West Germany have sought to encourage a European defense industry in order to spread research and development costs and to produce systems they could not have afforded alone.[36]

From 1982 to 1989, West Germany ranked seventh in exports of major weapons to the Third World.[37] It also supplied approximately the same dollar amount in arms exports to the industrial world, unlike France and the United Kingdom.[38] Between 1984 and 1988, West Germany exported $3.6 billion in constant 1985 prices of major weapons to the Third World and $3.1 billion of major weapons to the industrial world. Should sales to the latter decline, the German defense industry may seek other potential buyers.[39] In theory, Germany has highly restrictive arms export laws preventing it from exporting weapons to regions of conflict. Germany does, however, permit conventional arms sales through arms consortia of which it is a member -- such as Euromissile. This allows German weapons to be sold without Germany itself taking the lead in the sale.[40]

West German exports to the Middle East and South Asia have come under harsh criticism, with charges that equipment for chemical and nuclear weapons production have been transferred to a number of regional states. Such exports are illegal in Germany, and Bonn had agreed to prevent them through its membership in the London Suppliers Group (restricting nuclear exports), the Australia Group (restricting chemical exports), and the Missile Technology Control Regime (restricting missile exports).[41] Currently, the German government is investigating whether the country's third largest chemical company, Bayer AG, sold equipment to Iran in 1987 that might have been used to produce poisonous gas.[42] Furthermore, the former head of the West German firm Imhausen-Chemie, Juergen Hippenstiel-Imhausen, was convicted in June 1990, of selling Libya materials with which to construct its chemical weapons plant at Rabta.[43] Using the plans originally supplied for the Rabta plant, Libya has begun construction of a second facility at Sabha. Hippenstiel-Imhausen has testified that he suspected his exports conflicted with West German export laws but proceeded with his sales because he "didn't want to lose the business."[44]

East European Arms Sales

Eastern European countries have engaged in numerous arms transfers to the Third World, often serving as a proxy supplier for the USSR. From 1982 to 1989, Czechoslovakia was the eighth leading exporter of weapons to the Third World.[45] As the Soviet Union and United States cut back on their military might, arms buyers may continue to turn to suppliers in Eastern Europe. Countries such as Czechoslovakia, Hungary, and Poland, that have traditionally supplied weaponry to the Soviet Union are now turning to Third World countries to maintain sales.[46] Eastern European arms sales to the Third World peaked during the period from 1982-1986, but decreased considerably toward the end of the decade.[47] Post-Gulf war demand may now boost sales from these countries.

By far the strongest motivation for emerging Eastern European nations to sell arms will be to generate hard currency. Many of these states face severe economic problems, in part because they lack the resources and funds necessary to convert arms production facilities into civilian manufacturing. For most of them, the only means to acquire such resources is through arms sales to the Third World.

This problem is most evident in Czechoslovakia, a country that for generations has been regarded as the engineering mecca of Eastern Europe and whose arms industry has a long and impressive record. Although President Vaclav Havel has denounced his country's arms export policy and vowed to end arms sales and convert weapons production facilities to non-lethal production, the Czech government will find it extremely difficult, if not impossible, to do so. Most of the arms industry is located in Slovakia and the impact on employment of shutting down arms production would be unacceptable. Czechoslovakia is reportedly considering sales of T-72 tanks to both Syria and Iran.[48] President Havel discussed using the earnings from these sales to cover the cost of the infrastructure conversions, but has little power to enforce such a drastic and problematic change. Unless they receive foreign aid to help in similar conversions, Czechoslovakia and its neighbors may find it necessary to continue to sell arms to the Middle East and elsewhere in the Third World.[49]

With the relaxation in the West of high technology export controls to formerly communist regimes through the Coordinating Committee for Multilateral Export Controls (COCOM), Eastern European countries may provide a new transfer point for high technology goods to pass to the

Middle East unless new control agreements are established. For example, states may be able to use East European front companies to acquire unconventional weapons technology denied them by U.S. or European export laws.[50] The de-control of many COCOM regulations includes krytrons, industrial furnaces, spin machines used to make uranium gas centrifuges, and vacuum pumps, all of which Iraq acquired or was trying to obtain before the war to further its nuclear weapons program.[51] The problem was summarized by Representative Samuel Gejdenson of the House Foreign Affairs Committee: "This points to the need for Cocom to start looking at North-South proliferation. The real national security risk we now face is Iran, Iraq, Syria and Libya."[52]

Another potentially disturbing development involves the transfer of East European personnel. As economic disruption grows in Eastern Europe, well-trained cadres of unemployed engineers and scientists may be tempted to share their knowledge, for a price, with countries seeking arms technology and defense expertise.

Chinese Arms Sales

China's greatest motivation for selling arms to the region is the need for hard currency to pay for the "Four Modernizations" process, which began in the early 1980s and centered on improving agriculture, industry, science and technology, and national defense. To play a more active role in international politics and economics, especially in dealing with the United States, China needs foreign currency. According to one analysis: "The more relations improve, and the more Washington allows military technology to be sold to China, the more the Chinese need hard currency to pay for it; and the most direct way for China to obtain currency is to sell arms."[53] Increasingly, China is turning to the lucrative market in the Middle East and is working hard to build a strong economic relationship with the oil-rich countries in the Persian Gulf.[54]

Decisions on arms sales are made within the complex structure of the Chinese military command, the government, and the weapons-exporting corporations. "[The] locus of decisionmaking on arms sales resides in specialized corporations that exercise nearly autonomous authority because of their insulation within the system and their personal connections." Further, "the political-military system is not organized to convey, to the officials and companies who negotiate weapon sales, detailed instructions concerning issues such as what might constitute defensive weapons, constraints on specific weapons, regional stability, and domestic interference."[55]

Arguments for the economic and political benefits generated by Chinese arms exports, therefore, are not effectively countered by the implications of such sales. In the international arena, sales are justified by claiming that conventional arms in limited quantities "cannot upset regional military balances or political stability." Domestically, sales are seen as "mutually beneficial" in terms of technology transfers and the increase of Chinese political influence.[56]

China was the fourth leading exporter of major weapons to the Third World in 1984-1988.[57] The PRC gained attention in 1982 when its exports grew between two and three hundred percent.[58] In the period from 1984-1988, 90 percent of Chinese arms deliveries went to the Middle East and South Asia, primarily to Iran and Iraq. The Chinese, criticized by United States officials for their export policies, especially missile exports, defended themselves by indicating the political utility of the sales.[59] For example, China's sale in March 1988, of CSS-II ballistic missiles to Saudi Arabia paid off in the establishment of formal diplomatic relations between the two in July 1990.[60]

Since the end of the Gulf war, there has been increasing concern in Washington about rumored Chinese missile sales to Syria and Pakistan. While no missiles have been delivered to either at present, numerous reports followed the cease fire declaring that China had revived a formerly defunct deal with Syria for 600 km range M-9 SSMs, and was negotiating a deal with Pakistan for the sale of 300 km range M-11 SSMs.[61] China has repeatedly refused to yield to American pressure to halt such sales; yet at the same time, it joined the other permanent members of the UN Security Council in July 1991, in support of a zone free of mass destruction weapons in the Middle East.[62] Beijing appears to be engaging in a delicate balancing act between placating the concerns of the industrialized world while garnering influence with, and earning hard currency from states in the Middle East.

Economic Constraints on Arms Purchases

In addition to the economics of supply and demand for weaponry in the Middle East, the economic constraints on individual countries in the region will affect their decisions on arms purchases. The Gulf war has left each of the major actors in the Middle East with financial burdens that will limit their ability to buy new supplies of arms in the absence of increased military aid. An examination of each country shows that while they all may wish to rearm, none will find it financially easy to do so.[63]

Seven months of Iraqi occupation and the latter's scorched earth policy during the war have left the Kuwaiti oil-production facilities and Kuwait City in a shambles. Estimates predict that it will take at least eighteen months and between $45 and $60 billion for reconstruction of the Kuwaiti oil industry and other infrastructure damaged by Iraq. Kuwait has also promised $10 billion to help the allied coalition cover the costs of the war.[64] Kuwait will need to use its $100 billion in foreign assets as collateral for loans. If it places a priority on reconstruction, it will have less money to buy arms.

Saudi Arabia, like Kuwait, will need loans to cover its war costs. The Saudi government's pledged support, and funds spent as part of its war effort add up to $48 billion. Since it entered the war with $60-70 billion in reserves and continues to support Egypt and Syria financially, Saudi Arabia will not be able to spend money as freely as in the past. The Saudis have a number of ways to cover their costs besides loans. They can run down foreign currency levels, order state-owned corporations to increase their government dividends, slow down payment on bills, or simply decrease the amount they spend.[65]

Egypt faces a grave economic situation. The war affected three of Egypt's four main sources of revenue. Tourism in Egypt dropped by about 70 percent, equating to a loss of between $1.5 and $3 billion. Egypt also lost between $7-8 billion in remittances from nationals working in Iraq and Kuwait who were forced to leave. Traffic in the Suez Canal was greatly reduced by the war, translating into a loss of at least $1 million per day. A rise in oil prices during the war may have brought Egypt an additional $70-100 million, but this sum does not come close to offsetting the country's losses. To face its increased economic burdens, Egypt is relying, in part, on debt forgiveness. So far, the United States and its allies have agreed to forgive half of Egypt's $20.2 billion debt.[66]

Jordan has also suffered severe economic disruption as a result of the seven month conflict. Ninety-five percent of its agricultural exports had been to the Gulf states, as had been a majority of its manufactured exports. Shipping out of Aqaba, Jordan's only port, was greatly reduced, and the return of Jordanian workers from Kuwait and Iraq led to the loss of foreign currency remittances. Jordan also incurred some major costs in dealing with the flow of refugees across its border with Iraq. These costs have all tallied to approximately $1 billion. Perhaps the greatest financial impasse for Jordan has been the lack of foreign support due to its pro-Iraqi stance during the war. Saudi Arabia has refused to restore its preferential oil sales to Jordan, and American aid -- $50 million, broken down into $30 million in economic aid and $20 million in military assistance -- has been halted.[67] King Hussein has tried to make amends with the coalition members, but even if aid is restored, the Jordanian economy will face a slow recovery.

Unlike Jordan, Syria has not suffered financially from the Gulf war. Rather, the crisis gave Syrian President Assad an opportunity to obtain much-needed financial assistance in return for his cooperation in the anti-Iraq coalition. During the war, Syria received $500 million in promised development projects from Saudi Arabia.[68] Nevertheless, Syria's financial situation remains tenuous since it can no longer rely on the Soviet Union for military or other economic support.

Israel faced both direct and indirect costs as a result of the war. Estimates place Israeli losses at about $3.5 billion. These losses can be broken down as follows: $1.4 billion in lost production, $700 million in lost tourism, $400 million in supplementary military expenditures, $400 million in increased fuel prices, and at least $600 million in damages to housing and businesses as a result of Scud attacks. Furthermore, the war greatly weakened the Israeli economy; according to Finance Minister Yitzhaq Modai, "since August 1990, the Israeli economy has stopped growing."[69] Israel, however, has been able to make up for some of its losses through increased foreign aid. Even before the war, Israel faced great economic burdens in trying to absorb the influx of thousands of Soviet Jews. The United States has recently granted Israel $400 million in loan guarantees to offset the costs associated with the absorption of immigrants, although the Israeli government has argued that this sum does not come close to meeting these costs.[70]

Turkey, which has kept itself largely outside Middle East politics for many years, has reemerged as an important actor in the region due to its involvement in the war. Like Israel, this country may have faced economic costs, but gained politically from the conflict. Turkish losses from the war total between $3 and $6 billion.[71] The majority of these losses came from lost trade during the embargo against Iraq. On the other hand, however, the United States agreed to increase its foreign aid to Turkey from $533 to $700 million.[72]

Iran's costs during the war were minimal. However, Iran still faces huge reconstruction costs from its war with Iraq. Estimates of the cost of rebuilding the country's infrastructure and oil facilities are between $1 and $2 billion a year for the next few years.[73] Oil prices will be the main determinant of the pace at which Iran, OPEC's third largest producer, will recover.

At this point, there are few estimates on the overall damage incurred by Iraq during the war. One source estimates that rebuilding Iraq might cost over $100 billion.[74] Iraq faced severe financial burdens before the war due to debts incurred during the Iran-Iraq war; the post-war domestic uprising and the continued embargo will further delay reconstruction.

The price of oil will determine the extent to which the Arab members of OPEC will be able to use oil revenues to fund the region's recovery. Unless oil prices rise sharply and unexpectedly, even the rich Arab countries will have less money to spend on arms than in the past. This may be a more practical constraint on an unbridled arms race than restrictive supplier regimes.

Notes

1. Anthony Cave Brown, editor, *Dropshot: The American Plan for War With the Soviet Union in 1957* (New York: Dial Press, 1978), p. 156.

2. See Jeffrey Boutwell, "The Middle East Arms Bazaar," paper prepared for the American Academy of Arts and Sciences, June 1991.

3. For a pragmatic and bipartisan discussion of post-war U.S. Gulf policy, see *After the Storm: Challenges for America's Middle East Policy*, Report of the Washington Institute's Strategic Study Group (Washington, D.C.: Washington Institute for Near East Policy, 1991).

4. See Jim McGee, "Syria Said to Help Neutralize Terrorist Threat," *Washington Post*, March 3, 1991.

5. Esther B. Fein, "Office In Moscow Opened by Israelis," *New York Times*, January 4, 1991.

6. Peter Waldman and John J. Fialka, "Israel Explores Purchasing a Soviet Nuclear Reactor," *Wall Street Journal*, May 8, 1991.

7. See Bill Gertz, "Soviet Rebels Storm an A-Bomb Facility," *Washington Times*, February 19, 1990.

8. Some Indians, including communists, are now questioning Moscow's intentions. See Barbara Crossette, "Gorbachev in India to Reaffirm Ties," *New York Times*, November 19, 1988. See also Ross H. Munro, "Superpower Rising," *Time*, April 3, 1989, p. 14.

9. For details on the attack, see "U.S. Jets Hit Terrorist Centers in Libya," *New York Times*, April 15, 1986. The U.S.-run installation on Lampedusa was not damaged. See Judith Miller, "Italian Island, a Libyan Target, Escapes Unscathed," *New York Times*, April 16, 1986.

10. France, Italy, Portugal, and Spain have proposed a conference on Security and Cooperation in the Mediterranean to follow the model of the original CSCE concept. Hopefully, this could lead to a "Mediterranean Act" laying down rules of behavior for the region, and eventually including Middle East countries. See *After the Storm: Challenges for America's Middle East Policy*, p. 10.

11. See Boutwell, "The Middle East Arms Bazaar," p. 8.

12. See ibid., p. 2.

13. John W. Lewis, Hua Di, and Xue Litai, "Beijing's Defense Establishment: Solving the Arms-Export Enigma," *International Security*, Spring 1991, Vol. 15, No. 4, p. 105.

14. Anthony H. Cordesman, "After the Gulf War: The World Arms Trade and Its Arms Races in the 1990s," May 19, 1991, unpublished paper, p. 4.

15. Between 1986 and 1989, this region accounted for 66 percent of the total value of all Third World arms transfer agreements. France, Britain, West Germany, and Italy together accounted for 16 percent of the arms transfer agreements; the Soviet Union and United States accounted for 36 and 19 percent of transfers agreements, respectively; other suppliers made up the remaining 28 percent. Richard F. Grimmett, *Trends in Conventional Arms Transfers to the Third World by Major Supplier, 1982-1989* (Washington, D.C.: Congressional Research Service, 1990), p. 12 and p. 17.

16. Karen Pennar and Michael J. Mandel, "The Peace Economy," *Business Week*, December 11, 1989, p. 52.

17. See Boutwell, p. 2.

18. Mary H. Cooper, "Can Defense Contractors Survive Peace?" *Congressional Quarterly Editorial Research Reports*, September 29, 1989, p. 544.

19. Pennar and Mandel, "The Peace Economy," p. 54.

20. "Selling Weapons Abroad," *Washington Post*, May 13, 1991.

21. *SIPRI Yearbook 1989: World Armaments and Disarmaments* (New York: Oxford University Press, 1989), p. 198.

22. "...and for Soviet Defense Expenditures," *International Defense Review*, February 1989, p. 137.

23. See Andrei V. Shoumikhin, "Soviet Policy Toward Arms Transfers to the Middle East," in Shelley A. Stahl and Geoffrey Kemp, editors, *Arms Control and Weapons Proliferation in the Middle East and South Asia* (New York: St. Martin's Press, 1992 forthcoming).

24. Grimmett, *Trends in Conventional Arms Transfers to the Third World by Major Supplier, 1982-1989.*

25. See Shoumikhin, "Soviet Policy Toward Arms Transfers to the Middle East."

26. "Soviet Weapons in the Third World," *Proceedings*, U.S. Naval Institute, June 1990, p. 107.

27. Daniel Southerland, "China Seeks Technology from Soviet Military," *Washington Post*, July 17, 1990.

28. "Kozyrev Calls For Limiting Arms Trade," Tass, 1127 GMT, 16 May 1990, translated in *FBIS-SOV*, May 17, 1990, p. 3.

29. Grimmett, p. 56.

30. Ibid., p. 31.

31. Ibid., p. 42.

32. See John Chipman, "Europe and the Iran-Iraq War," in Efraim Karsh, editor, *The Iran-Iraq War: Impact and Implications* (London: Macmillan Press, 1989), p. 217.

33. Ian Davidson, "Pressure Grows in France for Defence Cuts," *Financial Times*, July 10, 1990.

34. Grimmett, p. 56.

35. See Susan F. Rasky, "Britain Signs Deal With Saudis, Replacing U.S. as Big Arms Supplier," *New York Times*, July 9, 1990; and Robert Pear, "Saudi Finesse on Arms," *New York Times*, July 11, 1988.

36. *SIPRI Yearbook 1989*, p. 204.

37. Grimmett, p. 56.

38. *SIPRI Yearbook 1989*, p. 198.

39. Ibid.

40. See Andrew J. Pierre, *The Global Politics of Arms Sales* (Princeton: Princeton University Press, 1982), pp. 109-116.

41. For details on these and other arms control and supplier regimes, See Chapter 7.

42. "Bonn Probes Firm's Sale of Gas Chemical to Iran," *Washington Times*, January 12, 1990.

43. Serge Schmemann, "German Is Jailed in Sale to Libya," *New York Times*, June 28, 1990.

44. Bill Gertz, "2nd Chemical Arms Plant Spied in Libya," *Washington Times*, June 18, 1990.

45. Grimmett, p. 56.

46. "East Bloc Arms Marketing," *Aviation Week and Space Technology*, May 28, 1990, p. 13.

47. Cordesman, "After the Gulf War: The World Arms Trade and Its Arms Races in the 1990s," p. 11.

48. See Mary Battiata, "Czechoslovakia Considers Selling Tanks to Syria, Iran," *Washington Post*, May 7, 1991.

49. "Hard-Pressed Czechs Retain Arms Trade," *New York Times*, May 3, 1991.

50. John J. Fialka and Eduardo Lachica, "Easing of Technology Export Controls May Boost Arms Smuggling in Mideast," *Wall Street Journal*, June 19, 1990.

51. Gary Milhollin, "Attention, Nuke-Mart Shoppers," *Washington Post*, July 22, 1990.

52. Fialka and Lachica, "Easing of Technology Export Controls May Boost Arms Smuggling in Mideast."

53. Lewis et al., "Beijing's Defense Establishment: Solving the Arms-Export Enigma," p. 107.

54. Mushtak Parker, "Oriental Attractions," *The Middle East*, March 1990, p. 45.

55. Lewis et al., pp. 98-99.

56. Ibid., p. 104.

57. *SIPRI Yearbook 1989*, p. 198.

58. Ibid., p. 207. SIPRI noted a doubling of exports while the U.S. Arms Control and Disarmament Agency noted a threefold increase.

59. Ibid., pp. 207-8.

60. See "China, Saudi Arabia Establish Formal Ties," *Washington Post*, July 22, 1990.

61. See John J. Fialka, "Pakistan Seeks Chinese Missile, U.S. Believes," *Wall Street Journal*, April 15, 1991; and Nicholas D. Kristof, "U.S. Feels Uneasy As Beijing Moves To Sell New Arms," *New York Times*, June 10, 1991.

62. See R. Jeffrey Smith, "U.S. to Press China To Halt Missile Sales," *Washington Post*, June 11, 1991; Keith Bradsher, "Baker Warns China Against Selling New Missiles," *New York Times*, June 13, 1991; David Hoffman, "Selling Missile Technology Would Risk U.S. Wrath, Baker Tells

China," *Washington Post*, June 13, 1991; and Sharon Waxman, "Nations Draw Mideast Arms Guidelines," *Washington Post*, July 10, 1991.

63. In the past, Middle Eastern countries have spent a greater percentage of their GNP on arms than countries in other parts of the world. Expenditures on defense (in percentage of GNP) are as follows: Syria and Israel, 10-15 percent; Iraq, 25 percent; Saudi Arabia, 20 percent; Jordan, 12 percent. These figures are high when compared to the 3-4 percent spent by most NATO members. See "Race to be Powerfullest," *The Economist*, February 9, 1991, pp. 22-23.

64. Steven Mufson, "Kuwait Shapes Plans to Rebuild Financial System, Fund Recovery," *Washington Post*, February 27, 1991.

65. Edward Cody, and Steven Mufson, "Saudi Arabia May Seek Bank Loans," *Washington Post*, February 13, 1991.

66. See Steven Greenhouse, "Half of Egypt's $20.2 Billion Debt Being Forgiven by U.S. and Allies," *New York Times*, May 27, 1991.

67. See Guy Gugliotta, "House Foreign Aid Bill Drops Jordan," *Washington Post*, June 20, 1991.

68. James LeMoyne, "Saudis Twist Much Harder Now," *New York Times*, September 22, 1990.

69. "Treasury Estimates Gulf Losses at $3.5 Billion," Tel Aviv, MAARIV, 1 March 1991, translated in *FBIS-NES*, 5 March 1991, p. 40.

70. "Israel to Ask $10 Billion in Loan Guarantees," *Washington Post*, May 6, 1991.

71. Robert S. Greenberger, "Turkey May Reap Major Rewards From Gulf War," *Wall Street Journal*, January 31, 1991.

72. Jonathan C. Randal, "Turkish Leader Bolstered by Role in Gulf Conflict," *Washington Post*, March 3, 1991.

73. Hossein Askari, "Restoring the Gulf's Health," *U.S. News and World Report*, March 18, 1991, pp. 60-61.

74. Ibid., p. 61.

CHAPTER FOUR

Regional Weapons Acquisition and Production

This chapter provides a factual review of the extent and pace of major weapons acquisition, including indigenous production capabilities.

Introduction

The Gulf war alerted the world to the extraordinary quantities of weapons acquired by the states in the Middle East over the past decade. Iraq was an example of a regional state that had amassed a significant arsenal, as well as much of the technology needed to expand and maintain it over time. This distinction is important in that a state that relies entirely on an outside supplier -- as does Syria -- cannot assure the quality and integrity of its arsenal without a guarantee of continued supply from its patron.

The following matrix indicates which of the regional states have progressed beyond importing weapon systems to modifying, producing, and developing their own systems. With regard to mass destruction weapons like nuclear, chemical, and biological, the programs in the Middle East are mostly a combination of indigenous design and production using foreign-supplied technology, as well as some foreign components and expertise.

Nuclear Weapons

In the Middle East, Israel is currently the only state that both possesses nuclear weapons and has the capability to produce them. Israel's nuclear arsenal is believed to contain at least fifty to sixty nuclear weapons.[1] Some of these devices are apparently far more sophisticated and technologically advanced than those used by the United States against Japan in the closing days of World War II.[2] Although Israel has never openly acknowledged the possession of nuclear weapons, it has relied on the veiled threat of their existence to deter the Arab states from a

71

Matrix of Weapons Production by Type

	Indigenous Development and Production	Modification and Co-Production	Import Only
SSMs	Israel India Pakistan	Iraq Egypt Iran	All others
Combat Aircraft	Israel India	Egypt	All others
Tanks	Israel India Pakistan	Egypt	All others
Artillery	Israel India Iran Iraq Pakistan		All others
Warships	Israel India		All others
Small Arms	All major countries		

combined assault.

While Israel's nuclear program is now virtually indigenous, its original technology came from France, which built the Dimona reactor for Israel in the early 1960s. Israel has also used other foreign-supplied items -- such as Norwegian heavy water -- in its nuclear program.

Aside from Israel, Iraq's nuclear weapons program was, prior to the Gulf war, the most advanced in the Middle East. Iraq suffered a major setback in 1981 when Israel bombed its French-supplied Osiraq research reactor, then under construction. Baghdad has remained intent on developing nuclear arms, however, as indicated by the revelations of its secret uranium enrichment facilities using calutrons for electromagnetic isotope separation.[3] This secret program is in addition to Iraq's much-publicized and often successful efforts to obtain nuclear technology illegally from West European and American sources.

Iran and Libya have also sought nuclear weapons in the past. Iran began a nuclear weapons program under the Shah, but the revolutionary government of Ayatollah Khomeini showed little interest in pursuing the program after he came to power in 1979. Following the Iran-Iraq war, however, Iran began a major rearmament program which is likely to have included a renewal of its nuclear weapons research.

By mid-1990, it was estimated that Iran was ten years from a nuclear weapon production capability.[4] At the same time, Tehran had concluded an agreement with the Soviet Union on technical cooperation in, among other fields, nuclear energy.[5] By the spring of 1991, new evidence had emerged pointing to attempts by Iran to acquire essential ingredients for a nuclear weapons program in Western Europe.[6] It is still too early to determine, however, how Iran's nuclear program will respond to the perceived outcomes of the Gulf war. While Iran's interest in nuclear weapons may be revived, its capabilities to pursue this goal will be impaired for many years as a result of its priorities for reconstruction and the lack of capital to purchase technology.

Instead of opting for indigenously developed devices, Libya attempted unsuccessfully to purchase nuclear weapons outright from China in the 1970s, and subsequently from the international black market in arms. Libya has also attempted to acquire nuclear technology by financing the programs of other countries, specifically Pakistan.[7] While its efforts have failed, Libya's leader, Colonel Muammar Qaddafi, has continued to assert his desire for Arab countries to produce nuclear weapons.[8] Libya still does not possess the technology to produce nuclear weapons, and it is unlikely that any other state will provide it with either an assembled weapon or the technology to produce one in the near future.

In the spring of 1991, it was revealed that China was building a nuclear reactor for Algeria. Since this disclosure, Algeria has announced that the reactor will be under IAEA safeguards.[9]

On the Indian subcontinent, a nuclear rivalry exists between India and Pakistan. India is believed to have enough plutonium for 50 to 75 nuclear weapons.[10] In testimony before the Senate Governmental Affairs Committee in May 1989, CIA Director William H. Webster asserted that the evidence suggested India was building a hydrogen bomb.[11]

Pakistan is believed to have enough nuclear material to produce ten to fifteen nuclear weapons.[12] Pakistan has, until recently, been highly dependent on the United States for economic and military assistance. It has, in turn, seen its nuclear program come under close congressional scrutiny in the U.S. and has been the subject of numerous legislative attempts in Washington to curb its growth.[13] American aid to Pakistan was, in fact, suspended in October 1990 when the President was unable to certify, as required by Congress, that Pakistan did not possess a nuclear explosive device.[14]

Chemical and Biological Weapons

Chemical weapons (CW) differ from other munitions because they directly affect living tissue and cause little damage to buildings and other structures. There are four basic types of chemical agents currently used as weapons. First, tissue irritants, such as mustard gas, burn or blister the skin and lungs. Mustard gas can be produced by any country with a modest petrochemical industry.[15] Due to the relative simplicity of the production process and the accessibility of its main components, mustard gas could be an attractive weapon for terrorist organizations, although there is no evidence at this juncture that any such group has used it. Second, blood gases, such as hydrogen cyanide, are chemicals that enter the circulation system through the lungs and block cell respiration. Third, lung irritants, or choking agents, irritate and damage lung tissue. Finally, nerve agents such as tabun, sarin, and soman, interfere with nerve impulse transmission and inhibit breathing and other vital functions.[16]

Iraq is the only country in the region that has admitted to producing chemical weapons, although Iran, Israel, Syria, and Libya are known to produce them as well.[17] Egypt, which used chemical weapons during its involvement in the civil war in Yemen in the 1960s, is believed to be improving its chemical weapons production capability by acquiring a chemical plant from a Swiss firm.[18] Both India and Pakistan are now categorized by the U.S. administration as probably possessing chemical weapons.[19]

Before the Gulf war, Iraq's chemical weapons capabilities were the most advanced in the region. According to CIA Director Webster, Iraq began producing chemical weapons in the early 1980s and accelerated their development during its war with Iran.[20] The first use of chemical weapons against Iranian troops took place in 1983. Iraq also used chemical agents, both lethal and nonlethal, against its own Kurdish population.[21] On April 18, 1991, in accordance with its obligaions under UN Security Council Resolution 687, the Iraqi authorities provided the UN Secretary-General with details on the existence of the Muthanna State Establishment, a major chemical weapons production facility, approximately 80 km northwest of Baghdad and 50 km southwest of Samarra. This is the facility that has been referred to in western media reports as the Samarra facility. At this site, the UN team found mustard gas and organophosphorus nerve agents, types GB and GF, both as bulk agent and in the form of munitions.[22] There was also speculation after Saddam Hussein's speech of April 2, 1990, in which he threatened Israel, that Iraq had acquired binary chemical weapons. UN inspections have revealed, however, that what was referred to as binary weapons were simply a mixture of two nerve agents, and not binary chemical munitions.[23]

Allied bombing during the Gulf war targeted Iraq's known chemical weapons facilities. It can be assumed, therefore, that Iraq's ability to produce these weapons has been severely hampered. The United Nations cease fire resolution requires that Iraq destroy its existing stockpiles of chemical weapons and its chemical weapons facilities. Resolution 687 also calls on Iraq to reaffirm its obligations under the Geneva Protocol of 1925, and maintains the embargo on the transfer to Iraq of all chemical weapons related materials.[24]

Although Iran may have begun a small chemical weapons program before the beginning of its war with Iraq in 1980, its chemical weapons industry was developed mainly to acquire a retaliatory capability against Iraqi chemical attacks during the Iran-Iraq war. The main production plant is near Tehran, and is believed to produce mustard gas, blood agents, and nerve agents.[25] Iran most likely obtained its precursor chemicals from the West, particularly from West Germany and possibly from the United States.[26] Iran used its chemical weapons in the Iran-Iraq war in response to Iraqi use.

Syria's chemical weapons program remains very secretive, although Damascus is believed to have been stockpiling chemical agents since it began their production in the early- to mid-1980s. It is believed that the Syrian chemical weapons program has been assisted by West Germany and other European countries.[27]

Libya was believed to possess the largest chemical weapons production plant in the Third World until a fire allegedly damaged part of the facility on March 14, 1990. The plant, located in Rabta, 100 km South of Tripoli, and built according to West German plans, is a large complex producing mustard gas and possibly the nerve agents sarin and tabun.[28] The extent of the fire's damage, as well as its causes, are unclear.[29] While initial satellite reports indicated that most of the plant was out of commission, later intelligence information did not support this conclusion.[30] Some analysts believe the fire at the Rabta plant may have been self-inflicted, or staged, as Qaddafi attempted to preempt a possible U.S. military strike against his facilities.[31]

Israel is also believed to possess chemical weapons, having first developed them in response to Egyptian possession and use of such weapons in the 1960s against Yemen. Israel is thought to maintain a fairly sophisticated arsenal, including nerve agents, and to have chemical warheads for its surface-to-surface missiles.[32] Israel has consistently refused to acknowledge its possession of chemical weapons.

In contrast to chemical weapons, biological, or as they are sometimes called, bacteriological weapons (BW), are comprised of living organisms that can cause often incurable diseases such as anthrax, plague, and tularemia.[33] Only tiny amounts of agent are necessary in order to create widespread infection and death.[34] Biological weapons have the potential to be much more deadly than chemical weapons, and, according to CIA Director Webster, yield the widest area coverage per pound per payload of any weapon system in existence.[35]

In March 1991, the Director of U.S. Naval Intelligence stated that Iraq had, prior to the war, and Syria has offensive biological weapons capabilities, and that at least five other states have biological weapons programs.[36] In 1989, an Israeli official stated that the Iraqis had developed a military capacity without having manufactured biological warfare agents, and that less-advanced Syrian biological research existed as well.[37] Libya reportedly also has attempted to buy information on biological warfare.[38]

Iraq admitted to UN inspectors in August 1991 that it had a biological weapons research facility at Salman Pak, but denied having any biological weapons.[39] The Salman Pak facility was heavily targeted by allied bombing during the Gulf war; Iraq's biological weapons are slated for destruction under Resolution 687.

Advances in biotechnology are also making possible the eventual mass production of toxins for weapons use. These are chemical substances found in living organisms that can be reproduced with genetic engineering techniques. The common example is rattlesnake venom -- an organic toxin, that if mass produced could act like a chemical weapon, and for which there is no antidote. According to Dr. Barry J. Erlick, Senior Biological Warfare Analyst with the U.S. Army, some toxins, such as those derived from some shellfish and botulinal toxins, have lethality rates of 50 and 60 percent with potency from 1000 to 10,000 times greater than some nerve gases.[40] Research into toxin production can be disguised as legitimate research into a potential vaccine against the agent. According to Dr. Erlick, "Most production facilities utilizing microorganisms, including pharmaceutical plants and even breweries, can be converted to produce biological or toxin agents in a matter of hours, with modest prior provision."[41] The development of toxin weapons represents a dangerous blurring of the distinction between chemical and biological agents.

Surface-to-Surface Missiles (SSMs) and Combat Aircraft

Surface-to-surface missiles and long-range combat aircraft are the two most likely instruments to be used for the delivery of nuclear, chemical, biological, or conventional ordnance to targets removed from the battle front.

There are significant differences between the delivery capabilities of SSMs and combat aircraft. Combat aircraft can carry larger, more diversified payloads than SSMs and, depending on the sub-systems, can deliver it more accurately. Aircraft are more flexible than missiles, performing multiple missions such as close air support, air defense, and deep strike. In addition, they can be used more than once, and they can be recalled or redirected to new targets of opportunity in the event of a sudden change in the battlefield scenario. They can be more easily protected on the ground because they can be moved around quickly, making them less vulnerable than SSMs to certain types of preemptive attack.

Ballistic missiles, on the other hand, have unique features that make them particularly attractive for certain missions in the Middle East and

South Asia. Because of their high speed, SSMs are not easily countered by enemy anti-air capabilities, although they are not invulnerable, as demonstrated by the successful use of the Patriot system during the Gulf war. They do not require highly trained and expensive pilots and navigators, nor do they require long concrete runways, which are vulnerable to interdiction. They can be located in, and fired from hardened silos or, if mobile, can be rapidly redeployed. Since SSMs are unmanned vehicles, they pose no risk of having air crews captured and used as pawns in political gamesmanship.

In comparison to aircraft, the unit cost of an SSM is likely to be much lower. A missile, however, can only be used once and most missiles currently in regional arsenals are relatively inaccurate. Both of these factors tend to degrade the military effectiveness of missiles unless they carry a nuclear or other high-yield warhead. In short, the multiplicity of functions, flexibility, accuracy, and extended command and control of aircraft are sacrificed for reduced operational costs, invulnerability to defense mechanisms, and psychological impact of missiles.

Surface-to-Surface Missile Proliferation

In the Middle East, Israel, Egypt, Iran, Iraq, Libya, Saudi Arabia, Syria, and Yemen all possess SSMs, while in South Asia, both India and Pakistan have developed and tested indigenous ballistic missiles.[42] The most common SSM in regional inventories is the Soviet-designed Scud-B. This missile can carry a 1000 kg payload to a range of 300 km with an estimated circular error probable (CEP) of 900 meters.[43] The Scud-B has found its way into the arsenals of Egypt, Iran, Iraq, Libya, Syria, Yemen, and Algeria.[44] In addition, some 1000 Scuds have been provided to the Afghan Army by the Soviet Union.[45] (See Appendix I for tables and maps showing SSM distribution and ranges. See Appendix II for a summary of SSM use in combat.)

Israel has by far the most sophisticated missile arsenal and production capability in the Middle East. Working originally with the French, Israel developed the Jericho I with a range of 450 km and a payload of 450-680 kg.[46] The Jericho II, believed to be first deployed in the mid-1970s, has a range of 640 km and is also believed to carry a nuclear warhead weighing approximately 100 kg.[47] A spin-off of the Jericho II, referred to in the press as the Jericho II or Jericho II-B, has been successfully tested to 800 km and is said to have a maximum range of up to 1440 km, putting both Baghdad and Tehran within Israeli range.[48] A possible test launch of the Jericho IIB may have taken place on September 14, 1989, when a 1300 km range missile is reported to have fallen in the Mediterranean, 400 km north of the Libyan city of Bengazi.[49]

Israel is also aggressively pursuing a space program that could easily be converted into a long-range ballistic missile program. On September 19, 1988, Israel launched its first satellite, the Ofeq-1, making it the eighth nation in the world to have achieved such a feat.[50] The rocket, named Shavit, was launched in the opposite direction from most space launches in order to avoid passing over Arab territory. On April 2, 1990, Israel put the 160 kg Ofeq-2, its second satellite, into orbit.[51] Depending on the estimates, an Israeli missile based on the Shavit could have a range from 5200 to 7200 km, both widely sufficient to hit Moscow and all targets within the Middle East.[52]

Israel is working on a new short-range rocket under production by Israel Aircraft Industries, the MAR-350, which was slated for completion by the end of 1989. The Israeli arsenal includes the American Lance, with a range of 100 km and a payload of 225 kilograms. Israel also produces the Have Nap, or Popeye, air-to-surface missile, which is being purchased by the U.S. Air Force for its strategic and tactical aircraft. The Have Nap is television-guided, carries a 340 kg warhead, and has a range of 80 nautical kilometers.[53]

Egypt, which had purchased FROG rockets and Scud-B missiles from the Soviet Union, has taken part in development programs to modify or replace these weapons. With French assistance, Egypt developed the SAKR-80 to replace its FROG-7s.[54] Along with Iraq, it took part in the Argentina-initiated Condor missile program which began in the mid-1980s. This program, using technology smuggled from West Germany and Italy, attempted to develop a ballistic missile with a range of over 900 km.[55] Egypt has also cooperated with North Korea on a modified version of the Scud-B. This indigenous version slightly increased the missile's range.[56]

Iraq's pre-war missile capability was extensive. Prior to the war, the Iraqi arsenal contained Soviet Scud-Bs and FROGs, and two Iraqi variants of the Scud-B -- the 640 km range al-Husayn, and the 900 km range al-Abbas. During the Gulf war, Iraq fired 81 modified Scuds, most, if not all, of which were al-Husayns. Fifty-three of these were directed at Saudi Arabia and the Gulf states, while 40 were directed at Israel.[57] All Iraqi missiles with a range over 150 km are to be destroyed under Resolution 687.

Iraq's missile development program had been active throughout the last few years. In early December 1989, Iraq test-fired a 48 ton, three stage,

25 meter long, satellite launching vehicle named Al-Abid. At the same time, Iraq claimed it had "come through the most complicated and important stages in the development and production of two different SSM systems, each of which has a 2,000 km range."[58] Both the satellite launching vehicle, the Al-Abid, and the missile system, named Tammouz-I, appeared to be little more than a number of Scud-B engines strapped together -- an ingenious but unsophisticated development.[59] However, despite its low accuracy, such a modified Scud system could reach all Israeli population centers, and many Arab capitals as well.

As noted above, Iraq was also believed to be involved in the formerly Argentine-Egyptian project to develop the Condor II ballistic missile.[60] Even though Egypt and Argentina have pulled out of the project, the evidence indicates that Iraq continued to push forward with the Condor II at its Saad-16 complex with the aid of German scientists and Italian loans.[61] The Iraqis were finally forced to give up the project due to a lack of sufficient funds. New questions have been raised since the end of the Gulf war, however, about the possibility that the Condor II project might continue in Argentina and whether new missiles could eventually be transferred to Iraq or Egypt.[62]

Iran also possesses Scud-B missiles, apparently acquired from North Korea.[63] Iran is producing a number of shorter-range unguided rockets, the 40 km range Oghab or Eagle (reported to be a modified Chinese Type-83 273mm rocket), and the 90 km Nazeat, as well as the 200 km range ballistic missile known as the Iran-130, produced with Chinese assistance.[64] In March 1990, Iran announced the testing of a 45 km range missile named Fajr-3 which, according to Tehran, "has reached the stage of mass production."[65]

Syria maintains an arsenal of Soviet FROG-7, SS-21, and Scud-B ballistic missiles. Syria was unsuccessful in its attempt to purchase the Soviet SS-23 in 1987.[66] In November 1989, the U.S. expressed concern over reports that China might be arranging to sell medium-range M-9 missiles, or the technology to make them, to Middle Eastern countries. Further reports surfaced at the end of 1989 that China was negotiating with Syria to sell it M-9 missiles. These allegations were dismissed by China as "utterly groundless."[67] New allegations have arisen over sales of Chinese M-9s to Syria following the Gulf war. Syria has also purchased North Korean modified Scuds and is working out a large arms deal with the Soviet Union that may include missiles.[68]

In spite of its lack of an indigenous missile industry, Saudi Arabia's missile arsenal is one of the most imposing in the Arab world. Its purchase in March 1988 of about 50 nuclear-capable Chinese CSS-II ballistic missiles helped to bring the issue of missile proliferation to the attention of the international community.[69] The missiles have given Saudi Arabia the ability to threaten Iraq, Iran, and Israel.[70] While Saudi Arabia's missiles, with a range up to 2700 kilometers, may be among the most threatening in the region in terms of reach, Saudi Arabia is believed to have acquired them for deterrent purposes. Following the accounts of the purchase, the Saudis made a number of concessions to the United States in this regard, such as agreeing to a range limit of approximately 1900 km, as well as signing and ratifying the Nuclear Non-Proliferation Treaty.[71]

In South Asia, India has developed its own SSM capability with the short-range Prithvi, and the Agni, an intermediate-range missile. The Agni, a two stage, 14-ton, 19 meter long rocket, was successfully tested on May 22, 1989, to a range of approximately 960 km, although it is believed to have a potential range of over 2500 km, and a payload capacity of 1000 kg.[72] India claims that the Agni is the result of indigenous engineering efforts. However, technology transfers in the fields of satellite launching vehicles and guidance systems from West Germany, France, and the U.S., are partly responsible for the success of the Agni program.[73]

India's Prithvi is a single-stage, liquid-fueled missile with a range of 250 km and a payload of 1000 kg. The Prithvi was test-fired in February 1988, in September 1989, and again in February 1991. It is slated to begin production in the middle of 1992.[74] Other tactical missiles developed by India are the Trishul and Akash SAM systems, and the Nag anti-tank missile system.

Pakistan has also continued to develop its missile program. In April 1988, Pakistan test-fired a nuclear-capable missile, reportedly developed with Chinese assistance.[75] In February 1989, then-chief of staff of the Pakistan Army, General Mirza Aslam Beg, announced that Pakistan had recently tested two indigenously developed surface-to-surface missiles, named Hatf-I and Hatf-II, with ranges of 80 and 300 km respectively. According to Beg, the missiles have a payload capacity of 500 kg.[76] In April 1990, U.S. intelligence sources believed that China was preparing to sell Pakistan M-9 missiles with a range of 600 km.[77] There has been no evidence that such a sale took place. In early 1991, however, Pakistan apparently received parts of the Chinese M-11 missile system with a range of 290 km and a payload of over 450 kg.[78]

Cruise Missiles. Cruise missiles represent another technological development with the potential to significantly alter the military balance in the Middle

East and South Asia. A cruise missile is an unmanned, self-propelled, guided weapon-delivery vehicle that can be launched from the air, the ground, or the sea, and sustains flight through aerodynamic lift.[79] Unlike ballistic missiles, cruise missiles can be controlled during both their ascent and descent, similar to an aircraft or drone.[80] Due to its versatility and ability to carry a variety of warheads, the cruise missile has both tactical and strategic significance, especially if used in a geographic region like the Middle East.[81]

Only in the last decade have highly accurate cruise missiles with long ranges become an important component of the arsenals of developed countries. Cruise missile technology is rapidly becoming available, through legal and illegal transfers, to both developed and developing countries. The combination of cruise missile technology and more sophisticated guidance systems makes this trend potentially very dangerous. One significant reason for this is the development of the Global Positioning System (GPS) which uses navigation signals from satellites to improve communications. This technology is inexpensive and, if applied to cruise missiles, could result in weapons with long-range accuracies below 100 meters.[82] Furthermore, the commercial applications of the GPS will make restrictions on technology transfer difficult, if not impossible, to obtain. While cost is a significant factor in obtaining cruise missiles, the increased accuracy and maneuverability they provide over ballistic missiles could make their procurement a high priority for states in the Middle East and South Asia.

During the Gulf war, the United States fired about 300 Tomahawk cruise missiles from both ships and submarines. These missiles achieved a hit rate of approximately 85 percent.[83] The success of the American cruise missiles will likely increase the desire of Middle Eastern nations to acquire or develop similar systems.

Advanced Combat Aircraft

Despite all the interest in SSMs and related technology, sales of advanced combat aircraft to the region remain high. There is no regime similar to the MTCR to control the transfer of aircraft to the Middle East, despite the region's virtual total dependence on outside suppliers for combat aircraft. This trade is supplemented by the aircraft modernization market which is attracting new arms exporters such as Brazil, Singapore, and India.[84] These countries sell the parts and technology with which countries can update their aging aircraft and increase their overall perfomance. Modernization offers a much more affordable alternative to purchasing new squadrons of expensive aircraft.

Israel has by far the most sophisticated air force in the Middle East, due in part to its strong ties to the United States. The decision to cancel the Lavi jet program for budgetary reasons resulted in even closer U.S.-Israeli cooperation (the U.S. supported cutting the expensive program that its foreign military aid to Israel had been financing) and the possibility of a co-production arrangement for the F-16.[85] As part of its post-Gulf war arms sales to its allies in the region, the United States is preparing to sell an additional 50 F-15s to Israel.[86]

Following the end of the Iran-Iraq war there were a number of important aircraft purchases in the region. Among the most significant was the sale of 15 Soviet Su-24 bombers to Libya in April 1989. The Su-24D's combat radius is 1285 km, with a maximum payload of 11,022 kg. Announced simultaneously was an agreement to convert a Soviet-made IL-76 transport plane to an aerial refueler.[87] A midair refueling capability for Libya's SU-24s would enable them to reach Israel while flying at low altitudes, thus increasing their chances of successfully evading defensive reconnaissance.[88]

Two of the largest combat aircraft sales to the region were completed between Saudi Arabia and Great Britain in 1986 and 1988. The two agreements, known as Al-Yamanah I and II, signed in February 1986 and July 1988, were worth $10 billion and $20 billion respectively. Included in the deals were 118 Tornado fighter jets, 48 Hawk light fighters, and 80 Blackhawk helicopters.[89] In addition to challenging the United States as Saudi Arabia's primary military supplier, the sale provided Saudi Arabia with the capability to launch offensive strikes against all of its regional adversaries, including Israel.[90]

In response to the Gulf crisis, the Bush Administration proposed to sell Saudi Arabia 48 additional F-15 fighters as part of a $6-8 billion arms package. This follows a significant sale of new weapons, including upgraded AWACS surveillance planes, to Saudi Arabia which was agreed to at the beginning of the crisis.[91] The plan to arm Saudi Arabia also includes a second phase worth $13 billion of American weapons, including F-15s and Apache helicopters. Phase II has been delayed due to opposition from Congress.[92]

Syria's aircraft inventory has also continued to grow. In addition to its fleet of Soviet MiG-23 and MiG-21 fighter aircraft, Syria acquired approximately 15-20 MiG-29s along with additional Su-22 fighter aircraft in 1988.[93] It has also been reported that an unspecified number of MiG-

31 fighters and Ilyushin Il-76 early-warning aircraft, top-of-the-line Soviet systems, were purchased in May 1989.[94] Syria has received Soviet Su-24 fighter bombers, and following the war is working out a large arms package with the Soviet Union that will likely include new advanced combat aircraft. Syria will pay for its new weapons with aid granted by Saudi Arabia and the Gulf states for Syrian participation in the coalition.[95]

Prior to its invasion of Kuwait, Iraq maintained a sophisticated air force with advanced Soviet Mig-29s and French Mirage F-1s. As a result of the Gulf war, however, the Iraqi air force has been left in a shambles. Many planes were destroyed on the ground during allied bombing. In addition, 115 of Iraq's military aircraft, including the majority of its best equipped and most advanced planes, flew to Iran during the war to avoid destruction.[96] The Iranian government has stated that it will not return any of the aircraft.[97]

India's air force includes a variety of Soviet combat aircraft -- the MiG-21, MiG-23, MiG-27, and MiG-29 -- the British Jaguar, the French Mirage 2000, and a number of new Sea Harriers.[98] India purchases the majority of its aircraft from the Soviet Union, but has begun development of its own Light Combat Aircraft (LCA).

Pakistan purchased 40 F-16 aircraft from the United States during the early 1980s, and in June 1989, the United States agreed to sell 60 additional F-16 fighters to Pakistan.[99] Pakistan also purchased 75 modern F-7 fighters from China in March 1989.[100] Most recently, Pakistan contracted with Australia in April 1990 to purchase 50 used Mirages.[101] The U.S. decision in Ocober 1990, to cut military aid to Pakistan because of its nuclear program will likely result in a cancelation of the planned sale of the 60 F-16s agreed to in 1989.

Air Defense: Surface-to-Air Missiles (SAMs) and Anti-Tactical Ballistic Missiles (ATBMs)

Air defense systems have been important elements in regional arsenals for many years. The majority of SAMs in the region are anti-aircraft weapons without the speed or accuracy to target incoming ballistic missiles. However, the introduction of the U.S. Patriot air defense system, with its limited ATBM capability, has marked a new era which is likely to see the proliferation of ATBM systems as long as the SSM threat continues.

The Soviet SA-7 SAM is a standard component of Arab arsenals, and the highly effective shoulder-fired U.S. Stinger SAM, supplied to the

Afghan rebels for use against the Soviets and Soviet-backed Afghan military, has begun to spread beyond Afghanistan.[102]   Stingers were apparently waylaid by Pakistan, which acted as a conduit for U.S. covert assistance to the Afghan mujaheddin, and others were sold to, or otherwise acquired by, Iran during the course of the conflict.[103]   In the Persian Gulf, Stingers are currently in the arsenals of Bahrain, Saudi Arabia, and Qatar, which acquired a number of them from an unspecified source.[104]

A major component of Syria's military buildup beginning in 1982 was the restructuring of its air defense systems.   In trying to reach strategic parity with Israel, Syria saw a credible air defense as a way to neutralize Israeli offensive air superiority.[105]   Since 1982, Syria has increased both the number and the sophistication of its surface-to-air missiles.   In 1983, Syria acquired Soviet long-range SA-5 batteries that could hit targets over Israeli territory.   Transfers from the Soviet Union also likely included the hand-held SA-14 (similar to the American Stinger).   Syria's military expansion has given it the largest air defense system in the region.[106]

Iraq's use of Scuds during the Gulf war, and the subsequent use of American Patriot defense systems demonstrated both the dangers of SSMs and the emerging technology being developed to counter them.   The Patriot is a medium-to-high altitude SAM system developed as an area defense against enemy aircraft.   The Patriots used against Iraqi Scuds in Israel and Saudi Arabia were the modified PAC-2 version.   This version allows the Patriot to track and destroy not only aircraft, but also cruise missiles and tactical ballistic missiles, enabling it to track several missiles at the same time.[107]

Israel, with financial assistance from the United States, is developing the Arrow ATBM. Under the agreement, which is officially part of the Strategic Defense Initiative, the United States paid 80 percent of the $158 million cost of the first phase of development of the Arrow and will own the technology, but Israel will be able to use it for defensive purposes.[108] The U.S. agreed in June 1991 to underwrite the second phase of the Arrow program, paying 72 percent of the cost, estimated at $300-340 million over four years.   Israel will pay the remaining 28 percent.[109]   Total costs for the project are estimated at $800 million and the expected year of completion is 1995.[110]

The Arrow will have greater speed, range, and maneuverability than the Patriot, allowing it to intercept more advanced SSMs at greater distances from civilian and military targets.   While the Patriot was first designed as an anti-aircraft system, the Arrow has been developed specifically to counter tactical ballistic missiles.[111]   The Arrow ATBM was first tested on

August 9, 1990.[112] On March 25, 1991, the Arrow underwent a second test, launched from an Israeli ship in the Mediterranean. The test was only partially successful; the missile encountered communications problems during the second stage. Two more test launches are planned for 1991.[113]

There have been reports that Iraq was developing its own ATBM, named the Al-Faw-1, which, like the Arrow, is designed to shoot down incoming short-range ballistic missiles. Iraq claimed to have successfully tested the ATBM on November 19, 1988. According to Iraqi Major General Hussein Makki Khammas, the development of the Al-Faw-1 was in direct response to the development of long-range Israeli missiles.[114]

Indigenous Conventional Arms Production

Despite the growing interest in unconventional weapons and weapons of mass destruction, countries in the Middle East and South Asia continue to direct most of their defense expenditures toward the acquisition of conventional weapons. While most of the regional states remain dependent on outside sources for their supply, a number of them have emphasized domestic development and production capabilities. The greater this capability, the more insulated a country is from outside efforts to restrict the arms race.

Within the Middle East, Israel has the most advanced defense industry. It is not only a major producer and importer of modern conventional weaponry, but also an emerging exporter of military technology to both Third World and western nations. During 1988, Israel exported $1.47 billion in arms to 61 states, and the first half of 1989 saw a 40 percent increase in the sales of Israel Aircraft Industries, 75 percent of which was accounted for by increases in exports.[115] In addition, Israel has a unique strategic and defense cooperation arrangement with the United States that allows for two way transfers and leasing of military equipment for weapons research and development.[116]

Within the Arab world, Egypt is one of the foremost domestic weapons producers. With 29 arms production companies producing close to $1.5 billion in weapons a year, indigenous arms production is an important component of Egypt's defense, although much of this weaponry is exported to other states in the region.[117] Egypt also engages in licensed production of foreign systems. The most significant development in Egyptian conventional weaponry is the 1987 United States-Egyptian agreement on Egypt's licensed production of the state-of-the-art M-1A1 main battle tank (MBT).[118]

86

Iraq's defense industry had also made independent progress prior to the Gulf war, ranging from production of all types of small arms and ammunition to developing upgrades for sophisticated missile systems. Iraqi engineers proved adept at upgrading and modernizing old weaponry. At the First Baghdad International Exhibition for Military Production in 1989, Iraq's Minister of Industry stated that the government was considering a program to export domestically-manufactured arms.[119]

Much of Iraq's military infrastructure, as well as its stockpiles of weapons, were destroyed during the Gulf war. Due to the continuation of sanctions on the transfer of military-related items to Iraq as outlined in Resolution 687, Baghdad will find it difficult to rebuild its military, either through arms purchases or domestic production in the near future.

Following the Iran-Iraq war, both Iran and Iraq emerged as regional weapons manufacturing centers. Iran's domestic arms industry includes co-production arrangements with China and North Korea.

Other major Arab countries in the region, particularly Libya, Saudi Arabia, and Syria, do not have extensive domestic weapons production capabilities. Both Syria and Libya are dependent on the Soviet Union as their main weapons supplier. Syrian exports of Soviet-made weapons have, however, made their way to other countries, primarily Lebanon, where 30,000 Syrian troops are stationed.[120]

Saudi Arabia's indigenous arms production capability is very limited, encompassing only licensed production of small munitions and APCs. Its large arms purchases and ability to give financial aid to other countries for military purposes, however, make Saudi Arabia a key player in the Middle East's arms market. Following the Gulf war, Saudi Arabia will be more limited in the amount and form of financial aid it can extend to its neighbors.

The Saudis are increasingly focusing on arms deals that include technology transfers and the development of local industry, both civilian and military. Contacts have been made between Saudi Arabia, other Gulf Cooperation Council nations, and India regarding defense cooperation and training. This is a switch from the Gulf countries' traditional cooperation with Egypt, Turkey, and Pakistan in the area of technical personnel.[121] Iraq's invasion of Kuwait, with the subsequent multinational military deployment in Saudi Arabia, may eventually increase its potential as a weapons producer, but for the foreseeable future, this capacity will be limited to relatively simple systems.

The other indigenous weapons producing giant in the region alongside Israel, is India. In addition to being a chief client of the Soviet Union in the Third World and one of the world's leading importers of weapons over the last decade, India possesses a highly sophisticated indigenous defense production capability.[122] These facts set India apart as one of the few nations in the Third World capable of acquiring, licensing, and developing state-of-the-art weapons systems. A new Indian pro-export policy was announced in February, 1989.[123] The Indian government decided to increase exports of its domestically produced weapons to finance imports of high technology weapons and upgrades.

Pakistan can be expected to continue its conventional arms buildup through imports as well as local and licensed production of weaponry. Pakistan's defense industry has fourteen branches and is self-sufficient in tank ammunition and artillery. China, in addition to being one of its principal suppliers, is involved in assisting Pakistan's defense industry through joint development projects.[124]

Conclusion

While most Middle East countries spend a greater percentage of their budgets on defense than any other Third World region and have larger weapons inventories than the major industrial powers in some instances, the most significant trend in weapons proliferation is that it is asymmetric. At one extreme, Israel and India have the indigenous capacity to build nuclear weapons and launch satellites. At the other extreme Libya, although rich, is highly dependent on external sources for its high technology weapons maintenance. This suggests that a military balance of power in the classical sense is not possible. Asymmetries in capabilities suggest that very different concepts of defense and deterrence are necessary to meet the individual security needs of the countries of the region.

Notes

1. See Leonard S. Spector with Jacqueline R. Smith, *Nuclear Ambitions* (Boulder, Colorado: Westview Press, 1990), p. 159.

2. Details of Israel's long-suspected nuclear arsenal were provided by former Israeli nuclear technician, Mordechai Vanunu, in an interview with

the London *Sunday Times* in the fall of 1986. See "Revealed: The Secrets of Israel's Nuclear Arsenal," *Sunday Times* (London), October 5, 1986.

3. See Trevor Rowe, "IAEA Head Says Iraq Could Have Enriched Uranium in 2 Years," *Washington Post*, July 16, 1991. See also William J. Broad, "Iraqi Atom Effort Exposes Weakness in World Controls," *New York Times*, July 15, 1991.

4. Spector and Smith, *Nuclear Ambitions*, p. 215.

5. "Calls Talks 'Fruitful,' Departs," Tehran, IRNA, 1252 GMT, 7 March 1990, in *FBIS-NES*, March 14, 1990, p. 38.

6. Leonard S. Spector, Jacqueline R. Smith, *Nuclear Threshold* (working title) (Boulder, Colorado: 1991 forthcoming).

7. For a detailed account of Libya's dealings with China, see Mohamed Heikel, *The Road to Ramadan* (New York: Quadrangle/The New York Times Book Co., 1975), pp. 76-77. For details on Libya's search for nuclear weapons and technology, see the section on Libya in Leonard S. Spector, *The Undeclared Bomb* (Cambridge, Mass.: Ballinger Publishing Co., 1988), pp. 196-201.

8. For example, in 1987 Qaddafi stated: "The Arabs must possess the atomic bomb to defend themselves until their numbers reach one billion, until they learn to desalinate seawater, and until they liberate Palestine. We undertake not to drop the atomic bomb on any state around us, but we must possess it." Quoted in "Al-Qadhdhafi Lectures University Students," Tripoli Television Service, 1958 GMT, 21 June 1987, translated in *FBIS-NES*, June 26, 1987.

9. See R. Jeffrey Smith, "Algeria to Allow Eventual Inspection of Reactor, Envoy Says," *Washington Post*, May 2, 1991.

10. Spector and Smith, *Nuclear Threshold*.

11. See David B. Ottaway, "Signs Found India Building An H-Bomb," *Washington Post*, May 19, 1989.

12. Spector and Smith, *Nuclear Threshold*.

13. For a summary of nuclear proliferation-related restrictions against aid to Pakistan in U.S. legislation, see Appendix G, "Non-Proliferation Restrictions on Aid to Pakistan," in Spector, *The Undeclared Bomb*, pp. 474-480.

14. President Bush sought, unsuccessfully, to win congressional support for a waiver of the Pressler Amendment requiring a cut-off of aid to Pakistan if it was found to possess a nuclear explosive device. See, for example, Neil A. Lewis, "Key Congressman Urges Halt in Pakistan Aid," *New York Times*, October 3, 1990; and R. Jeffrey Smith, "Administration Unable to Win Hill Support for Continued Aid to Pakistan," *Washington Post*, October 10, 1990.

15. For a list of the necessary items for mustard gas production, see Robert D. Shuey, et al., *Missile Proliferation: Survey of Emerging Missile Forces* (Washington, D.C.: Congressional Research Service, 1988), p. 32.

16. For a detailed description of the characteristics of existing chemical warfare agents, see Testimony of Mr. David Goldberg, Foreign Science and Technology Center, U.S. Army Intelligence Agency, before the Senate Committee on Governmental Affairs, February 9, 1989.

17. For details on the chemical weapons programs of Iraq, Syria, Iran, and Libya, see the Statement of the Honorable William H. Webster, Director, Central Intelligence Agency, before the Senate Committee on Governmental Affairs, February 9, 1989; and Statement of Rear Admiral Thomas A. Brooks, USN, Director of Naval Intelligence, before the Seapower, Strategic, and Critical Materials Subcommittee of the House Committee on Armed Services, March 7, 1991. For a description of the Israeli chemical weapons program, see W. Seth Carus, "Chemical Weapons in the Middle East," *Policy Focus*, Washington Institute for Near East Policy, December 1988, p. 3. For a description of the Iraqi chemical weapons program see W. Seth Carus, *The Genie Unleashed: Iraq's Chemical and Biological Weapons Program* (Washington, D.C.: Washington Institute for Near East Policy, 1989).

18. On the history of Egyptian chemical weapons, see W. Seth Carus, "Chemical Weapons in the Middle East," pp. 2-3. On allegations of renewed Egyptian activity in the chemical weapons field, see Michael R. Gordon with Stephen Engelberg, "Egypt Accused Of Big Advance In Gas for War," *New York Times*, March 10, 1989.

19. See Brooks testimony, March 7, 1991.

20. See Webster testimony, February 9, 1989.

21. Helga Graham, "Poisoned Kurds Put Blame on Iraqi Chemicals," *Observer*, 4 February 1990. For a different interpretation of the Halabja massacre asserting that Iran may have been equally to blame, see Patrick E. Tyler, "Both Iran and Iraq Gassed Kurds in War, U.S. Analysis Finds," *Washington Post*, May 3, 1990.

22. See United Nations press release, "Special Commission Conducts Exploratory Inspection at Muthanna State Establishment, Iraq's Chemical Weapon Facility, 9-14 June," June 24, 1991.

23. Ibid.

24. UN Security Council Resolution 687 For a Formal Cease Fire in the Gulf War, April 3, 1991, UN Document S/RES/687. For details of the Geneva Protocol, see Chapter 7.

25. See Webster testimony, February 9, 1989.

26. See Testimony of W. Seth Carus before the Senate Committee on Governmental Affairs, February 9, 1989.

27. Ibid.

28. Bill Gertz, "Chinese Move Seen as Aiding Libya in Making Poison Gas," *Washington Times*, July 12, 1990.

29. See Webster testimony, February 9, 1989; and Michael R. Gordon, "Libyan Plant Said to Make Poison Gas, Is Ablaze," *New York Times*, March 14, 1990.

30. Michael R. Gordon, "Libyan Plant Said to be Out of Action Indefinitely," *New York Times*, March 15, 1990.

31. Michael R. Gordon, "U.S. Says Evidence Points to Hoax in Fire at Libyan Chemical Plant," *New York Times*, June 19, 1990.

32. See Carus testimony, February 9, 1989; and "NRDC Says Jericho IRBM Is Nuclear, Chemical Armed," *Jane's Defence Weekly*, 25 November 1989, p. 1143.

33. Shuey, et al., *Missile Proliferation: Survey of Emerging Missile Forces*, p. 31.

34. For details on the effects of biological weapons use, see Gary Thatcher, "Poison on the Wind: The New Threat of Chemical and Biological Weapons," *Christian Science Monitor*, December 15, 1988; and ABC World News Tonight with Peter Jennings, January 17, 1989, reported by Charles Glass, in *Current News Early Bird*, Special Edition on Chemical Weapons, February 28, 1989.

35. See Webster testimony, February 9, 1989.

36. See Brooks testimony, March 7, 1991.

37. See Stephen Engelberg, "Iraq Said To Study Biological Arms," *New York Times*, January 18, 1989; David B. Ottaway, "Official Denies Iraq has Germ War Plant," *Washington Post*, January 19, 1989; and "Iraq has Developed Biological Weapons, Says Israeli Official," *Financial Times*, January 19, 1989.

38. "Iraq has Developed Biological Weapons, Says Israeli Official," *Financial Times*, January 19, 1989.

39. See R. Jeffrey Smith, "Iraq Admits to Germ Warfare Research," *Washington Post*, August 6, 1991.

40. See Testimony by Dr. Barry J. Erlick, Senior Biological Warfare Analyst, U.S. Army, before the Senate Committee on Governmental Affairs, February 9, 1989.

41. Ibid.

42. See Appendix I on Selected Rockets and SSMs in the Middle East and South Asia, pp. 185-190.

43. *The Military Balance 1989-90* (London: International Institute for Strategic Studies, 1989), p. 221.

44. Shuey, et al., p. 37.

45. Robert Pear, "U.S. Asserts Soviet Advisers are Fighting in Afghanistan," *New York Times*, October 10, 1989. Moscow continues to make Scuds available to the Kabul regime as long as the United States

continues to supply the Afghan rebels with weapons. See testimony of W. Seth Carus before the House Foreign Affairs Subcommittee on Arms Control, International Security and Science, and the House Foreign Affairs Subcommittee on International Economic Policy and Trade, July 12, 1989; and Pratap Chakravarty, "Army Begins Firing Soviet-made Missiles," Hong Kong, Agence France Presse, 3 November 1988, in *FBIS-NES*, November 4, 1988, p. 47. And on Soviet re-assurances see "Joint Soviet-American Statement" released by Tass, Moscow, February 10, 1990.

46. Martin S. Navias, "Ballistic Missile Proliferation in the Middle East," *Survival*, International Institute of Strategic Studies, May/June 1989, p. 227; and Aharon Levran and Zeev Eytan, *The Middle East Military Balance 1987-88* (Tel Aviv: Jerusalem Post Press, 1988), p. 459.

47. On deployment of original Jericho II, see "Israel Said to Deploy Improved Jericho Missile," *Aerospace Daily*, May 1, 1985, p. 5; and George D. Moffett III, "Questions About Nations' Nuclear Ability Make US Policy Making Complex," *Christian Science Monitor*, May 23, 1985. On nuclear payload and range, see Shuey, et al., Table 3, p. 39; Thomas Netter, "Israel Reported to Test New, Longer Range Missile," *New York Times*, July 22, 1987; and Arthur Manfredi, Jr., "Third World Ballistic Missiles: The Threat Grows," *National Defense*, March 1987, pp. 51-54.

48. See Thomas W. Netter, "Israel Reported to Test New, Longer-Range Missile;" "Israeli Missile Worries Soviets," *Jerusalem Post International Edition*, August 1, 1987; Ian Mather, "Israelis Plan A-Bomb for New Rocket," *Observer*, August 13, 1987; Aaron Karp, "The frantic Third World quest for ballistic missiles," *Bulletin of the Atomic Scientists*, June 1988, p. 15; and "The missile trade in launch mode," *U.S. News and World Report*, July 25, 1988, pp. 32-38.

49. "Soviets claim Israel has launched ballistic missile," *Jane's Defence Weekly*, 23 September 1989, p. 549.

50. See Glen Frankel, "Israel Launches Its First Satellite Into Orbit," *Washington Post*, September 20, 1988; and John Kifner, "Israel Launches Space Program and a Satellite," *New York Times*, September 20, 1988.

51. "Official Communique Issued," Jerusalem Domestic Service, 1500 GMT, 3 April 1990, translated in *FBIS-NES*, April 4, 1990, p. 26.

52. Different estimates of the range of the Shavit by the Lawrence Livermore Laboratories and the Defense Department were cited in Stephens Broening, "Israel could build missiles to hit Soviets, U.S. thinks," *Baltimore Sun*, November 23, 1988. See also Yezid Sayigh, "The Middle East strategic balance," *Middle East International*, June 22, 1990, p. 16, stating that the range is between 3000-7200 km.

53. See "USAF Awards Rafael Contract to Certify Have Nap for B-52," *Aviation Week and Space Technology*, June 27, 1988, p. 24.

54. W. Seth Carus, "Trends and Implications of Missile Proliferation," paper prepared for the International Studies Association, April 13, 1990, p. 5.

55. Janne E. Nolan, *Trappings of Power: Ballistic Missiles in the Third World* (Washington, D.C.: The Brookings Institution, 1991), pp. 53-54.

56. Carus, "Trends and Implications of Missile Proliferation," p. 10.

57. Department of Defense Fact Sheet, June 7, 1991.

58. See, "Hussayn Confers Names on Rocket, Missile Systems," INA, 1125 GMT, 9 December 1989, translated in *FBIS-NES*, December 12, 1989, p. 20; and "Satellite Carrier System Tested," Voice of the Masses, 1230 GMT, 7 December 1989, translated in *FBIS-NES*, December 8, 1989, p. 23.

59. See W. Seth Carus, "Trends and Implications of Missile Proliferation," pp. 19-20; and "Iraq's Heavy Missile Launch 'Definitely' not Condor II," *Defense & Foreign Affairs Weekly*, January 29-February 4, 1990, p. 1.

60. Don Oberdorfer, "U.S. Seeks to Curb Argentine Missile Project," *Washington Post*, September 19, 1988. See also Simon Henderson and David Goodhart, "Prosecutor launches inquiry into MBB's Condor missile link," *Financial Times*, April 12, 1989.

61. For reports on Egypt's withdrawal from the program see David B. Ottaway, "Egypt Drops out of Missile Project," *Washington Post*, September 20 1989; and "Egypt 'has pulled out of Condor programme'," *Jane's Defence Weekly*, 30 September 1989, p. 630. On MBB & SNIA's involvement, see Barbara Starr, "Ballistic Missile Proliferation, a Basis for Control," *International Defense Review*, March 1990, p. 267. Argentina formally dropped out of the project between March and April 1990. See Spector and Smith, *Nuclear Ambitions*, p. 232 and p. 393.

62. Nathaniel C. Nash, "Argentina's President Battles His Own Air Force on Missile," *New York Times*, May 13, 1991.

63. On Iran's involvement in the North Korean Scud program, see Joseph S. Bermudez, Jr. and W. Seth Carus, "The North Korean 'Scud-B' Programme," *Jane's Soviet Intelligence Review*, April, 1989, pp. 177-181; and Joseph S. Bermudez, Jr., "New Developments in North Korean Missile Programme," *Jane's Soviet Intelligence Review*, August 1990, pp. 343-345.

64. See "Defense Industries Manufacture New Missile," IRNA, 1535 GMT, 17 April 1989, in *FBIS-NES*, April 18, 1989, p. 52.

65. This is probably another unguided artillery rocket. "Fajr-3 Missile Reaches Mass Production Stage," Tehran, 1930 GMT, 3 March 1990, in *FBIS-NES*, March 8, 1990, p. 51.

66. SS-23s are now proscribed under the INF Treaty between the U.S. and Soviet Union. *SIPRI Yearbook 1990: World Armaments and Disarmament* (Oxford: Oxford University Press, 1990), p. 389 and p. 391.

67. See David B. Ottaway, "China Warned Against Selling Syria Missiles," *Washington Post*, June 23, 1988; and "Syria is Studying New Missile Deal," *New York Times*, June 22, 1988. On Chinese denials, see Martin Sieff, "U.S. Takes China's Word On Missiles," *Washington Times*, January 12, 1990.

68. See Charles Lane, "Arms For Sale," *Newsweek*, April 8, 1991, pp. 22-27; and "'Concern' Voiced about Syrian-Soviet Deal," Qol Yisra'el, 1700 GMT, 9 May 1991, in *FBIS-NES*, May 10, 1991, p. 16.

69. *The Military Balance 1988-89* (London: International Institute for Strategic Studies, 1988), p. 94. See also "Satellite Captures First Views of Saudi CSS-2 Missile Sites," *Jane's Defence Weekly*, 1 October 1988, pp. 744-745.

70. In fact, Israel made a number of veiled threats against the Saudi missiles. See for example, "Fallout from Saudi Missiles," *Christian Science Monitor*, March 30, 1988. See also Yosi Ben-Aharon, quoted in "Shamir Aide Discusses 'Removing' Saudi Missiles," Jerusalem Domestic Service, 20 March 1988, translated in *FBIS-NES*, March 21, 1988, p. 26; and Dr. Alexander Bly, quoted in "Shamir Adviser on Need to Monitor Saudi Missiles," Jerusalem Domestic Service, 4 May 1988, in *FBIS-NES*, May 5, 1988, p. 38.

71. See Adel Darwish, "The Shape of Wars to Come," *The Middle East*, August 1988, p. 13; and John M. Goshko, "Saudis to Cut Ties with Iran," *Washington Post*, April 26, 1988.

72. See Barbara Crossette, "India Reports Successful Test of Mid-Range Missile," *New York Times*, May 23, 1989; Richard M. Weintraub, "India Tests Mid-Range 'Agni' Missile," *Washington Post*, May 23, 1989; and "Advanced Surface-to-Surface Missile Tests Planned," Hong Kong, Agence France Presse, 1550 GMT, 26 May 1989, in *FBIS-NES*, May 30, 1989, p. 60.

73. Gary Milholin, "India's Missiles -- With a Little Help from Our Friends," *Bulletin of Atomic Scientists*, November 1989, pp. 31-35.

74. See "Usefulness of Newly Tested Missile Noted," Delhi Domestic Service, 1530 GMT, 11 February 1991, in *FBIS-NES*, February 12, 1991, pp. 72-73.

75. "Pakistan Accused of a Nuclear Move," *New York Times*, May 24, 1988.

76. See "Army Chief: Surface-to-Surface Missiles Tested," Islamabad Domestic Service, 1100 GMT, 5 February 1989, in *FBIS-NES*, February 6, 1989, p. 72; Barbara Crossette, "Pakistan Claims Major Gains In Developing Its Own Arms," *New York Times*, February 6, 1989; and "Parade Day debut for Pakistani missiles," *Jane's Defence Weekly*, 15 April 1989, p. 635.

77. "China Selling Ballistic Missiles to Pakistan: U.S.," *News India*, April 27, 1990.

78. Bruce W. Nelan, "For Sale: Tools of Destruction," *Time*, April 22, 1991, p. 44.

79. See *SIPRI Yearbook 1990*, p. xviii.

80. See W. Seth Carus, *Ballistic Missiles in the Third World: Threat and Response*, The Washington Papers (Washington, D.C.: Center for Strategic and International Studies, 1990), pp. 2-3.

81. For more on the various capabilities of the cruise missile, see Richard K. Betts, *Cruise Missiles Technology, Strategy, Politics* (Washington, D.C.: The Brookings Institution, 1982), p. 2.

82. See Carus, *Ballistic Missiles in the Third World: Threat and Response*, p. 39.

83. "Systems That Won the War," *Jane's Defence Weekly*, 6 April 1991, pp. 544-51.

84. Robert Salvy, "Updating Older Combat Aircraft: a Fiercely Contested Market," *International Defense Review*, December 1988, pp. 1590-91.

85. Aaron Karp, "The Trade in Conventional Weapons," in *SIPRI Yearbook 1988: World Armaments and Disarmament* (Stockholm: SIPRI, 1988), p. 182. See also "The Middle East and North Africa," *The Military Balance 1988-89*, pp. 94-95. For specifics on the linkage between the two, see O. Erez, "The Arab-Israel Air Balance," in Levran and Eytan, *The Middle East Military Balance 1987-88*, p. 183.

86. Stephen Budiansky, "Back to the Arms Bazaar," *U.S. News and World Report*, April 1, 1991, pp. 20-22.

87. Stephen Engelberg with Bernard E. Trainor, "Soviets Sold Libya Advanced Bomber, U.S. Officials Say," *New York Times*, April 5, 1989.

88. Michael R. Gordon, "Libya Takes Key Step to Extend Range of Bombers," *New York Times*, March 29, 1990.

89. Ian Curtis, "Saudi Arabia's European Connection," *Defense and Foreign Affairs*, January 1989, pp. 15-16. See also "Saudi Arabia's jumbo prize," *The Middle East*, August 1988, p. 37; and *The Military Balance 1988-89*, p. 94.

90. The ADV Tornados have a combat radius of 1850 kilometers, while the IDS Tornadoes have a combat radius of 1390 kilometer. See Table B: Nato and Warsaw Pact Combat Aircraft Key Characteristics, *The Military Balance 1988-89*, pp. 238-241.

91. Patrick E. Tyler, "Major Sale of U.S. Arms To Saudis Set," *Washington Post*, August 8, 1990.

92. Barbara Starr, "Phase II of Saudi Sale Delayed," *Jane's Defence Weekly*, 12 January 1991, p. 37.

93. "The Syrian-Soviet Connection," *Contemporary Mideast Backgrounder*, Number 252, November 1988, p. 8.

94. "Weekly Arms Transfer Tables," *Defense and Foreign Affairs Weekly*, June 19-25, 1989, p. 8.

95. "Syria's Scuds," *Wall Street Journal*, April 25, 1991.

96. "Number, Type of Planes in Iran Reported," INA, 1745 GMT, 12 April 1991, translated in *FBIS-NES*, April 15, 1991, p. 26.

97. See William Drozdiak, "Iran Reasserts Influence in Gulf," *Washington Post*, March 24, 1991.

98. *The Military Balance 1989-90*, p. 160; and "Sea Harriers for India," *Aviation Week & Space Technology*, January 1, 1990, p. 25.

99. See David B. Ottaway, "Administration May Sell F-16s to Pakistan," *Washington Post*, June 6, 1989.

100. "Pakistan Buys More F-7s and F-16s," *Defense and Foreign Affairs Weekly*, March 13-19, 1989, p. 3.

101. "Mirage Fighter Aircraft Arrive From Australia," The Nation, 29 November 1990, in *FBIS-NES*, November 29, 1990, p. 72.

102. According to a U.S. Army report on the use of the Stinger by the Afghan guerrillas, the weapon "changed the nature of combat" in the Afghan conflict and was "the war's decisive weapon." The Stinger, which weighs approximately 16 kg and has a maximum range of over 4.8 km, is considered so adaptable to terrorist use that the Joint Chiefs of Staff initially resisted providing it to the Afghan guerrillas. See David B. Ottaway, "Stingers Were Key Weapon in Afghan War, Army Finds," *Washington Post*, July 5, 1989.

103. In one report, U.S. officials were said to have known of and allowed Pakistani diversion of Stingers for their own use, calling it "a kind of commission they cut for allowing us to transport them through their territory." Quoted in Ricard Sale, "Missiles for Afghan Rebels Believed Waylaid by Pakistan," *Philadelphia Inquirer*, July 13, 1987.

104. *The Military Balance 1989-90*, p. 97, pp. 111-112.

105. Shai Feldman, "Security and Arms Control in the Middle East: An Israeli Perspective," in Shelley A. Stahl and Geoffrey Kemp, editors, *Arms*

Control and Weapons Proliferation in the Middle East and South Asia (New York: St. Martin's Press, 1992 forthcoming).

106. See Hirsh Goodman and W. Seth Carus, *The Future Battlefield and the Arab-Israeli Conflict* (New Brunswick: Transaction Publishers, 1990), pp. 30-31; and Charles B. Perkins, *Arms to the Arabs: The Arab Military Buildup Since 1973* (Washington, D.C.: AIPAC, 1989), pp. 19-20.

107. David Hughes, "Patriot Antimissile Successes Show How Software Upgrades Help Meet New Threats," *Aviation Week & Space Technology*, January 28, 1991, pp. 26-28.

108. See Elaine Sciolino, "U.S. and Israel to Build Defensive Missile," *New York Times*, June 30, 1988. See also Arie Egozi and Cheryl Pellerine, "U.S. and Israel Conduct Tests for SDI," *Defense News*, August 1, 1988, and Dore Gold, "Star Wars' Little Brother," *Jerusalem Post International Edition*, December 3, 1988.

109. See Bradley Burston, "U.S. to Cover 72% of Arrow Costs," *Jerusalem Post*, June 8, 1991.

110. Neal Sandler, "Israel Seeks More Cash for Arrow," *Jane's Defence Weekly*, 6 April 1991, p. 519.

111. Sharon Parnes, "Anti-Missile Rockets High on the Agenda," *Jerusalem Post International Edition*, April 13, 1991.

112. "Israel Successfully Launches First Antiballistic Missiles," *Aviation Week & Space Technology*, August 13, 1990, p. 23. See also Joel Brinkley, "Israelis Test Fire A Defense Missile," *New York Times*, August 10, 1990.

113. See "Test Flight of Arrow Missile Successful," Jerusalem Domestic Service, 1650 GMT, 25 March 1991, translated in *FBIS-NES*, March 26, 1991, p. 35; and Neal Sandler, "Israel Seeks More Cash for Arrow."

114. "Iraq says it has tested anti-missile missile," *Financial Times*, December 1, 1988. See also David B. Ottaway, "Iraq Reports Successful Test of Antitactical Ballistic Missile," *Washington Post*, December 19, 1988.

115. See "Israel Defence Export Figures," *Jane's Defence Weekly*, 24 June 1989, p. 1299; and "Export boost for IAI," *Jane's Defence Weekly*, 21 October 1989, p. 887.

116. David B. Ottaway, "Pact Allows U.S. to 'Lend' War Material to Israel," *Washington Post*, September 27, 1989.

117. Martin Sieff, "Egypt's Military Posturing Worries Israel," *Washington Times*, April 4, 1988.

118. *Reuters* news wire report, cited in *Current News*, Department of Defense, May 30, 1989, p. 5; and "Plant's Production to Replace U.S.-Built Tanks," Cairo, Al-Ahram, 23 January 1990, translated in *FBIS-NES*, January 26, 1990, pp. 7-8.

119. Christopher Foss and Tony Banks, "'Candid' AEW one of Baghdad show surprises," *Jane's Defence Weekly*, 13 May 1989, p. 837.

120. *The Military Balance 1989-90*, p. 115.

121. "Saudi Military Team Visiting Indian Defense Establishments," *Defense and Foreign Affairs Weekly*, July 3-9, 1989, p. 2.

122. Aaron Karp, "Trade in Conventional Weapons," *SIPRI Yearbook 1988*, p. 178.

123. "Indian Minister Calls for Manufacture of Export Weapons," *Defense and Foreign Affairs Weekly*, February 20-26, 1989, p. 3. See also Gregory Copley, "Inevitable India, Inevitable Power," *Defense and Foreign Affairs*, December 1988, p. 52.

124. Pakistan and China are working together to develop a new main battle tank. "New Sino-Pakistani MBT Project," *International Defense Review*, December 1988, p. 1553. See also "Pakistan Takes Delivery of First Home-Built Tank and APC," *Defense and Foreign Affairs Weekly*, April 2-8, 1990, pp. 2-3.

CHAPTER FIVE

Proliferation and Regional Security

This chapter examines the impact of the arms race on the propensity for and against hostilities, and the relationship between proliferation and the security problems facing the key regional players.

Arms Races and War

While intuition suggests regional arms races will result in more wars, it is not easy to demonstrate a simple causal relationship. Rather, what is at issue is the impact of new weapons on the stability of regional military balances and the relationship between these balances and other variables that contribute to regional conflict. It is impossible to isolate certain weapon systems as contributing specifically to an increase in the potential for armed conflict.

Weapons, including weapons of mass destruction, do not cause wars by themselves any more than handguns alone are responsible for murders in American cities. Rather, what must be considered is the political-military environment into which the new weapons are introduced. If the environment is unstable, and adversaries have a predilection to resolve disputes by force, certain types of new weaponry will increase threat perceptions and provide a catalyst for war. However, if the political-military environment is more stable and the climate is one of reconciliation and peaceful dialogue, or, alternatively, if the likely casualties resulting from a new war are believed to be unacceptable to both adversaries, the impact of new weapons may be less dangerous and could even contribute to stability. Furthermore, weapons trends that may be judged destabilizing in one regional context may be deemed stabilizing in another.[1]

On some occasions, weapons proliferation has led to greater caution between adversaries, and may have strengthened deterrence. For example, Syria and Israel have a healthy respect for one another's arsenals and have

101

refrained from provoking one another in recent years. That India and Pakistan did not go to war over the crisis in Kashmir in the spring of 1990 may be attributable in part to their undeclared nuclear weapons. And even at the most dangerous moments of the Gulf war, Iraq desisted from using its chemical weapons against Israel and the allies, presumably out of fear of massive retaliation.

These examples strengthen the argument that when adversarial states possess nuclear or chemical weapons, they may be more aware of the dangers of using them. In this case, such weapons may act either as a deterrent to war or as a cause for constraint on the use of force during a war. Some might argue that this confirms the controversial thesis put forward by Kenneth Waltz in 1981, that a multi-nuclear world would be a more stable world.[2]

On the other hand, Israel's attack on Iraq's nuclear reactor in 1981, and Iraqi threats in the spring of 1990 to retaliate against Israel for any future attack, point to the highly destabilizing potential of nuclear weapons and missile development in the Arab-Israeli context. While Israel's monopoly on nuclear weapons may be perceived as a deterrent to war, it also provides an incentive for Arab states to seek access to the bomb. Once this becomes a serious possibility, the probability of Israeli preemptive action, including a preventive war, increases.

As to whether trends in high technology weapons proliferation hinder efforts to find a diplomatic solution to regional conflicts, the evidence is also inconclusive. For years Syria has insisted that peace with Israel can only be negotiated once the Arabs achieve strategic parity, suggesting that it is the imbalance of arms in Israel's favor that is the major stumbling block. In contrast, Israelis believe that only when the Arabs understand that there is no realistic military option against the Jewish state will they come to the peace table.

On the Indian subcontinent, some Indians argue that it would be easier for India and China to compromise on territorial disputes once India has an open nuclear weapons program and can negotiate from a position of equality. It is argued that as long as China has a nuclear monopoly, no Indian politician will dare compromise on territorial issues. Similarly, Pakistan argues that India will not take it seriously until in can match New Delhi's nuclear capability.

The characteristics of specific weapon systems may also affect decisions on territorial concessions, particularly in Israel. One proposition is that the new technology and the improved strategic reach of weapon systems call into question the need for defense in depth. After all, if Iraq could bomb Tel Aviv with long-range missiles, this would appear to obviate Israel's preoccupation with territorial defense.

While the extended reach of many new weapons expands the arena in which conflict can take place, it does not follow that the traditional concepts of defense in depth and control of the high ground play a less important role in modern warfare. In fact, a case can be made that these geographical components of strategy are more important precisely because of the new technologies. For example, early warning and command and control systems are more vital to detect fast flying missiles and aircraft; such detection systems are best located on high ground. The extreme lethality of small, man-portable surface-to-air missiles, such as the Stinger, increases the need for area defense perimeters. The high speed of modern aircraft increases the premium on secure air space for training missions. In addition, the more accurate means of interdicting missile forces on the ground with combat aircraft increases the demand for mobile missile systems that can be rapidly redeployed and hidden in different types of terrain. In sum, the evidence is not persuasive that modern weapons override geography.

Alternatively, the most persuasive argument that current trends in proliferation may assist in conflict resolution is a negative but powerful one. Precisely because the new trends are so dangerous, it is argued, a way must be found to tackle the problem, irrespective of the status of political relations between the adversaries. This is particularly true in the intractable conflicts found in the Middle East and South Asia.

The Arab-Israeli Conflict

Israel and the Arab states have radically different concepts of security deriving from the different threat perspectives discussed in Chapter 2. As long as Israel perceives itself as surrounded by hostile, or potentially hostile Arab states, it must insist on a qualitative military edge over all potential adversaries. To maintain its edge requires two ingredients: well-trained and highly motivated military forces, and open and guaranteed access to high technology. The latter can only come from the United States, which has pledged to maintain Israel's qualitative edge.[3]

The Arab states, on the other hand, believe that Israel's access to U.S. military technology and financial assistance leaves the Jewish state with little incentive to negotiate a final peace settlement, one which most Arab countries argue they are now ready to join. According to the Arab

103

argument, one way to bring Israel to the negotiating table is for the Arabs to bargain from a position of parity, or equality, in the military arena. It is this struggle between the perceived needs for superiority on the one hand, and parity on the other, that determines the nature and pace of the Arab-Israeli arms race and the military doctrines each side pursues.

Israel's Defense Policy

Israeli defense strategy is influenced by several unique constraints and advantages. Its small population is located in a vulnerable and narrow piece of land that, itself, is bitterly contested. Israel's pre-1967 borders have few natural defensible frontiers, and at one point the old border between the West Bank and the Mediterranean is separated by only nine miles. Thus, the debate about whether Israel should give up land for peace in order to live in harmony with its Arab neighbors is intimately tied to the issue of security. The use of missiles in the Gulf war, far from diminishing the perceived need for strategic depth, has made most Israelis more cautious about returning the territories occupied in 1967. On the other hand, the presence of a significant and hostile Palestinian population in their midst points toward some separation or autonomy for parts of the country, which, in turn, raises other important security issues.

Before the Gulf war, Israeli military strategy relied heavily on a conventional preemptive counterforce capability. The aim of this strategy was to preclude the enemy from using its air and ground forces in the early days of an operation, and to carry the brunt of the war immediately to Arab territory. During the 1980s, there was a debate in Israeli defense circles as to how much this capability was being systematically undermined by a much-publicized Arab offensive buildup in aircraft, missiles, and chemical weapons, as well as by the strengthening of Arab defenses for air, anti-air, and anti-tank operations.[4]

Israel's superiority in its wars with Arab states has been based on a combination of better technology, more motivated and better trained manpower, and superior tactics and battlefield management. While there is no evidence that Israel was losing its superiority in any of these categories prior to the Gulf war, there were concerns that it might be losing the degree of superiority it had enjoyed for the past decade. Over time, and with massive arms transfers, the Arab armed forces would have been able to improve their technical competence so as to reduce the qualitative edge upon which Israel had relied to overcome any combination of hostile powers. It was this edge that provided the Israeli Defense Forces (IDF) with its deterrent.

Different nuances exist as to the meaning of deterrence in the Israeli context. But in practice, it means the development of forces capable of preemptive operations designed to keep the war zone as far away from Israeli population centers as possible. Because the citizen army requires 48-72 hours of full-scale mobilization to reach full strength, the air force, which is comprised of regular forces, has been assigned a critical role in the early hours of a war. Hence, any military trends that threaten the superiority of the Israeli air force undermine not only the defense of the country, but its concept of deterrence as well.[5]

The IDF's counterforce offensive capability was demonstrated most spectacularly on the first day of the 1967 War. On June 5, 1967, the Israeli air force conducted a highly successful preemptive attack against the air forces of Egypt and Syria, effectively eliminating them from the war. With the Arab air threat removed, the IDF was able to win the ground war in six days. In subsequent wars, the air force was similarly prominent in hostilities, although its preemptive capability was not used so dramatically.

During the 1980s, the most worrisome trends were the growth of the Arab capability to launch offensive air operations over Israel, the much strengthened depth of Arab anti-air capabilities, and the ability of Arab surface-to-surface missiles (SSMs), cruise missiles, and long-range rockets and artillery to threaten Israel's air bases. Before the Cold War ended, some western military experts believed that non-nuclear, surface-to-surface missiles with improved guidance, more sophisticated conventional munitions, and possibly chemical warheads could provide an effective, non-nuclear first-strike capability in the European theater.[6] If this was true, Israel would have much to fear from upgraded Arab SSMs in view of its geography and smaller number of vulnerable targets.

Israeli concerns about an Arab coalition were reinforced following Iraq's victory in the Iran-Iraq war, and Saddam Hussein's increasingly vocal threats to Israel. During the months prior to Iraq's invasion of Kuwait there was talk in Israel about the possibility of an eastern front resulting from the massive movement of Iraqi armored units into Jordan or Syria. If the Israeli air force were unable to stop or blunt such movement, ground force operations would be necessary with a commensurate rise in Israeli casualties.

The Gulf War and its Aftermath. Because of the allied victory over Iraq, Israel's military position has been strengthened and it currently enjoys military superiority over a much weakened Arab military coalition.

However, the Arab military threat has not diminished sufficiently from Israel's viewpoint to allow it to relax its military posture. Israeli defense planners believe that in the absence of a peace settlement, Arab military capabilities will continue to grow. While the existence of the Jewish state may not be threatened, a new war will likely be longer, more difficult to win, and involve higher casualties.

During the Gulf war, two critical lessons emerged for Israel. First, Saddam Hussein was not deterred from attacking Israel with conventionally-armed Scud missiles. In fact, the reverse was true: he wanted to draw Israel into the war. A case can be made that Saddam was deterred from using chemical weapons against Israel for fear of Israeli retaliation with nuclear weapons. If Israel's nuclear weapons played a role in deterring a chemical attack, this suggests that a key element of future Israeli deterrence must be its nuclear weapons capability. However, as everyone, including Saddam Hussein and the Israelis realized, use of the nuclear option was unthinkable in response to a conventional attack. Perhaps if Israeli casualties from the Scud attacks had been significantly higher, a nuclear threat might have been explicitly issued. It is more likely, however, that Israeli ground and air forces would have entered the war.

The nagging question for Israel, then, is how to deter future conventional attacks with conventional forces whose relative superiority is being increasingly eroded, while Arab surface-to-surface missile capabilities grow. Israel must weigh the impact of dependence on the United States for the active measures taken to cope with the SSM threat during the Gulf war (the deployment of Patriots in Israel and the massive allied air effort against the Scud sites) on its future deterrence posture. On the one hand, Israeli passivity during the war may be interpreted by some as weakness. On the other hand, the fact that the United States came to Israel's aid with its own forces suggests that its support of Israel is strong and that American deterrence is credible.[7]

Coping with the SSM Threat. There are several ways for Israel to counter the future SSM threat, assuming that arms control limitations on missiles are not in effect or are not believed to be verifiable. One way would be to rely on a more explicit strategy of deterrence to persuade a potential aggressor that the costs of using SSMs would be unacceptable. This may prove difficult, however, as radical Arab regimes would likely be deterred only by overt threats of nuclear weapons use. Furthermore, since those Arab states would likely launch a conventional attack, the threat of a nuclear response would lack credibility. At the other extreme would be a strategy that relied on defensive measures designed to destroy SSMs in flight and that was backed up by passive defenses in the event that some warheads did penetrate. The more comprehensive alternative would be a combination of the first two: deterrence combined with both active and passive defense measures.

Israel's experience with Scud attacks during the Gulf war strengthened the arguments for developing a sophisticated defensive system, but left uncertainties about the preferred choice of system. First, there remain questions as to the performance of U.S. and allied forces against the Scuds during the war.[8] Only 40 Scuds out of Iraq's inventory of hundreds were fired at Israel. If greater numbers had been launched against Israel, its defenses would have been hard-pressed to shoot at every incoming missile and the casualties would have been much higher, almost certainly precipitating Israeli offensive action. In sum, even a crude, inaccurate missile like a Scud could, if fired in sufficient numbers, pose a threat.

An additional factor in countering the missile threat involves financing. Ultimately, Israel's decisions about theater missile defense (TMD) will rest with the United States. Israel does not have the resources to develop its only active anti-missile system, the Arrow ATBM and Arrow follow-ons, without continued major U.S. financial support. The program is controversial for several reasons, including its financial cost, the extent to which it compromises U.S. efforts to restrict missile proliferation under the MTCR, and potential ABM treaty implications. A great deal will depend on the results of the Arrow tests.[9] If it can be demonstrated that the system is far superior to any current competitor program in the U.S., Washington may show interest in procuring the system for its own forces. Indeed, the survival of the Arrow follow-on may depend on U.S. procurement decisions.

In its entirety, Israel's highly sophisticated defense planning, including its defense industries, has made great progress in modernizing Israel's ground and air forces to meet the new challenges posed by the steady buildup of Arab inventories.[10] In the long term, however, and discounting a more explicit nuclear deterrence strategy, the outlook for Israel is not good. Although the Arab countries face enormous problems themselves, if they were ever to act in unison, their combined resources in money, population, and geography could overwhelm the Jewish state.

Arab Responses to Israel's Qualitative Edge

The Gulf war may have strengthened Israel's case for a nuclear deterrent, but from the Arab perspective, Israel's nuclear weapons arsenal far exceeds its needs for defense. Rather, it is seen as evidence of Israel's determination to remain the predominant military power in the region and to retain control of the West Bank, the Gaza Strip, the Golan Heights, and East Jerusalem.[11] Arab leaders view their acquisition of chemical weapons, as well as ballistic missiles, as legitimate in the face of the Israeli nuclear threat. While chemical weapons are not viewed as correcting the imbalance in capabilities, they provide a deterrent against Israeli nuclear blackmail. Furthermore, since Arab nuclear capabilities are limited and are unlikely to match Israel's for many years, emphasis on chemical weapons as a counterpoint seems logical.[12]

Concerning the conventional military balance, achieving a strong, unified Arab eastern front is essential to counter Israel's overall superiority. In reality, however, Arab unity is further away than ever, and Iraq's present impotence only adds to overall Arab frustrations toward Israel's military strength. Even if some form of Arab unity were to reemerge in the coming decade, any strategy that increased the risk of full-scale war would carry enormous risks. Given the costs Israel would face in such a war, the Arabs would have to assume that Israel would only fight if military victory were to be total. That would mean the destruction of key units of the Arab armies, the crippling of the Arab economic infrastructure, and a direct military threat to the regimes themselves. Arab military analysts view the Israeli occupation of the Golan Heights, parts of southern Lebanon, and the West Bank as providing ideal forward positions from which the IDF could launch offensive operations against the eastern front countries.

Egypt. Unlike other states in the region, Egypt's leaders do not openly discuss threats from specific countries. They argue, instead, that the key threats Egypt faces are, at this juncture, threats to regional peace. Peace is jeopardized by tension and instability; one key to peace would be a political agreement between Israel and the Palestinians.

While Egypt's primary focus is not on building up a major military force to confront Israel or any of its neighbors, it has used Israel's nuclear program as a justification for its possession of chemical weapons and ballistic missiles. In July 1988, the former head of Egypt's chemical warfare department, Mamdouh Ateya, argued that the Arab countries should acquire chemical and biological weapons as a counter to the Israeli nuclear threat, and should strive for an Arab nuclear capability as a longer-term goal. He stated, "A chemical and biological Arab force could provide a temporary protective umbrella until we can achieve nuclear parity with Israel," and argued that the resulting balance would be stable.[13] In October 1988, then-Defense Minister Abu Ghazala responded to a question regarding the spread of ballistic missile systems to the Middle East by noting that the missiles are only the means of delivering a weapon. "The arguments should revolve around the nuclear warheads in the region. These are the destructive force [sic] that should not be deployed in the region in order to protect world peace and stability."[14]

Syria. Syria's strategic position in the conflict with Israel is extremely vulnerable. Israel's occupation of the Golan Heights and the enclave in southern Lebanon provides it with strong forward positions from which to defend against a Syrian attack, or to launch a two-pronged attack into the Syrian heartland. Damascus is only 40 kilometers from the demilitarized zone along the cease fire line in the Golan, and is within range of Israel's long-range rockets and Lance SSMs.

Syrian defense policy has focused on the need to overcome its inferiority to Israeli military power. According to Syria's argument, Israel has been able to dominate the Mideast, both on the battlefield and in the conference halls, because of its military superiority. Thus, rather than bowing to Jerusalem as Egypt's late-President Anwar Sadat was seen to have done, the Arabs need to build up their military power in order to confront Israel from a position of strategic parity.[15]

Accordingly, Syria has sought to deter Israel's perceived expansionist aims and its potentially overwhelming force, including its nuclear weapons. This deterrent posture explains Syrian emphasis on building up its surface-to-surface and surface-to-air missile capabilities, and its increasing references to chemical warfare capabilities. Syria's second goal is to provide for adequate defense in the event of an Israeli attack. This requires that Syria hold ground on the Golan and in southern Lebanon, protecting the flanks to Damascus. Third, the Syrians believe that the level of their military strength is directly related to how seriously they will be regarded in the political arena. Hence, strategic parity is a political weapon. Finally, Syria has developed its military capabilities so that, if the opportunity arose, it could launch a lightning, surprise offensive against Israel with relatively limited objectives, such as the early capture of a section of the Golan Heights. Syria faces problems, however, in planning an effective offensive strategy against Israel, in large part because its primary supplier, the Soviet Union, is no longer interested in supporting an Arab military solution to the Arab-Israeli conflict.[16]

Jordan. Jordan remains the weakest of the frontline Arab states caught between stronger players who have used its territory in the past as the battleground for regional conflict. Jordan cannot confront, let alone defend itself against Syria or Israel. It has no SSMs or chemical weapons, and is rapidly falling behind its neighbors in the acquisition of other categories of advanced arms. Its one major asset is a well-trained and disciplined army that has served as a model for other Arab states, particularly the small Gulf countries.

Precisely because Jordan sees itself as so weak vis-à-vis Israel and Syria, it was difficult for King Hussein to resist Iraqi offers of defense cooperation in the late 1980s. Coordination between the two air forces followed, and in 1989, Iraqi and Jordanian fighters flew joint reconnaissance missions along the Israeli border. One purpose may have been to signal to Israel that the Arabs could attack vulnerable targets such as the Dimona reactor in the Negev if Israel were tempted to repeat its 1981 attack on Iraqi nuclear facilities. There were other reasons why the Jordanian air force benefited from such cooperation. Due to a lack of equipment, including spare parts, the number of flying hours of the Jordanian air force had fallen over the years, and cooperation with Iraq was a good way to make up for training deficits.

The subsequent crisis in the Gulf demonstrated the danger of this situation for Jordan. King Hussein found himself in a dilemma created by his own politics and geography. Jordan's defense dilemma has not been resolved by Saddam Hussein's defeat. Because of the unresolved Palestinian problem and the importance of Jordan's geographical location, any improvement in Jordan's military capabilities are seen by Israel to be potentially part of an Arab eastern front. Thus, despite its legitimate need for defense against Arab aggression -- such as from Syria, for example -- any attempt by Jordan to upgrade its arsenal with modern air defenses will appear threatening to Israel.

Iraq. Before the Gulf war, Iraq had the most powerful and experienced military force in the Arab world. Its weapons modernization program and its military doctrine were derived from the eight-year war with Iran. Iraq emerged from the war with a vastly increased, battle-tested army and an air force that was beginning to exploit its quantitative and qualitative advantages. Most important, Iraq demonstrated a formidable capability for static defense, tactical surprise, and the logistic mastery of maintaining an army of 1.25 million men over several years in an intense combat environment. Iraq also gained experience with the use of attack helicopters, in-flight refueling of its combat aircraft, and the integrated use of chemical weapons delivered by mortar, helicopter, rockets, and aerial-delivered bombs and artillery.[17]

Iraq's efforts to build up its high technology weapons capabilities -- including chemical and biological weapons, ballistic missiles, and nuclear weapons -- were designed to guarantee Iraq's status as the preeminent Arab military power, and to provide it with a strategic deterrent against Iran and Israel. Ironically, Iraq wished to adopt an Israeli model of military planning. This required not only that it maintain a qualitative edge over Iran, but that it eventually establish a reserve system. Efforts to reduce the size of the standing army, estimated to be approximately 1.25 million strong in mid-1990 (Iraq only had 300,000 before the war), were underway and there had been a reorganization of army units.

After the cease fire in the Iran-Iraq war, Iraq simultaneously increased its military capability and its rhetoric against Israel, while strengthening, in appearance, its ties to the Arab world. For example, the Iraqi Culture and Information Minister, Latif Nusayyif, stated in July 1989: "Any attempts by Israel to launch an aggression against Iraqi territory will be met with all firmness and strength. We will reply to such an attempt.... We hope the Israelis will not commit any foolish act for which they will be sorry."[18] Following revelations in April 1990 of Iraqi attempts to smuggle nuclear weapons components from the United States, both Foreign Minister Tariq Aziz and Iraqi President Saddam Hussein clarified their intentions toward Israel and the Arab world. On April 3, 1990, Saddam Hussein stated "...we will make the fire eat up half of Israel if it tries to do anything against Iraq....We do not need an atomic bomb, we have the dual chemical. Whoever threatens us with the atomic bomb, we will annihilate him with the dual chemical." And on April 19, 1990, Saddam added: "He who launches an aggression against Iraq or the Arab nation will now find someone to repel him, because Iraq is part of the Arab nation, and we will repel him from Iraq."[19]

In justifying the development of high technology weapons such as chemical and nuclear weapons and missiles by the Arab world in general and by Iraq in particular, Iraqi Foreign Minister Tariq Aziz stated on April 5, 1990: "While Israeli supremacy is maintained in the industrial, military and technological spheres, Israel will continue to occupy our territory, deny us our rights, and will be able to carry out its expansionist plans at the expense of its Arab surroundings."[20] And Foreign Undersecretary Nizar Hamdoon stated that "as long as Israelis keep developing their system and their [nuclear] weapons, Iraq and others in the area feel they have the same right."[21]

The allied victory in the Gulf war resulted from a number of military advantages that included tactical surprise, the destruction of Iraq's command and control system, air supremacy and control of tactical intelligence, superiority in every dimension of technology, and better trained, motivated, and disciplined armed forces. In addition, the UN cease fire resolution called for the destruction of Iraq's nuclear, chemical, and biological capabilities, as well as most of its SSMs.[22] Nevertheless, Iraq's post-war army remains large, reasonably well-equipped, and capable of a renaissance if sanctions are ever lifted. Iraq's ability to use military power in the future to intimidate its neighbors, then, will depend on its access to money and the willingness of outside suppliers to provide arms and technology for financial reward.

The Iran-Iraq Conflict

Iran has emerged as the key strategic player in the Gulf. The destruction of the Iraqi military during the Gulf war has removed a significant security threat in the short term, and will allow Tehran to concentrate its energy and resources on reconstruction necessitated by the Iran-Iraq war. In addition to the lessons it learned from its own war with Iraq during the 1980s, Iran has drawn a number of lessons from the Gulf war. Recognizing the increasing importance of the quality of weapons, Iran is focusing on acquiring or developing new, sophisticated weaponry. Most importantly, Iran seeks to modernize its air force, largely destroyed during the Iran-Iraq war. (The acquisition of defecting Iraqi aircraft during the war has already partially filled this need.) Iran has also placed a priority on the development of its air defense system and is debating the value of SSMs in fighting a war.

However, new security alignments in the Gulf and the Middle East, as well as the heightened presence of the U.S. in the region may mitigate any tendency in Iran to favor regional arms control agreements.[23] While the Iranian leadership has shown great caution in confronting the United States, and notwithstanding its new friendship with Saudi Arabia, Iran and the Arab states of the Gulf have been adversaries for longer than their modern states have existed. Iran is unlikely to view the events of 1991 as evidence of a seachange in Arab attitudes toward their Persian rival, and is therefore likely to pursue a slow but deliberate effort to procure a major deterrent capability.

The Arms Race in South Asia

While most of the emerging literature on the dangers of weapons proliferation has focused on the Middle East, some important developments are taking place on the Indian subcontinent, including a debate about the correlation between the development of nuclear weapons in India and Pakistan over the last two decades and the absence of full-scale war since 1971. This argument has several dimensions.

112

First, it can be argued that to further stabilize their deterrence relationship, both states should be more explicit about their possession of nuclear weapons and proceed to integrate them into their armed forces inventories. They should establish well-tested command, control, and communications procedures. One of the most frightening prospects in a future conflict is the possibility that both sides might deploy bombs literally 'out of the basement' for the first time during a crisis or war. If nuclear weapons are to be part of the Indo-Pakistani military balance in the future, then, it could be argued, it is better to get them out of the basement and establish secure methods for their deployment.[24]

A second, and contradictory view is that precisely because nuclear weapons remained in the basement during the 1990 Kashmir crisis, they should stay in the basement and not be acknowledged as part of each side's inventory. According to this argument, the knowledge of their potential existence served as a deterrent to escalation by either side. However, by remaining undeclared, neither side was forced to react as they would have had to if explicit mention of nuclear capabilities had been made. Neither was the international community forced to intervene because of the danger of overt nuclear threats.

Third, the events of 1990 will reinforce the belief long held in both India and Pakistan that chemical weapons are of little utility in the Indo-Pakistani conflict. Neither side has shown publicly any interest in developing them, in part, because they already have nuclear weapons. But if the message here is that countries with nuclear weapons do not need chemical weapons, this will reinforce the Arab argument that Israel's nuclear capability is far more threatening than any Arab chemical capacity.

Finally, it is possible to argue that Pakistan's nuclear capability was of greater utility in the Kashmir crisis than was India's. India could hardly threaten a nuclear strike in response to local insurrection. Yet, Pakistan's nuclear capability may have deterred India from using its conventional superiority to put down the revolt more forcefully. If this is the case, arguments for proportional nuclear deterrence in Pakistan may be strengthened.

If this concept gains credence in the region, the most predictable result will be a strengthening of India's resolve to acquire all the military attributes of great power status, including thermonuclear weapons, intercontinental ballistic missiles, and significant regional power projection capabilities. While immediate attention has been focused on the prospects for a new Indo-Pakistani war, India's other rival, China -- acknowledged as a great power in part because of its nuclear weapons -- remains the key to understanding Indian concerns and aspirations in the high technology weapons arena.

From an Indian perspective, the silence in western circles concerning the Chinese nuclear weapons program and its impact on regional and international security is politically motivated. In 1971, when the United States decided that a rapprochement with China would be a strategic benefit, much of the rhetoric decrying the dangers of Chinese nuclear weapons disappeared. The Defense Department, which had routinely used the Chinese nuclear program as a benchmark for sizing U.S. nuclear forces, ceased to emphasize the dangers of the Chinese threat. Yet during this period of Sino-American rapprochement, China has systematically improved its intercontinental capabilities and poses a far greater threat now than at any time in the past. Indeed, in view of the alarm sounded in the U.S. Congress in 1989, when India first tested the Agni missile, an objective observer might well have thought that India, rather than China, posed the greater threat to the United States.

As long as China remains an accepted nuclear power, and the border disputes between them remain unresolved, India will not give up its nuclear ambitions. The Pakistani bomb may provide the political fuel for pressures on the Indian government to continue the program. However, fundamentally, India regards itself as a competitor with China, not with Pakistan. Pakistan is a dangerous irritant, but China is a regional superpower.

Since China exploded a nuclear device in 1964, India has refused to participate in discussions on nuclear non-proliferation on the grounds that nuclear disarmament must be comprehensive, not selective by region or state. India will not allow itself to be put into the category of a Third World state while China receives honorary superpower status based on its weapons technology. India's strategic relationship with China conditions its response to Pakistan; while India feels threatened by Pakistan in many ways, both direct and indirect, Indians bristle at being paired with Pakistan on the subcontinent.

Conclusion

The continued proliferation of advanced weapons to the Middle East and South Asia inevitably increases the demand for weapons to match or counter them. Furthermore, items such as nuclear weapons, chemical weapons, SSMs, and advanced combat aircraft carry important political baggage. Prestige, status, and the fear of appearing weaker than one's neighbors are central elements of national security. Thus, it is not possible to weigh the costs and benefits of weapons proliferation solely on a rational scale of military utility. Arab objections to Israel's nuclear weapons, like India's preoccupation with Chinese nuclear capabilities, goes far beyond the weapons' physical characteristics. Until the political dimensions of the proliferation problem are taken into account, regional arms control will remain elusive.

Notes

1. For a discussion of the factors that contribute to making a weapon stabilizing or destabilizing, see W. Seth Carus, "Weapons Technology and Regional Stability," in Shelley A. Stahl and Geoffrey Kemp, editors, *Arms Control and Weapons Proliferation in the Middle East and South Asia* (New York: St. Martin's Press, 1992 forthcoming).

2. Kenneth N. Waltz, *The Spread of Nuclear Weapons: More May Be Better*, Adelphi Papers #172 (London: International Institute for Strategic Studies, 1981).

3. In a speech in June 1990, Secretary of Defense Richard Cheney stated: "[The] U.S. commitment to Israel remains absolutely solid and unalterable.... [The] United States remains committed to insuring Israel's security, and we will continue to support Israel's qualitative military edge in the region." Remarks of Defense Secretary Dick Cheney to the American Israel Political Action Committee (AIPAC) Policy Conference on U.S. Middle East Policy and Israel, Washington, D.C., June 11, 1990.

4. For a sampling of opinions see Ze'ev Schiff, *Israel's Eroding Edge in the Middle East Military Balance* (Washington, D.C.: Washington Institute for Near East Policy, 1985); and Shai Feldman, "Security and Arms Control in the Middle East: An Israeli Perspective," in Stahl and Kemp, *Arms Control and Weapons Proliferation in the Middle East and South Asia*. For more optimistic views during this period see O. Erez, "The Arab-Israeli Air Balance," in Aharon Levran and Zeev Eytan, *The Middle East Military Balance 1987-88* (Jerusalem: Jerusalem Post Press, 1988), p. 196; and Hirsh Goodman and W. Seth Carus, *The Future Battlefield and the Arab-Israeli Conflict* (New Brunswick: Transaction Publishers, 1990).

5. See Avner Yaniv, *Deterrence Without the Bomb: The Politics of Israeli Strategy* (Lexington, Mass.: Lexington Books, 1987), p. 200.

6. One report states that only three Soviet SS-23s with submunitions would be required to knock out an American air base. See W. Seth Carus, "NATO, Israel, and the Tactical Missile Challenge," *Policy Focus*, Washington Institute for Near East Policy, May 1987, p. 2.

7. Both before and after the Gulf war, an intense debate has raged among Israeli specialists as to the role of deterrence in Israeli political-military doctrine. The issues at stake include: the extent to which Israeli deterrence relies on nuclear weapons, despite the official refusal to acknowledge their existence; how nuclear deterrence was affected by the war; how conventional deterrence is being undermined by new technology; and the costs and benefits of an overt nuclear policy.

A sampling of this debate can be found in the following texts. In addition to the works cited in this book by Evron, Yaniv, Gold, Harkavy, and Schiff, see Shai Feldman, *Israeli Nuclear Deterrence: A Strategy for the 1980s* (New York: Columbia University Press, 1982); Gerald M. Steinberg, *Deterrence, Defense, or Arms Control? Israeli Perception and Responses for the 1990s* (Santa Monica, California: California Seminar on International Security and Foreign Policy, 1990); Gerald Steinberg, "Does Deterrence Work?" *Jerusalem Post*, March 13, 1991; and Avner Cohen and Marvin Miller, "How Close to Midnight? A Retrospective View of the Gulf War Nuclear Threat," *Bulletin of the Atomic Scientist*, July/August 1991.

8. Raytheon, the Patriot's manufacturer, claims the missile was more effective in achieving catastrophic kills against Scuds aimed at Saudi Arabia than against those aimed at Israel. It claims that the missile enjoyed an 85 percent success rate against Scuds fired at Israel, and a 90 percent success rate against those fired at Saudi Arabia. However, Israeli officials claim that the success rate was only 50 percent since those missiles whose warheads were only hit by the Patriots and not destroyed caused considerable damage to Israeli buildings. In the Israeli estimate, these were not counted as kills. Raytheon's definition of success was similiar to that of the U.S. Army: the Patriot was successful if it demolished the warhead or pushed it out of the 15 mile area defended by the Patriot. Israel, on the other hand, used damage on the ground as the measure of a successful intercept, not whether the incoming Scud was hit.

One reason given by Raytheon for the variance in performance between Israel and Saudi Arabia is that the batteries sent to Israel were deployed hastily and were not optimally positioned for most effective interceptions. Raytheon also claimed that Israeli crews working with the American crews were not fully proficient in operating the system. Apparently, many of the Scuds fired against Israel broke up in reentry due to poor engineering by Iraq, with their fragments causing as much damage as the conventional warheads.

See "Raytheon Defends Its Patriot Missiles' Performance in War," *Wall Street Journal*, April 26, 1991; and R. Jeffrey Smith, "Patriot Missiles Less Effective in Israel," *The Washington Post*, April 26, 1991.

9. For more information on the Arrow program see pp. 85-86 in Chapter 4.

10. For more on the modernization of Israeli forces, see Goodman and Carus, *The Future Battlefield and the Arab-Israeli Conflict.*

11. For a strong statement of the impact of the Gulf war on Arab elite opinion see Walid Khalidi, "The New Middle East Security Environment," paper prepared for the American Academy of Arts and Science Conference on Restraining the Middle East Arms Race: Post-Gulf War Prospects, June 6-8, 1991.

12. For an indepth look at Arab strategies against Israel, see Abdel Monem Said Aly, "Quality vs. Quantity: The Arab Perspective of the Arms Race in the Middle East," in Stahl and Kemp.

13. Quoted in "Egyptian Says Arabs Should Acquire Chemical Weapons," Reuters, July 27, 1988, PM cycle.

14. Quoted in "On Mideast Nuclear Warheads," Cairo, MENA, 1400 GMT, 6 October 1988, translated in *FBIS-NES*, October 7, 1988, pp. 14-15.

15. The concept of strategic parity was developed after Sadat's 1977 journey to Jerusalem and is seen as a dynamic strategy, including military, political and economic factors. For an elaboration see Moshe Ma'oz, *Asad: The Sphinx of Damascus* (New York: Weidenfeld and Nicolson, 1988), pp. 178-183.

16. In April 1987, Mikhail Gorbachev was quoted as stating that "the reliance on military force in settling the Arab-Israeli conflict has completely lost its credibility." Quoted in Efraim Karsh, *The Soviet Union and Syria: The Asad Years* (London: Routledge, 1988), p. 92. In November 1989, the Soviet Ambassador to Syria, Alexander Zotov, remarked that Soviet arms sales to Syria would be based on the latter's "ability to pay" for the weapons, and "due observance" to the principle of "reasonable

defense sufficiency." Quoted in Caryle Murphy, "Syria Urged to Stress Defense," *Washington Post*, November 20, 1989.

17. Stephen C. Pelletiere, Douglas V. Johnson II, and Leif R. Rosenberger, *Iraqi Power and U.S. Security in the Middle East* (Carlise Barracks, Pennsylvania: Strategic Studies Institute, U.S. Army War College, 1990), pp 38-39.

18. "Jasim Interviewed on Israeli Threats, Kurds," Al-Ra'y, 23 July 1989, translated in *FBIS-NES*, July 24, 1989, pp. 14-15.

19. "President Warns Israel, Criticizes U.S.," Baghdad Domestic Service, 1030 GMT, 2 April 1990, translated in *FBIS-NES*, April 3, 1990, pp. 32-36. See also Alan Cowell, "Iraq Chief, Boasting of Poison Gas, Warns of Disaster if Israel Strikes," *New York Times*, April 3, 1990; and "Hussein Vows Retaliation," *New York Times*, April 19, 1990.

20. Quoted in "Iraq's 'Aziz Arrives in Amman, Makes Statement," Baghdad, INA, 1105 GMT, 4 April 1990, translated in *FBIS-NES*, April 5, 1990, p. 23.

21. Quoted in Caryle Murphy, "Iraqi Leader Presses Drive For Regional Dominance," *Washington Post*, March 23, 1990.

22. UN Security Council Resolution 687 For a Formal Cease Fire in the Gulf War, April 3, 1991, UN Document S/RES/687.

23. See Shahram Chubin, "Iran and the Lessons of the War with Iraq: Implications for Future Defense Policies," in Stahl and Kemp.

24. Former Indian Army Chief, General Krishnaswami Sundarji, argued this in April 1990 at the height of the most recent tension between India and Pakistan over Kashmir. See the interview with General Sundarji, "If pushed beyond a point by Pakistan, we will retaliate," in *India Today*, April 30, 1990, pp. 74-75.

CHAPTER SIX

Regional Arms Control: Origins and Precedents

Arms control can be a confusing concept. It is regarded with suspicion in the Third World because arms denial was one instrument the great powers used to colonize Africa and much of Asia. Modern arms control is a child of the nuclear age, and of the efforts to reduce the risks of war between the superpowers. The breakthroughs in conventional arms control in Europe hold some lessons for the Middle East, but the differences between the two regions exceed the areas of commonality.

Regional Arms Control: Historical Perspectives

The colonial powers were able to establish their vast empires in Asia, Africa, and Latin America between the fifteenth and nineteenth centuries in part by retaining a monopoly on sophisticated technology. When the Portuguese pioneered the sea-route to Asia via the Cape of Good Hope, they had a major advantage over the local populations along that long littoral: guns. Hand guns and, more important, big ship guns enabled them to force the submission of local potentates and to establish extremely favorable trading relations which, in turn, led to the establishment of fortified enclaves to combat the local population and to defend against attacks from other colonial powers.

Over the next three centuries, as more and more European powers joined in the scramble for colonies, firearms became widely available locally and were a less important factor in the acquisition of land than the organizational abilities and extraordinary self-confidence of the colonial powers. However, by the 1800s rapid changes in technology once more became the most decisive factors in enabling small colonial forces to control vast areas and huge populations. Railways, the telegraph, and more sophisticated military hardware were the keys to successful administration of empires.[1]

Weapons In the 'Wrong Hands'

A constant worry for the colonial powers was the lucrative trade in arms to native tribes and non-subjugated peoples located within or near colonial borders. This trade threatened to undermine the foundations upon which the empires rested. In the early nineteenth century, uprisings began to occur in various parts of Africa, and particularly West Africa, as a result of the introduction into the region of muskets, muzzle-loading guns, and later breech-loading rifles. The transfer of new breech-loaders in the late 1800s began to have a serious impact on the status quo. Wars became shorter and bloodier as a result of the effectiveness of breech-loaders in the hands of native groups.[2]

Thus, it was the colonial powers' fear that this new high technology was falling into the wrong hands that led to the first efforts at regional arms control in Africa and Southwest Asia. The Brussels Act of 1890 dealt with the African problem. It was part of a broader agreement on the slave trade and was signed by 13 European states, together with the United States, Iran, Zanzibar, and the Congo Free State. The relevant section of the act dealing with limitations on arms sales called for the prohibition of transfers into Africa between latitudes 20' North and 22' South of all firearms and ammunition. The exceptions were for flintlock guns and gunpowder, as well as for imports directly controlled by the great powers that included guarantees concerning the end use of the weapons.

Although the Brussels Act was ineffective in preventing the arms trade to Africa -- in large part because of the long coast lines and the ease with which controls could be circumvented -- the passage of the Act is highly significant. First, it reflected a consensus among the great powers that it was not in their interests to permit a free market in arms to Africa where many of the signatories had ongoing and competitive claims for colonial real estate. Second, the area of Africa covered by the Treaty conforms with what today would be called Black Africa. Excluded were the Arab countries of North Africa and the British stronghold in Southern Africa.[3]

Weapons in the 'Right Hands'

As long as high technology weapons remained in the hands of the colonial power at a time of rapid technological change, dominance over local groups was relatively easy to achieve. Perhaps the most stunning example of how this technological superiority operated in practice was the British military campaign in the Sudan in the last years of the nineteenth century.

On January 20, 1885, the British General 'Chinese' Gordon was murdered on the steps of his quarters in Khartoum, as the city was being looted by Mahdist armies.[4] With this victory, the Sudan was to remain under the control of the Mahdists until September 2, 1898, when an expeditionary force of 25,000 British and Egyptian troops under the command of Sir Herbert Kitchener defeated a Mahdist army of 60,000 men and occupied the capital city of the Mahdist empire, Omdurman.[5]

The one-sided victory of the numerically inferior British-Egyptian forces at Omdurman was made possible by the technological superiority of their weapons. Not only did Kitchener's forces have superior rifles and artillery, but they were also armed with the first modern machine gun, the Maxim gun.[6] The Maxim gun was used extensively in the battle of Omdurman, both as a combat support piece for infantry formations and mounted in gunboats to fire on the Mahdist forces, while remaining out of their range.

The British victory highlighted the importance of maintaining a technological edge in colonial wars. The success of the Maxim gun is apparent from the final 200 to 1 casualty ratio. By one account, less than 50 of Kitchener's men died, and 400 were wounded, compared to approximately 10,000 dead in the Mahdist army.[7] The battle of Omdurman was, in the words of Winston Churchill, "...the most signal triumph ever gained by the arms of science over barbarians. Within the space of five hours the strongest and best-armed savage army yet arrayed against a modern European Power had been destroyed and dispersed, with hardly any difficulty, comparatively small risk, and insignificant loss to the victors."[8]

The legacy of the colonial period remains strong in the contemporary world. Parallels between attempts by the great powers to limit arms to the natives in the 1880s and present efforts to limit arms to the Third World are frequently drawn. Similarly, one could draw an analogy to the battle of Omdurman when examining the extraordinarily asymmetric casualties in the Gulf war against Iraq. Thus, whether alluding to European efforts in the nineteenth century to keep breech-loading rifles out of the hands of the natives, or to more recent attempts to stop the spread of supersonic jet aircraft, nuclear weapons, and now surface-to-surface missiles, these policies result in discriminatory regimes pitting the technical 'haves' against the technical 'have-nots.'

Duplicitous Arms Suppliers

A more contemporary criticism of external power behavior concerns their willingness to turn the arms flow on and off in times of crisis. Thus, at various times over the past 40 years, western suppliers have severely restricted arms transfers to Israel, most of the Arab states, Iran, India, and Pakistan. For example, in September 1965, Britain and the United States placed an arms embargo on India and Pakistan during the war that broke out between them that month.[9]

The record is replete with examples of specific arms sales being denied, delayed, or placed under restrictions concerning end-use. This has been most apparent with regard to U.S. arms sales to Arab countries. The major suppliers have also shown a marked proclivity to increase arms sales and military assistance when it serves their strategic interests, as, for example, with the U.S. arms relationship with Pakistan. The Soviet Union has also displayed similar behavior toward its traditional clients, most recently when arms transfers to Syria were abruptly reduced in late 1984.

Because of their mixed track record, recipient countries have an inherent suspicion of supplier behavior. This is quite aside from questioning the relevance of arms control to their problems, particularly with regard to the example of recent arms control agreements reached between NATO and the Warsaw Pact countries in Europe.

Modern Arms Control As A Concept

Arms control, as currently known, came into vogue in the late 1950s as a result of the nuclear arms race. Early advocates were mostly drawn from the defense community, which included within its orbit many academic institutions and research centers that embraced academic disciplines increasingly associated with military strategy, such as economics, pure mathematics, physics, and political science.[10]

The involvement of these disciplines was a result of changes in strategy that evolved once thermonuclear weapons entered the U.S. and Soviet inventories. From this time the underlying purpose of nuclear weapons was to deter, rather than to fight wars. Nuclear deterrence theory provided strategists with a new military exchange model they could analyze using the rigorous tools of their disciplines. A nuclear war between the United States and Soviet Union was not expected to last more than a few days, making it very different from the protracted conflict of World War II. It would be a more quantifiable war: it could be 'gamed out.'

122

Furthermore, since the purpose of the strategy was to deter, not to fight, many of the more interesting questions concerned the deterrence phase: how to design and deploy nuclear weapons and nuclear forces to deter the adversary without using them in anger.

Arms control analysts were not interested in utopian schemes for general and complete disarmament such as those being proposed in the United Nations. Rather, they were concerned with ways to change the prevailing U.S. military doctrine which called for massive retaliation, or all-out thermonuclear war with the Soviet Union in the event of a Soviet attack on vital western interests. Explicit in the prevailing doctrine was an assumption that the West would, if necessary, initiate nuclear escalation against Soviet cities and industry if western conventional forces were on the verge of defeat.

A second stimulant for arms control was the nature and pace of the arms race. Since changes in military technology were occurring rapidly, the equation of power between the United States and Soviet Union could shift very quickly. Under these circumstances, it was feared that one side might be tempted to launch a preemptive surprise attack against the other's nuclear forces in the hope of either achieving a knockout blow, or assuring parity in a post-nuclear environment.

The objectives of the early arms control advocates were, in order of priority: first, to reduce the risks of thermonuclear war; second, to limit the effects of war if it occurred; and third, to reduce the financial burden of the arms race. These classic goals have survived the passage of time but other goals, including arms control as a confidence-building incentive, have since been added.[11] Some contradictions between the first and the third of these goals occurred in the U.S.-Soviet relationship. For example, the best way to reduce the risks of war was to reduce the incentive for surprise attack. This meant buying a new generation of hardened, more secure nuclear delivery vehicles; in the U.S. case, this resulted in the land-based, Minuteman intercontinental surface-to-surface missile (SSM), and the submarine-based, shorter-range Polaris missile. Thus, reducing the risk of war was associated with modernizing strategic nuclear forces at considerable cost.

Early arms control initiatives were almost entirely linked to the central arms race between NATO and the Warsaw Pact. Emphasis was placed on nuclear issues, and arms control initiatives included support for secure second-strike systems, and new techniques for crisis management, such as the establishment of the U.S.-Soviet hot-line (argued to be essential if accidental war was to be avoided).

Interest in arms control was given a favorable boost as a result of the American experience during the Cuban missile crisis of October 1962. To most Americans, the missile crisis ended as a defeat for the Soviet Union and a success for American crisis management techniques. The United States had prevailed by applying force indirectly, while simultaneously talking to the Soviets. The lessons were clear: the orchestrated, rational, and gradual application of military power in the nuclear age, combined with restraint and dialogue, could prevent a nuclear war. Furthermore, since one likely route to a nuclear exchange came from escalating regional conflict, efforts to apply arms control techniques to the Third World were explored. The conceptual underpinnings of arms control came to embrace the broader idea of the control of local conflict, the argument being that it was difficult to find a way to control a regional arms race unless one also addressed the sources of conflict.[12]

The confidence inspired by the handling of the Cuban missile crisis was shattered by the Vietnam war, an event that not only led to a massive anti-war movement in the United States, but also cast deep suspicions on American motives and policies, including arms control initiatives, throughout the Third World.

Arms Control in Europe: How Relevant for the Middle East?

The United States, the Soviet Union, and the Europeans have spent more than twenty years discussing, negotiating, and finally signing agreements on nuclear and conventional arms limitations. Over this period of time, a cottage industry of analysts came into being; some specialists have devoted much of their adult careers to issues such as strategic arms limitations and conventional force structure controls. It is not surprising, therefore, that the end of the Cold War and the parallel breakup of the Warsaw Pact, together with the signing of the Treaty on Conventional Armed Forces in Europe (CFE) in Paris in November 1990, have raised the possibility that the European experience of arms control may have applications for other conflict regions, especially the Middle East.

A comparison of Europe and the Middle East and their respective experiences with arms control suggests some useful lessons. For instance, while Europe has evolved a series of formal arms control and confidence-building measures, the Middle East and South Asia, despite their reputations for conflict, are replete with examples of practical restraint -- including the highly sophisticated demilitarization agreements between Israel, Syria, and Egypt regarding the Golan Heights and the Sinai.

Nevertheless, at the political level, the differences between the two regions are great. The most important difference is that the idea of using military force in post-World War II Europe to achieve political ends was considered an unacceptable risk given the presence of large numbers of nuclear weapons in the European theater, and the explicit linkage between the use of conventional arms and the use of nuclear weapons. The Cold War debate about the role of weapons and the use of military forces concerned their non-use, or their deterrent value. True, there were scenarios where such conflict was possible and, on occasions, the Europeans, Americans, and Soviets used military forces for political ends outside the European theater. But a NATO-Warsaw Pact war was considered a remote possibility, primarily because no one could see how either side could win.

In contrast, Middle Eastern countries have amply demonstrated their belief that force, as a last resort, is a necessary instrument of national policy. Indeed, victory in war has historically brought rewards, at least in the short run, to the winning side. Israel, for instance, has been able to buy itself many years of security by defeating the Arabs in a number of wars. However, the Arabs have not been deterred from fighting Israel. Instead, they considered the 1973 war against Israel a necessary conflict to redeem their pride and improve their bargaining position with the outside powers. Syria and Iraq have displayed a willingness to use force on numerous occasions, and the wars in North Africa indicate that military conflict remains an acceptable, albeit painful method of coercive diplomacy elsewhere in the region.

Further differences reveal the chasm separating the European experience from the Middle East. Initial confidence-building and security measures, and arms control agreements were reached in Europe before the Gorbachev era, at the height of the Cold War. First, there was a pre-existing balance of power. Two major offsetting alliances, NATO and the Warsaw Pact backed up by the nuclear weapons of the superpowers assured that no small country or group of countries within the European arena could fundamentally upset this balance. In addition, while there were border disputes between the European powers, it was generally agreed that force not be used to resolve them.

There have also been full diplomatic relations between the adversaries. Even at the height of the Cold War, American and Soviet diplomats were meeting regularly. This was the case as well for the countries of East and West Europe. There has also been a long history of cooperation between the European powers, the Soviet Union, and the United States since

World War II on a host of political, economic, and military issues. While these relations did not stop the Cold War, at no point during this period were relations so bad that all communications ceased.

In the military arena, there has been a basic standoff in force levels and types of weaponry on each side despite arguments about which side was stronger. Neither were there outstanding conflicts between the alliances, or within them, for that matter, during the period of arms negotiations. This absence of inter- or intra-alliance conflict combined with its strictly bipolar nature, provided a positive environment for consensus building and, ultimately, decision-making.

Finally, the NATO and Warsaw Pact countries came to appreciate that arms and troop reduction would translate directly into enhanced security for all parties. This was the basis of commonality that drove the process forward, at least at the planning level, before political decisions were taken to implement concrete measures.

The final progress on European arms control can be attributed to the strength of the NATO alliance, to Gorbachev's reform policies, and to the subsequent relaxation of East-West tensions. There was political will on both sides to push forward for reductions. There was a mutual desire for domestic retrenchment. Enhanced diplomatic relations had further relaxed Cold War tensions. There were no imminent security threats to either alliance, or to any individual member of either alliance. Sources of tension had begun to break down, particularly as glasnost and perestroika removed many of the fears and misperceptions on both sides. Finally, the ideological aspects of the Cold War were no longer seen as a zero-sum struggle between the two parties.[13]

It is difficult to find counterparts to these trends in the Middle East. As noted earlier, most countries in the region face multiple threats from their neighbors. While there are some major conflicts (Arab-Israeli, Iran-Iraq) that have widespread regional significance, other bilateral conflicts are also intense and dangerous. Hence, there is no single military standoff between two groups like NATO and the Warsaw Pact. Furthermore, the infusion, or alternately the withholding, of new arms capabilities from outside the region could rapidly change the balance of power.

By reducing the Iraqi military threat, the Gulf war has altered the regional power structure. But for many Arab countries, this has given more prominence to Israel as the dominant regional hegemon. In particular, Israel's nuclear capability is seen by the Arab states as unilaterally skewing the balance of power and demonstrating the gross asymmetries in military capabilities. It is as if NATO and the Warsaw Pact had existed with only the United States possessing nuclear weapons. The result would have been a totally different relationship requiring very different politics, and certainly different defense doctrines and force structures. In the Middle East, there is no basic parity in force levels or in types of weaponry; the region is characterized by massive asymmetries in force structure, including quality and quantity of arms.

In marked contrast to Europe, secure and accepted legal boundaries remain another key source of antagonism in the Middle East. The Gulf war highlighted the problems of historical boundaries; some current borders are not recognized, and contested de facto frontiers exist throughout the region. The territorial issue between Israel and all of its neighbors except Egypt remains unresolved. There are territorial disputes between Syria and Lebanon, with Syria claiming it has rights over all of Lebanon. The Iran-Iraq war began as a battle over the delineation of the boundaries along the Shatt al-Arab waterway.

The absence of diplomatic relations between Israel and all the Arab nations except Egypt is also a major stumbling block to the peace process. This problem is directly related to the question of Palestinian rights. There can be no open Arab-Israeli political dialogue, except for crisis management purposes, until the issues of Israel's borders, its right to exist, and the political rights of the Palestinians are resolved.

Unlike in Europe, there are no accepted geographic parameters of the region for arms control agreements or political dialogue. For example, Turkey has become a major player in the Middle East since the Gulf crisis, but it is also a member of NATO and, thus, will likely be excluded from regional arms restraints. Some might view Pakistan as a key Middle East player given its Islamic ties to the Arab states; its nuclear weapons are often referred to as the Islamic bomb. But restraints on Pakistan would have to include India, which, in turn, would insist on including China. In short, to set geographical limits on the Middle East is extraordinarily complicated, particularly as the dynamics of the region change. It will become even more complex in the future as new Muslim states may emerge if the Soviet Union disintegrates.

An important factor in the success of European arms control was an acknowledgement by both sides of its benefits. In the Middle East, there is no recognition at this time that arms control, or arms reductions, will serve national or mutual interests. While there is agreement that arms control issues may have some utility, particularly between Israel, Egypt, and Jordan, there has been no movement toward negotiations. Arms control is more often seen as a vehicle to hinder military capabilities -- capabilities both the regional countries and their outside suppliers argue are needed for self-protection.

To comply with the European model, there must be a shared desire to promote stability and improve relations. There must also be an absence of imminent security threats. None of these conditions applies in the Middle East, and none is likely to emerge in the absence of some breakthrough on one or more of the diplomatic fronts. It is for this reason that major new arms control initiatives for the Middle East have taken the form of supplier agreements to impose more transparency and limitations on military procurement.

Conclusion

The industrial powers' new-found enthusiasm for Middle East arms control provides an opportunity to address some of the more dangerous problems of the regional arms race. However, it must be understood that the European experience cannot be simply transplanted into the Middle East. Effective arms control in the region will take years to implement, and will depend, in large part, on compliance by the regional parties.

Notes

1. William H. McNeill, *The Pursuit of Power* (Chicago: The University of Chicago Press, 1982), pp. 257-58.

2. For more detail on the changes in rifle technology, see Michael Howard, *War in European History* (Norwich: Oxford University Press, 1976), pp. 102-103; Michael Howard, *The Franco-Prussian War* (London: Collins, 1961), pp. 4-8; and McNeill, *The Pursuit of Power*, pp. 231-245.

3. Another problem the colonial powers in Africa faced concerned the behavior of independent states with access to the sea, such as Ethiopia. Weapons were transferred from these coastal nations to countries further inland. Colonial powers tried constantly to control the sale and transfer of weapons in this region, particularly the sale of rifles. Concern with the sale of modern rifles and weaponry in the area continued until August 21, 1930, when Britain, France, and Italy signed an agreement regulating the sale of arms and munitions.

The British also had trouble in Southwest Asia, where the local tribesman began to acquire modern breech-loading rifles from Europe, via the Middle East. To curb this trade, the British took measures in three fields: multilateral action in cooperation with other colonial powers, bilateral action with regional powers and protectorates, and unilateral military action.

For more information on attempts by the colonial powers to control the arms trade, see Franz Amadeus Dombrowski, "Some Ideas About the Historical Role of Ethiopia's Access to the Sea," *Northeast African Studies*, Vol. 6, Nos. 1-2, 1984, pp. 171-177; R. W. Beachey, "The Arms Trade in East Africa in the Late Nineteenth Century," *Journal of African History*, Vol. III, Nos. 1-3, 1962, p. 453; and R.M. Burrel, "Arms and Afghans in Makran: An Episode in Anglo-Persian Relations 1905-1912," *Bulletin of the School of Oriental and African Studies*, Vol. 49, No. 1, 1986, p. 8.

4. The Mahdist movement was an Islamic religious movement around the figure of the Mahdi, the divinely guided one, and waged war against the British and Egyptians in Sudan.

5. Robert O. Collins, "History of the Nolitic Sudan," *Encyclopedia Britannica*, 15th Edition, 1981, Vol. XIII, pp. 112-113.

6. The Maxim gun was the first modern machine gun, designed by Hiram Stevens Maxim (1824-1899), an American-born inventor. The Maxim gun needed no external source of power. Instead it used the recoil from the explosion as its source of energy in order to reload. Versions of the Maxim gun were adopted by Britain, Germany, and by the U.S. Navy in the 1890s. See *Weapons* (New York: St. Martin's Press, 1980), pp. 206-209.

7. Richard H. Berg, "Soldiers of the Queen," *Strategy and Tactics*, Issue 95, January/February 1984, p. 23.

8. Winston S. Churchill, *The River War* (London: Eyre and Spottiswoode, 1899) p. 300.

9. On the cut-off of aid to India and Pakistan in 1965, see G.W. Choudhury, *India, Pakistan, Bangladesh, and the Major Powers* (New York: The Free Press, 1975), pp. 119-122.

10. Gene M. Lyons and Louis Morton, *Schools for Strategy: Education and Research in National Security Affairs* (New York: Praeger, 1965).

11. See Joseph Nye, "Arms Control After the Cold War," *Foreign Affairs*, Vol. 68, No. 5, Winter 1989/90, pp. 42-64.

12. For a pioneering, and still relevant, study on the importance of understanding the linkage between regional conflict and arms control possibilities, see Lincoln P. Bloomfield and Amelia C. Leiss, *Controlling Small Wars: A Strategy for the 1970s* (New York: Alfred A. Knopf, 1969).

13. For more detail on European arms control initiatives, including the CFE, see Ivo H. Daalder, *The CFE Treaty: An Overview and an Assessment* (Washinton, D.C.: The Johns Hopkins Foreign Policy Institute, 1991).

CHAPTER SEVEN

Arms Control Regimes

The lack of trust among the regional countries and the control of most high technology by the industrial powers means that most arms control regimes are de facto supplier regimes. While multilateral efforts to secure a global ban on chemical and biological weapons have attracted political support from the regional countries, problems of verification remain unresolved. Supplier controls on nuclear and missile technology, and embryonic attempts to limit conventional weapons transfers raise many technical problems, and are seen by some key regional countries as discriminatory. However, a freeze on missile sales is both desirable and feasible. The most positive boost to regional arms limitations would be the successful implementation of UN Security Council Resolution 687 banning all unconventional arms and related technology in Iraq.

Multilateral Regimes

The major weapons suppliers have initiated arms control regimes to deal specifically with those weapon systems deemed unconventional. Although there is still no international regime to control the transfer of conventional arms, an increasing awareness of the importance of this problem has developed in the wake of the Gulf war. The following paragraphs outline the background, content, and status of existing multilateral regimes as well as the reactions of key countries to them.[1]

Chemical and Biological Weapons

The 1925 Geneva Protocol was established to prevent the use of chemical and biological weapons in war, and currently has 125 member states. The Protocol stemmed from the universal horror at the heavy use of chemical weapons by all sides during World War I. Its weakness lies in the fact that the Protocol does not prohibit the production, stockpiling, or transfer of chemical or biological weapons. In addition, it contains a provision stating that the Protocol ceases to be binding if a state's enemy fails to observe the prohibition against chemical use. An added complication for the Middle East was the decision by a number of Arab states to specify that their ratification of the Geneva Protocol did not imply a recognition of Israel. This leaves open the possibility that these states may not consider the no-use prohibition in force with regard to the Jewish state.[2]

The Biological Weapons Convention (BWC) of 1975 seeks to reinforce the 1925 Geneva Protocol prohibition against the use of biological weapons in war. The BWC prohibits the development, production, stockpiling, or other acquisition of biological weapons and toxins, and places a prohibition on delivery systems for biological weapons. Currently 112 states are full parties to the treaty. In the Middle East, Israel and Algeria are not members, while Egypt, Iraq, Morocco, Syria, and the United Arab Emirates have signed but not ratified the agreement. The BWC has been criticized from its inception for having no requirement for inspection or verification.

In a similar attempt to reinforce the Geneva Protocol against chemical weapons use, and wary of the mistakes made in negotiating the BWC, the UN Conference on Disarmament in Geneva has been negotiating a global chemical weapons convention (CWC) for over 20 years. The goal of a future CWC will be the complete elimination of chemical weapons from the world's arsenals combined with effective verification and inspection mechanisms to ensure compliance. The use of chemical weapons in the Iran-Iraq war reinvigorated the Geneva negotiations. A conference on chemical weapons held in Paris in January 1989 was attended by representatives of 149 states. The final document of the Paris conference reaffirmed the Geneva Protocol's commitment not to use chemical weapons and urged a speedy conclusion of a CWC.[3]

As the two parties most affected by a future CWC, the U.S. and Soviet Union have been steadily refining their view of a CWC over the last few years. In 1987, the Soviet Union accepted the U.S. demand for anytime/anywhere challenge inspections of chemical sites as the necessary standard for an effective verification regime. Recently, the U.S. made an important concession in its stand with regard to the CWC negotiations, abandoning its previous insistence on maintaining two percent of its chemical stockpile even after a CWC was negotiated.[4]

The principal criticism of the CWC negotiations in the Middle East comes from Arab states that insist the problem of chemical weapons in the region is linked to Israel's nuclear weapons arsenal. At the 1989 Paris conference, virtually every Arab state represented maintained that the two issues could not be addressed separately.[5]

In addition to the formal regimes outlined above, a number of industrial states formed the Australia Group in January 1987 to officially coordinate chemical export controls. The Australia Group grew out of informal export controls in the member countries in place since the spring of 1984 out of concern for chemical weapons use in the Iran-Iraq war. The Australia Group is based on the assumption that "relevant [chemical weapons] technologies are so highly developed, or rare, that they can be controlled by a relatively small number of governments through their export-control policies."[6] Membership includes the member countries of the European Community, Australia, Canada, Japan, New Zealand, Switzerland, the United States, and the Commission of the European Community.

The Australia Group targets 50 chemicals that could be used in the production of chemical weapons. These are subject to export licensing in each member country in order to prevent sales that will benefit chemical weapons programs. Over the last few years, several members of the Group -- specifically Germany, Switzerland, and Japan -- have come under attack for disregarding their obligations under the Australia Group by allowing chemical weapons-related exports to Third World countries. Chemical weapons technology and materials are also increasingly available from non-western sources. Nevertheless, the experience of the UN boycott of Iraq may give a boost to the export control restrictions approach embodied in the Australia Group by maintaining the boycott in place for chemical and other weapons technologies.[7]

Surface-to-Surface Missiles (SSMs)

A group of seven states -- the United States, Canada, France, Italy, Japan, Britain, and West Germany -- formed the Missile Technology Control Regime (MTCR) in April 1987, to deal with the growing threat posed by the spread of ballistic missile technology. The MTCR focuses narrowly on those missiles considered nuclear-capable, defined as having a range of at least 300 km and a payload capability of at least 500 kg. Like the Australia Group, the MTCR consists of a set of parallel export controls to slow the development of Third World SSM programs. The agreement prohibits the transfer of conventional SSMs, space-launch vehicles, key subsystems for SSMs, and facilities and equipment to produce SSMs. Other items to be limited are on-board computers, inertial navigation systems, liquid and solid rocket fuel, testing equipment, flight control equipment, materials for rocket body parts and engine parts, and technology and know-how for the above items. Any of these items sold must be accompanied by assurances that they will not be diverted to rockets.

Since its inception, Spain, Belgium, Luxembourg, the Netherlands, Australia, Denmark, and Norway have joined the regime. Sweden, Switzerland, and most importantly, the Soviet Union have agreed to abide by the MTCR export guidelines. China, however, has not agreed to abide by MTCR guidelines and appears to be continuing its policy of missile sales to the Third World, despite repeated pressure from the U.S. administration to halt such sales.

One of the principal faults of the MTCR is its definition of nuclear-capable missiles. The range and payload guidelines that it sets are not necessarily relevant limits for Third World conflicts. In the Middle East, for example, adversarial states are quite close together geographically, making shorter-range missiles strategically significant. Similarly, the 'nuclear-capable' designation leaves open the possibility that suppliers may sell missiles that fall within the MTCR's scope if the supplier is assured that they will not carry nuclear weapons. In addition, Third World states subject to the export restrictions complain that the regime is inherently discriminatory while being unverifiable and unenforceable.

Nuclear Weapons

The Nuclear Non-Proliferation Treaty (NPT) of 1968 divided the world into the nuclear 'haves' and 'have-nots' with the purpose of halting the spread of nuclear weapons technology in exchange for promoting the spread of peaceful nuclear energy technology. The NPT obliges its nuclear weapon state parties to refrain from providing nuclear weapons to non-nuclear states, and to assist in the development of peaceful nuclear energy in non-nuclear states. It further obliges the nuclear weapon states to work toward global nuclear disarmament. The NPT obliges its non-nuclear state members to refrain from acquiring nuclear weapons and to open all of their nuclear-related facilities to inspection by the International Atomic Energy Agency (IAEA) to ensure compliance. With 142 member states, including three nuclear weapon states -- the U.S., Soviet Union, and Britain -- the NPT is the most sweeping, comprehensive, and probably most successful technology control regime in existence. Both France and South Africa have announced their intention to join the NPT -- France as a nuclear weapon state, and South Africa as a non-nuclear state.[8] China announced in August 1991 its decision "in principle" to sign the NPT.[9]

To supplement the prohibition on military nuclear trade in the NPT, the Zangger Committee and later the London Club of nuclear suppliers developed a common trigger list of export items that would require an

IAEA inspection agreement before they would be sold.[10] The London Suppliers Club thus ressembles both the Australia Group and the MTCR. However, supplier export controls on nuclear material supplement a rigid global treaty, whereas there are currently no such treaties for chemical weapons or ballistic missiles.

Despite its success in formalizing the non-nuclear status of most of the countries of the world, the NPT has not succeeded in halting the spread of nuclear weapons altogether, nor has it been entirely successful even among its own member states. Israel, India, Pakistan, Brazil, and Argentina all remain non-members with significant nuclear programs. Iraq is a party to the NPT but has nevertheless been engaged in a sophisticated clandestine program to develop nuclear weapons, causing deep concern over the effectiveness of IAEA inspection procedures.[11] The discriminatory nature of the NPT has come under criticism in the Third World, particularly from India which accuses the nuclear weapon states of trying to prevent the developing world from gaining access to sophisticated technology. The NPT has also been criticized for not taking into account the regional security motivations of nuclear weapons acquisition in some states, such as Israel. The Treaty comes up for formal renewal in 1995.

Supplier Regimes in the Post-Gulf War Era

Arms Control and Iraq

The test case for whether international cooperation to control unconventional weapons proliferation can work in the Middle East will be the success of the UN sanctions against Iraq. One of the coalition's goals in the Persian Gulf war was to remove the military threat Iraq posed to the region. Although the air and ground campaigns destroyed a great deal of its conventional and unconventional capabilities, Iraq has emerged from the war with enough military power intact to continue to pose a threat, albeit a greatly diminished one, to some of its neighbors.

The terms of the United Nations cease fire resolution are aimed at containing and removing this threat.[12] This is the most severe resolution ever passed by the UN Security Council against a member state. In order to promote stability in Iraq and to prevent any new aggression, a UN observer mission will be deployed in a demilitarized zone along the Iraq-Kuwait border. To combat Iraq's continued conventional threat, and to prevent any near-term buildup in these weapons, the resolution calls on all states to continue sanctions on arms and related materials. Thus, the responsibility for preventing the transfer of arms to Iraq is placed on the supplier nations and not on the Iraqi regime. In fact, nowhere in the resolution is Iraq prohibited from purchasing conventional weapons or related materials.

While Iraq's conventional threat is important, the Security Council was concerned foremost with Iraq's unconventional weapons, specifically with its longer-range missiles, its chemical and biological weapons, and its nuclear weapons-usable material and development facilities. The resolution requires Iraq to destroy or remove, under international supervision, all chemical and biological weapons and stocks of agents, and all surface-to-surface missiles with a range greater than 150 kilometers. The resolution established a special commission to carry out on-site inspections of each of Iraq's chemical, biological, and missile capabilities. The resolution also prohibits Iraq from acquiring or developing nuclear weapons or nuclear weapons-usable material, and calls for the removal by the IAEA of all such material now in Iraq's possession. If the UN resolution is implemented and verification and permanent monitoring procedures work, and if the destruction of all relevant equipment is carried out, Iraq's ability to rearm covertly should be seriously degraded and its threat to the region weakened.

Implementing and verifying the terms of the resolution will not be easy; the task itself poses technical problems, and Iraq is known to be untrustworthy with regard to compliance, as evidenced by the pattern of partial disclosures and repeat inspections in UN efforts to enforce Resolution 687 during the summer of 1991. Furthermore, success will take time, and there are as yet no agreed upon mechanisms for enforcement other than keeping economic sanctions in place.[13] There is also a danger that other countries in the region, especially Israel, will not be convinced that the UN resolution is being effectively implemented. In this case, Israel may resort either to military operations to destroy Iraqi capabilities -- what has been called coercive arms control -- or, equally likely, it may refuse to subscribe to regional arrangements that call for restrictions on its own forces.

It is worth comparing Resolution 687 with the terms of the Versailles Peace Treaty following World War I. At Versailles, the Allies agreed to disarm Germany to ensure that German militarism would never again threaten European security or world peace. The terms were extremely harsh, even in comparison to those now levied against Iraq. Detailed restrictions were placed on the German army, navy, and air force, and Germany was forbidden to produce or import most weapons. Yet, over the years, Germany was still able to rearm covertly and keep alive its arms industry. The extent and thoroughness of Germany's ability to deceive the allies has become a case study in the methods a determined country can use to avoid what it considers unfair and discriminatory treatment.[14]

The German lesson should not be forgotten. It must be assumed that there are many patriotic Iraqis who, while having no love for Saddam Hussein, are appalled at the humiliation their country has suffered and are determined to redress the grievances. While Iraq does not possess the industrial skills available to Germany in 1919, the full extent of Iraq's ability to infiltrate the economic structure of the West, particularly western Europe, in order to gain access to very high technology is just becoming known. Similarly, the ineffectiveness of established export controls, particularly in Germany, to stem the flow of high technology has been dramatized by the Iraqi case.[15] The danger is that once Iraq begins to export oil and gains access to hard currency, it will be able to hide a portion of its revenues for covert purposes. Once it has accumulated a sizable hard currency account, it could once more use its financial resources to penetrate the arms market and buy the services of unemployed technicians and engineers in Europe, including East Europe and the Soviet Union.

Regional Options and Outlook

A supplier regime restricting the transfer of arms and technology to the Middle East would have a greater impact on those countries on the verge of reequipping or modernizing their forces than on those that had just completed major purchasing cycles. The following matrix breaks the countries of the region down into four classes based on two factors that help or constrain their efforts to override a cartel: access to hard currency, and the technical skills of their indigenous population.

In view of the leakage that is inevitable in any supplier regime, countries with access to hard currency will, over time, find ways around constraints through black market suppliers, or by tapping the potential of East European and Soviet specialists who may be seeking work as technological mercenaries in the future. A regional country with a large budget and a sense of purpose will not find it difficult to overcome some of the effects of a supplier restraint regime, particularly if it continues for many years. Furthermore, states outside of the five major arms suppliers, such as Brazil, Argentina, South Africa, or the Koreas, might well be tempted to break the rules of the cartel if a lucrative order was available. While the smaller suppliers currently do not produce the most advanced weapons, they can provide a wide array of less sophisticated systems, and could possibly increase production for the right price. In this sense, the

Vulnerability to Supplier Arms and Technology Cartel

	Significant Indigenous Technical Skills	Limited Indigenous Technical Skills
EASY ACCESS to Hard Currency	**1** • Iraq (in future) • Iran (in future)	**2** • Saudi Arabia • Libya • Kuwait • United Arab Emirates • Other GCC nations
LIMITED ACCESS to Hard Currency	**3** • Israel • India • Egypt • Pakistan • Turkey * • Iran (at present) • Iraq (at present)	**4** • Syria • Jordan • Yemen • Afghanistan

1 = Least vulnerable   4 = Most vulnerable

rich countries of the Persian Gulf are in a much better position to bypass a supplier regime than are those with very limited access to hard currency, such as Egypt, Israel, or Turkey.

However, when one takes skills into account, some of those countries with limited access to hard currency are also very technically adept, such as Israel, India, and, to a lesser extent, Egypt and Turkey. Here, the question is whether they could bypass the embargo by using their own indigenous skills, perhaps supplemented by commercial products from the open market where the clear-cut rules of the regime are not so readily applied.

The most vulnerable countries are those that have limited access to hard currency and few indigenous technical skills. Into this category would fall Syria, Jordan, Yemen, and Afghanistan. It is difficult to see how they could circumvent supplier restraints without greater access to hard currency. In the cases of Syria, Jordan, and Yemen, such access could be obtained from the Gulf Cooperation Council (GCC) countries. Indeed, this is how Syria is proposing to fund its own reequipment program. But, this is a perilous foundation on which to base national security.

While no country falls into the least vulnerable category at this time, both Iraq and Iran could move into this box if their oil production is brought back to capacity, if they pay off their debts, and if they start to exploit their abundant resources. Over a ten-year period, for example, they could emerge once more as formidable military powers, precisely for these reasons.

A Freeze on All New Arms Sales. The strictest conventional arms supplier regime would be one that instituted a freeze on all new arms and military-related technology requests for an indefinite period. To be effective, the freeze would have to be acceptable to all key suppliers. At minimum, ten European countries, the U.S., Soviet Union, China, North and South Korea, South Africa, Argentina, and Brazil would have to be parties. The chances of reaching a consensus among these disparate players is low, especially since it would mean foregoing lucrative export earnings. With aggressive leadership, the United States might be able to persuade most suppliers to join, especially if the U.S. itself were prepared to forego aid to friends and the revenues from arms sales. But even if the key supplier countries agreed to such a freeze, an active black market in some of the proscribed items would likely emerge, unless rigorous enforcement mechanisms could be found.

A moratorium on all arms sales to the Middle East might require the

United States to freeze not only new arms sales, but also its on-going cooperative military agreements with allies, such as Israel and Egypt. It can hardly be expected that the other major suppliers would hold back on sales if, for example, the U.S.-Israeli Arrow anti-missile missile program were to receive large amounts of additional funding. Washington might also be required to put limits on military assistance funds for Egypt and Israel that could be used to strengthen domestic arms production. If the U.S. refused to stop its military aid programs and joint cooperative ventures it is unlikely that any of the other suppliers would take the freeze seriously.

Restrictions on Specific Conventional Weapons. Restricting access to select weapons and technologies holds more promise, provided that there is a consensus on the items that should be proscribed. In theory, the focus should be on those weapons and technologies that pose the greatest risks to stability in the Middle East and are produced by the fewest suppliers. This might include the latest generation of aircraft, missiles, and heavy tanks, along with certain categories of warships.

The following matrix lists four categories of weapons based on the danger they pose to Middle East stability and the number of possible suppliers. While the matrix does not take into account the difficulty of controlling access to weapons components, which are as important as complete weapon systems, it nevertheless provides a reference to judge which categories of weapons should be the easiest and most difficult to control.

Small arms, for instance, have been responsible for hundreds of thousands of deaths in Middle East wars but are virtually impossible to control due to the number of potential sources. On the other hand, some of the very latest generation weapons are currently produced only by the United States. For example, only the United States makes Tomahawk cruise missiles, Stealth fighters, Patriot missiles, and some of the more sophisticated electronic warfare systems. Thus, Washington has the power to restrict the flow of these technologies without consulting with other suppliers. However, cooperation between the key suppliers is essential to limit the transfer of older technology aircraft and missile systems.

Suppose, for example, that sales of Soviet, American, French, and British advanced combat aircraft were prohibited for a year or more. This arrangement raises a number of problems. While aircraft such as the U.S. F-15, the British Tornado, and the French Mirage have formidable performance profiles, their potential effectiveness depends, in part, on pilot skills and the specific electronics, munitions, and computer software that

Focus of Arms Control Initiatives		
	More Dangerous	Less Dangerous
EASIER TO CONTROL (Few Suppliers)	• Nuclear weapons • Heavy surface warships • Submarines • Surface-to-surface missiles • Advanced rockets • 4th/5th generation SAMs/AGMs/AAMs • 4th/5th generation jet combat aircraft • Long-range cruise missiles • Heavy armed helicopters • Abrams class heavy tanks • Exotic munitions (FAEs)	• ATBMs (Patriot) • Reconnaissance satellites and aircraft
DIFFICULT TO CONTROL (More Suppliers)	• Chemical and biological weapons • Light surface warships • 3rd generation jet combat aircraft • 3rd generation SAMs/AGMs/AAMs • Medium-range artillery and rockets • Medium and light tanks • Cluster munitions • Mines	• Transport aircraft • Jet trainer aircraft • Light helicopters • Small arms and munitions • APCs and trucks • Patrol boats

are provided along with the basic platform. A pair of identical F-15s becomes two very different combat aircraft if one is fitted with long-range conformal fuel tanks and the latest electronics and missiles and the other has no conformal fuel tanks and less sophisticated sub-systems and software. Thus, unless all the sub-systems are included in the list of proscribed items, limiting the platforms may create as many problems as it solves. It would, for instance, give every recipient country an incentive to upgrade its existing inventory of combat aircraft with the latest sub-systems and thereby achieve a considerable jump in capability without having to buy a new fleet of jets. Furthermore, putting the sub-systems on the proscribed list would raise other problems since some countries -- such as South Korea and Brazil -- that do not produce the basic combat air platforms have sophisticated capabilities in electronics and missile production.

Another difficulty is that the Middle East playing fields would not be level when the restraints were initiated. Countries with the largest existing air forces (Israel, Saudi Arabia, Egypt, and Syria) would be better equipped to endure a moratorium than those countries on the verge of upgrading their inventories, or rebuilding depleted forces, (Jordan, Kuwait, Iran, and Iraq). Israel has the additional advantage of having its own advanced aerospace industry.

Nevertheless, a supplier agreement to slow down delivery of top-of-the-line combat aircraft would be an important political statement of intent. If coupled with active diplomacy to resolve regional disputes, such an agreement might win grudging approval from the key regional countries that have their own financial reasons to slow down force modernization.

Limitations on SSM Transfers. Limitations on ballistic missile sales offer more promising results, in part because their indiscriminate use against civilian targets in the Iran-Iraq war, in Afghanistan, and in the Gulf war has led to the widespread belief that they are dangerous weapons that should be banned like nuclear, chemical, and biological weapons. The United States has proposed an eventual ban on SSMs to the Middle East. Some observers believe a ban should be sought immediately. The Intermediate-Range Nuclear Forces Treaty (INF) signed by the super-powers on December 8, 1987, set in motion the systematic destruction of an entire class of missiles in the superpower arsenals. If the INF Treaty were extended to include all countries, it would require the removal of all the SSM systems with ranges between 500 and 5500 kilometers currently deployed in the Middle East.[16]

Nevertheless, a total ban on intermediate-range SSMs is unrealistic at this time. The INF Treaty, if applied globally, would put an end to programs under development in Israel and India, and would eliminate most Chinese and the principal French land-based missiles already deployed. These countries can make plausible arguments for continuing their missile programs. Nuclear deterrence for France and Israel, and probably India, is built around SSM capabilities. It is unlikely that an extension of the INF would be acceptable to countries in the region that already have SSMs. In addition, a total ban on SSMs would favor those countries that retained strong air forces, because of the overlap in mission capability. For example, it would give Israel an added advantage over Syria.

A freeze on SSM sales is more viable, and is, in large part, already in effect. The MTCR provides an institutional framework for expanding its membership and providing precise guidelines as to what items and technologies fall within its purview. Although full membership is currently limited to western countries, as noted earlier the Soviet Union has indicated its willingness to abide by the regime's guidelines with the exception of Scud transfers to Afghanistan. The problem countries are China and North Korea; the latter has already delivered modified Scud missiles to several Middle East states. In order to obtain compliance from these countries, significant diplomatic pressure will be necessary. The price may be a more relaxed attitude toward sales of less provocative items such as artillery and ammunition, which attract much needed hard currency.

There are also problems posed by the short-range SSMs that fall outside the guidelines of either the MTCR or the INF treaty. In some of the key Middle East conflicts, the distances between targets are so short that a missile with a range of 300 km has major strategic significance. For instance, Damascus, Amman, and Tel Aviv are all less than 70 km from enemy borders. New generations of cruise missiles, stand-off missiles, and multiple launch rocket systems may pose greater military threats than SSMs in view of their relatively low costs, and the ease with which they can be rapidly deployed to different sectors of a military theater.

The impact of a missile moratorium on regional stability and regional security would vary from case to case. In the context of the Persian Gulf, it would give the GCC countries time to reorganize their defenses, and allow them to escape the shadow of potential Iraqi and Iranian missile rearmament. It would also allow Israel to relax somewhat its military relations with Syria. While Syria already has an impressive missile force, Israel fears an increased Syrian missile capability that would enable it to launch a massive preemptive strike against Israeli military targets, crippling Israel's conventional offensive deterrent capability.

On the other hand, a freeze on SSM inventories would leave intact a number of existing offensive missile forces that could be used to intimidate neighbors. From an American perspective, Israeli and Saudi missiles pose no security problems, but to others they are provocative. On the Indian subcontinent, a missile freeze would have a more negative impact on Pakistan than on India, since China would have to be part of the arms restraint regime and its support for Pakistan's missile program has been more important than have the supplies by the industrial powers to the Indian program.

Limits on Offensive or Aggressive Weapons. Defining a weapon as offensive or aggressive is difficult, and often deceptive. It might be said that the Scud is obviously an offensive terror weapon while the Patriot missile interceptor, and other theater missile defense (TMD) systems, are defensive: therefore, the former should be banned, but not the latter. By this same logic, sales of the much smaller, defensive Stinger anti-aircraft missile should also be permitted. However, the Stinger has been one of the most tightly controlled weapons in modern history precisely because it is small, man-portable, and can shoot down aircraft. Stingers in the wrong hands, i.e. anti-western terrorists, can be used in very aggressive and offensive ways.

Scuds and Stingers are both considered offensive weapons though they have very different performance characteristics. The Patriot system can be used against aircraft and, depending on its deployment mode and its integration into the force structure of the recipient, can support offensive operations by providing tactical battlefield protection for offensive military units. The operational concept for a TMD system calls for an offensive capability to attack enemy launchers and missiles at the source, while active and passive defenses limit damage if the missiles are fired.

On the other hand, the case for TMD might be strengthened by an SSM freeze that left in place a small number of SSMs in the hands of countries such as Syria, Libya, Iraq, or Iran. Thus, there would be greater assurance that the adversary could not overwhelm anti-missile defenses by sheer numbers. Under these circumstances, the transfer of Patriot and follow-on defensive systems might be most sensible if restrictions on SSMs have been implemented.

Controlling Arms Transferred

End-use limitations are a means for suppliers to exercise restraint over recipients once a decision to sell arms has been made. The most common practices -- aside from simply limiting the quantities sold -- are to downgrade a particular weapon system or, alternatively, not to provide top-of-the-line sub-systems that fit on a basic weapon system platform. For instance, over the years, recipients of American combat aircraft have been denied access to the most advanced air-to-air missiles currently in service with the United States air force (the exception being NATO air forces).

Other control methods involve prior agreements between the supplier and the recipient on deployment. For example, Saudi Arabia agreed not to deploy any of its F-15s to its northern air base of Tabuk, owing to its proximity to Israel. While in a time of crisis the United States would be hard-pressed to stop such deployment if the Saudis insisted, Washington would have the capacity then to cut off follow-on equipment, particularly electronic spare parts, not produced in Saudi Arabia. Hence, the supplier, under these circumstances, has a certain amount of leverage that most recipients are prepared to accept.[17]

A variant of this control mechanism would be to limit the provision of advanced ground and support systems, such as radars and electronic warfare aircraft, thereby limiting an offensive platform's flexibility. For instance, one of the strongest arguments against supplementing the transfer of F-16s to Pakistan with the provision of AWACS aircraft was that the latter would act as a force-multiplier, thereby provoking extreme concern in India.

More exotic variants of the qualitative control approach are the development of permissive action links (PALs) including 'double key' systems, and so-called 'poison pills' that involve tampering with the electronic brains of military hardware to prevent certain kinds of use. The PAL/poison pill option is based on the fact that the electronic components of modern weapon systems are so complex that only the supplier, i.e. the manufacturer, really knows what occurs inside the brain of the weapon system. Accordingly, it is possible to design sub-components of the electronic brain that require positive approval from the supplier before they can be used, or that require frequent replacement, thereby providing the supplier with an ongoing veto on weapons use. Another alternative would be to place a kind of computer bug in a system that, given a certain electronic signal, would disable the weapon.

The problem with these approaches is that they are operationally unsound. The primary reason for transferring weapons to friendly countries is that they may need to use them in a crisis. It might be counterproductive, for instance, to provide Saudi Arabia with highly sophisticated weapons that required frequent upgrading by the United

States, for fear that a crisis might arise and the upgrading would coincide with the crisis. In such a case, the Saudis might not be able to use their weapons, in which case both U.S. and Saudi goals would be undermined.

The poison pill may never amount to a credible policy option, but as technology becomes increasingly sophisticated and certain capabilities are restricted to a limited number of suppliers, an argument can be made that supplier control over a client's arsenal is increasing, not diminishing. While this never eliminates the possibility that weapons can be used on a one-time basis without permission, and in ways that would elicit supplier disapproval, all the evidence from recent wars indicates that, with the exception of an initial first strike by aircraft and missiles, most weapons systems must be used repeatedly if they are to fulfill their mission.

The Problem of Dual-Use and Obsolescent Technology

Another problem facing a supplier restraint regime is the broader question of technology transfers, especially dual-use systems that have applications for both military and civilian purposes. It is understandable that proposals for conventional arms control focus on finished products, such as missiles and aircraft. But in the modern market place, the transfer of supposedly innocent items can, over time, have as serious an impact on the local military balance as can the transfer of finished products. Brookings Institution analyst Janne Nolan has argued that a symbiotic relationship between the advanced countries and the Third World has evolved over the years. In order to sustain the costs of developing new technologies, the major countries in the industrial world need to sell less sophisticated technology to raise revenues. As high technology items become obsolescent, it becomes less risky to export them to non-allies.[18] Iraq's use of calutrons -- now considered low technology and readily available in the technology market place -- for its nuclear program is a case in point.

Conclusion

Supplier attempts to establish arms control regimes that cover all military-related high technology items in the Middle East are unlikely to succeed. Rather, supplier efforts should focus on those technologies that are most relevant for weapons of mass destruction and advanced delivery systems. Within these parameters it may be possible to slow down or even stop the further proliferation of nuclear weapons and surface-to-surface missiles.

Notes

1. For a detailed account of these regimes, see Zachary S. Davis, *Non-Proliferation Regimes: A Comparative Analysis of Policies to Control the Spread of Nuclear, Chemical and Biological Weapons and Missiles* (Washington, D.C.: Congressional Research Service, 1991). Specifically on chemical weapons, see Brad Roberts, "The Strategic Implications of Chemical Weapons Proliferation," and "Chemical and Biological Weapons and Regional Arms Control," in Shelley A. Stahl and Geoffrey Kemp, editors, *Arms Control and Weapons Proliferation in the Middle East and South Asia* (New York: St. Martins Press, 1992 forthcoming).

2. See Davis, *Non-Proliferation Regimes*, p. 19.

3. See "Text of the Declaration From the Paris Conference on Chemical Weapons," *New York Times*, January 12, 1989.

4. See Fact Sheet on Chemical Weapons Initiative, U.S. Arms Control and Disarmament Agency, May 13, 1991.

5. See James M. Markham, "Arabs Link Curbs On Gas And A-Arms," *New York Times*, January 9, 1989.

6. See *SIPRI Yearbook 1988: World Armaments and Disarmament* (Stockholm: SIPRI, 1988), p. 104.

7. Elisa Harris of the Brookings Institution argues that neither export controls nor a non-proliferation treaty will halt the spread of chemical weapons. She states that the best solution is a total ban on chemical weapons. See Elisa D. Harris, "Stemming the Spread of Chemical Weapons," *The Brookings Review*, Winter 1989/90, pp. 39-45.

8. See Alan Riding, "France Will Sign 1968 Nuclear Pact," *New York Times*, June 4, 1991; and David B. Ottaway, "South Africa Agrees To Treaty Curbing Nuclear Weapon," *Washington Post*, June 28, 1991.

9. See Sheryl WuDunn, "China Backs Pact On Nuclear Spread," *New York Times*, August 11, 1991.

10. For a summary of the nuclear suppliers export control regime, see Davis, p. 10.

11. It was discovered in early August 1991 by UN inspectors that Iraq had secretly extracted plutonium from nuclear fuel under IAEA safeguards. See R. Jeffrey Smith, "Baghdad Surreptitiously Extracted Plutonium," *Washington Post*, August 6, 1991.

12. UN Security Council Resolution 687 For a Formal Cease Fire in the Gulf War, April 3, 1991, UN Document S/RES/687. For deployment of the observer force, see section B. For chemical, biological, and nuclear weapons, and long-range missiles see section C. For continued sanctions against the sale of conventional arms, see section F.

13. See Elaine Sciolino, "The Dauntingly Expensive Task of Imposing Arms Control," *New York Times*, April 28, 1991. While Resolution 687 includes the phrase "by all means necessary" in reference to enforcement, there is still disagreement among the Security Council members and the regional states as to whether a new resolution would be needed to authorize renewed hostilities. The Bush Administration has stated that it views Resolution 687 as providing sufficient authority if military action were necessary to enforce Iraqi compliance. See, for example, Gary Lee, "Bush Warns Iraq Over Atom Sites," *Washington Post*, July 29, 1991; and Helen Dewar, "Dole Seeks Vote To Allow Force Against Iraq," *Washington Post*, July 30, 1991.

14. For an excellent study on the German case, see Barton Whaley, *Covert German Rearmament 1919-1939: Deception and Misperception* (Frederick, Maryland: University Publications of America, Inc., 1984).

15. For more on Iraq's access to missile technology, see Janne E. Nolan, *Trappings of Power: Ballistic Missiles in the Third World* (Washington, D.C.: The Brookings Institution, 1991); and W. Seth Carus, *Ballistic Missiles in the Third World: Threat and Response*, The Washington Papers (Washington, D.C.: Center for Strategic and International Studies, 1990).

16. See Kenneth L. Adelman, "How to Limit Everybody's Missiles," *New York Times*, April 7, 1991; and Max M. Kampelman and Edward C. Luck, "Ban Missiles in the Middle East," *Washington Post*, April 18, 1991.

17. It is worth remembering that the most successful arms embargo in recent history was Operation Staunch, the international effort directed by the United States to prevent advanced arms and spare parts from reaching Iran after the overthrow of the Shah and the initiation of the Iran-Iraq war. Iran's air force was made up entirely of top-of-the-line U.S. equipment when the revolution occurred, including F-14 and F-4 fighters. As a result of the embargo, Iran's ability to use its air force was severely

curtailed from the start of the war. By 1988, it was not even a serious factor in the fighting. An indicator of Iran's desperation was the use of Oliver North and the Israelis to obtain U.S. weapons from their most avowed enemies.

18. See Nolan, *Trappings of Power: Ballistic Missiles in the Third World.*

CHAPTER EIGHT

Arms Control and Conflict Resolution

Far-reaching arms control agreements among the Middle East countries will depend on progress to resolve regional conflicts. Confidence-building measures and limited arms control initiatives are possible prior to negotiations on conflict resolution. In the Arab-Israeli conflict, arms control will have to be a key component of any peace agreement. However, the elimination of major classes of weapons and production capabilities will probably have to wait until regional peace has weathered the test of time.

Introduction

Suppliers agreements can provide a structure for more active and intrusive arms control regimes. While such agreements have clear benefits, over time they should be regarded as interim measures. Comprehensive regional arms control agreements must eventually have the cooperation of the key regional players. This, in turn, assumes that arms control, in its various guises, is perceived to be in the interests of the regional parties. Until some progress has been made in resolving sources of regional insecurity, it is unrealistic to expect local countries to endorse far-reaching constraints on their military options. This is not to rule out interim confidence-building measures prior to, or as part of conflict resolution; indeed such initiatives may work to reinforce political dialogue on broader questions of peace and security which lie at the heart of conflict resolution.

The precise relationship between an arms control process and a peace process will vary according to the status of the conflict and the level of political dialogue among the parties. In this chapter, the relationship between arms control and the Arab-Israeli, Persian Gulf, and Indo-Pakistani conflicts will be examined. The primary focus is on the Arab-Israeli conflict for two reasons. First, as a result of the Gulf war, an arms control regime has been imposed on Iraq by the United Nations, subsuming any immediate prospects for regional dialogue on arms restraint between Iraq and its neighbors. Second, India and Pakistan have recently initiated a series of bilateral confidence-building measures without the participation of the external powers. Furthermore, they have a better political relationship with one another than do the countries involved in the Arab-Israeli dispute, with the exception of Egypt and Israel.

The Arab-Israeli Peace Process and Arms Control

The agenda of issues that would need to be resolved before a comprehensive Arab-Israeli peace were possible is formidable. Aside from procedural questions as to how to initiate a dialogue, the most difficult questions relate to geographic borders, political legitimacy, the right of return of the Palestinians, reparations and compensation, access to resources such as water, the status of Jerusalem, relations between Israel, a Palestinian entity and the Arab countries, and security questions, including arms control and mutual force and weapons limitations.

Arms control covers a wide variety of initiatives -- unilateral, bilateral, and multilateral -- and can cover the gamut from informal, confidence-building measures such as 'red lines' establishing military ground rules between adversaries, to formal, multilateral treaties to eliminate entire classes of armaments, such as nuclear and chemical weapons. The peace process refers to a complicated series of negotiations between adversaries that passes through at least three distinct, but integrally-linked stages. These can be identified as: pre-negotiations, negotiations, and post-negotiations. At each phase different agreements are necessary to move the process forward and different arms control initiatives are appropriate. The interaction between these three stages of the peace process and arms control options is shown in the following matrix.

The Pre-Negotiations Phase

An Improved Climate for Limited Arms Control. The Egyptian-Israeli Peace Treaty, finally consummated in April 1982, had its origin in agreements negotiated between the United States, Israel, and Egypt between 1974 and 1979, and in Egyptian President Anwar Sadat's historic trip to Jerusalem in 1977. One reason the treaty has survived is because there exist complex arms control agreements limiting military activity in the Sinai Peninsula and along the Egyptian-Israeli border. If Egypt and Israel were the only parties to the Arab-Israeli conflict, by now they might have begun discussions on regimes to restrict weapons of mass destruction and their delivery systems, including advanced conventional arms. However, due to

Matrix of
Arab-Israeli Arms Control Initiatives
and the Peace Process

PRE-NEGOTIATIONS

- Measures to prevent war
  by miscalculation
- Transparency
- "Red-lines"
- Deployment limitations
- Weapons testing limitations
- Multilateral talks on
  CBW/Nuclear
- External restraints on supply

NEGOTIATIONS

- Territorial compromise
- Demilitarized zones
- Peacekeeping forces
- Deployment limitations
- Enhanced surveillance
  and verification
- Israeli-Palestinian security
  regime

POST-NEGOTIATIONS

- CBW/Nuclear agreements
- Conventional force reduction
- Inspection of arms production
- Regional arms supply agree-
  ments

Egypt's wider involvement in the Arab world, and the absence of substantive peace talks, it is premature to expect substantial progress on such issues at this time. This is not to diminish the role of international efforts to negotiate a chemical weapons or nuclear weapons ban. But in the last resort, the regional parties are unlikely to accept global weapons restrictions until peace has been achieved.

This creates a Catch-22 situation. Arms control initiatives between Israel and the Arabs to ban or limit major items prior to, or even during, an on-going peace process are unlikely to succeed. However, the political problems of reaching a peace settlement and deciding where Israel's security ends and Arab insecurities begin are so complex that a decision to postpone major arms control initiatives encourages a continued arms race. The practical approach to reconciling these two positions must be to pursue confidence-building measures prior to Arab-Israeli reconciliation, and to accept that substantive progress on resolving the difficult issues of nuclear and chemical weapons and long-range delivery systems must wait until the political environment has improved.

The overall Arab-Israeli conflict is still in the pre-negotiations phase; that is to say, all parties have shown some interest in a peace settlement but remain in disagreement as to how to proceed. Limited confidence-building measures already exist and new ones might contribute to an atmosphere conducive to negotiations.

There have been indications, discernable before the Gulf war, that both Egypt and Israel regard further arms control proposals as a legitimate issue for discussion. There are several reasons for this new attitude. First, given the nature of the arms race, there is concern that if military procurement trends continue, the dangers of war and the costs of deterrence will grow. The lack of progress on an Israeli-Palestinian dialogue need not rule out limited arms control if the parties believe they will benefit from constraints. Indeed, a dialogue on specific security issues under the rubric of arms control might provide a vehicle for more substantive talks on other sources of conflict. In the best of circumstances, arms control talks themselves might be the precursor for wider-ranging peace talks.[1]

Second, the dramatic developments in the East-West dialogue on conflict resolution have put pressure on regional leaders to take similar steps. Otherwise, in their new spirit of cooperation to resolve regional conflicts, the superpowers may initiate regional arms control regimes that the regional powers find intrusive.

154

Third, in terms of regional politics, it is sensible to be publicly supportive of arms control, which is difficult to oppose in the abstract. Furthermore, advocating arms control can potentially serve each country's interests. For instance, by supporting a ban on all weapons of mass destruction, the Arabs achieve two goals: they force Israel to be more open about its nuclear weapons program, and they help diffuse international criticism of their chemical weapons programs. On the other hand, by agreeing to participate in regional discussions on weapons of mass destruction, and by supporting a separate conference on conventional weapons, Israel puts pressure on the Arabs to either enter direct negotiations or be seen as the obstacle to progress.

Fourth, both sides may conclude that since the chance of any progress on regional arms control is remote, there is little to lose by appearing conciliatory and willing to discuss the highly complex issues in their security relationships.

Fifth, while few political leaders in Egypt, Jordan, or Israel believe that a full-scale premeditated Arab-Israeli war is imminent, all agree that the danger of a major crisis, or war by miscalculation, is cause for concern. Thus, while the wisdom of arms restraints may be questioned, there is a consensus on the need for measures to prevent wars by miscalculation and to limit the consequences if such wars occur.

With these new attitudes in mind, there are a number of confidence-building measures that warrant careful examination in the hope that a substantive Arab-Israeli dialogue may eventually be convened. Some of these ideas attracted interest in the region prior to the Gulf war, and might be resurrected at the appropriate time.

Measures to Reduce the Risks of War by Miscalculation. Israel, and those Arab neighbors with whom it is still technically in a state of war, must find ways to avoid miscalculations about one another's military intentions. There have been two incidents over the past few years that could have led to inadvertent war: the first between Israel and Syria, and the second, between Israel and Iraq.

In April 1986, Nizar Hindawi, a Syrian terrorist originally from Jordan, attempted to smuggle explosives onto an El Al flight leaving London's Heathrow airport bound for Israel. The explosives were detected and removed, and Hindawi, after approaching the Syrian embassy in London for help, turned himself in to the British police.[2] It remains unclear whether the Hindawi operation was typical of Syrian terrorist operations and was personally supervised by Syrian President Hafez al-Assad, or whether this and other Syrian terrorist acts are an outgrowth of rivalries or misunderstandings within the Syrian security apparatus. Nevertheless, the conclusion must be that if the El Al plane had been destroyed with over 200 killed, Israel would almost certainly have taken harsh military measures against Syria that could have led to all-out war. If it is assumed that Assad did not want a war and was unaware of the Hindawi plot, then one way to avoid future incidents would be some form of tacit Israeli-Syrian cooperation to strengthen intelligence-gathering on terrorist operations that could be damaging to both countries.

The second event concerned an explosion that took place in Iraq in September 1989, when it was reported that a missile production facility outside Baghdad had blown up.[3] On March 15, 1990, an Iranian-born journalist working for the *London Observer* who had been caught illegally investigating the site of the explosion was hanged in Baghdad. At that time, it was feared that another accident in an Iraqi munitions plant might be attributed by Saddam Hussein to Israel. Under certain circumstances, this could have caused him to launch an attack against Israel in the expectation that if he did not, he would lose all his forces in an Israeli attack. Mechanisms to convey information about such a crisis to each side might dispel fears of a surprise or preemptive attack. Before the Gulf crisis there was some talk of exploring ways to establish an Israeli-Iraq 'hot-line,' possibly using the good offices of Egypt.[4]

Transparency Issues. Transparency, a term that has come into vogue in the European arms control context, refers to efforts that seek to remove doubts and fears, and build trust by generating an expanding process of openness. By calling for both sides to reveal information on military practices and exercises, the European countries hope to develop East-West ties that help remove the misunderstandings and misperceptions that fueled the Cold War. A number of proposals have been offered to create this openness, including annual exchanges of military information, notification of military activities, and exchanges of annual military calendars.[5]

It remains to be seen whether these options have a place in the Arab-Israeli context. As long as the states in the region believe that the use of force is legitimate and, under the right circumstances, beneficial, transparency measures can be used for deceptive purposes. For example, the 1973 Arab-Israeli war began with what was announced as a training exercise. On the other hand, during the summer of 1989, Israel was alarmed by joint Iraqi-Jordanian air training flights along the Jordan valley. Prior notification might have downgraded this concern.

The most difficult transparency problem concerns Israel's nuclear weapons program. The post-Gulf war arms control debate has focused attention on Israel's nuclear arsenal and regional nuclear proliferation. President Bush's May 1991 initiative offered a cautious but sensible approach to dealing with these issues. By calling for a freeze on the further nuclear proliferation in the region rather than out-right abolition, the initiative attempted to deal with the threat that the spread of nuclear weapons poses while also respecting Israel's security requirements. It is plausible that Israel would agree to a halt on further production of nuclear weapons provided it were convinced that the Arab states would not acquire the same weapons.[6]

While greater transparency in Israel's nuclear weapons program is demanded by the international community, there are strong countervailing arguments to keep Israel's bomb 'in the basement' and not to disclose too much information about its capabilities. For instance, if Israel were to announce an explicit doctrine of nuclear deterrence and provide details of its nuclear forces -- analogous to what is known about British and French nuclear forces -- the Arabs would be under great popular pressure to acquire their own nuclear device. Similarly, it is difficult to see how the U.S. could avoid some painful choices in its relationship with Israel in view of strict U.S. laws and administration policies regarding proliferation in other countries in the Third World.

Red Lines. Red lines usually refer to informal agreements between adversaries concerning limits on the deployment and use of armed forces in given geographic regions. Red lines have been an integral part of both formal and informal force separation agreements in the Arab-Israeli conflict. They have been used in two ways. First, in the literal sense, red lines can refer to a geographic line or boundary. This line can be agreed upon by the parties and established as a marker beyond which one or both sides will not deploy forces. Second, red lines, in a conceptual sense, refer to conditions that prohibit certain actions. These, like the geographic lines, can be mutually agreed upon, or simply laid out by one party.

In April 1976, Syria and Israel reached a secret agreement through U.S. mediation to minimize the chances for confrontation in Lebanon. Syria agreed to Israeli red line conditions allowing Syrian military intervention in Lebanon provided that it was restricted to ground forces and that these did not move South of a line between the Zaharani estuary on the Mediterranean and the village of Mashki in the Bekka Valley. As part of this agreement, Syria was to respect Israel's legitimate security concerns in southern Lebanon and to avoid air attacks against Christian targets.[7]

Israel and Jordan also have an informal red line agreement. Since historic attack routes suggest an invading Arab army would attack from the East through Jordan, Israeli military strategists have consistently viewed Jordan's eastern and northern borders as red lines. If Iraqi or Syrian forces entered Jordan in significant numbers, Israeli forces would automatically respond. Understandings between Jordan and Israel on this condition have benefited both countries. For Israel, such a policy bolsters against its deterrence posture. For Jordan, this form of agreement bolsters national sovereignty and protects against Syrian and Iraqi intervention. Israel and Jordan also have informal understandings concerning their shared border along the Jordan valley. These understandings have dealt mostly with attempts to combat the infiltration of terrorists into Israel, thereby reducing the potential for political tension between Amman and Jerusalem.

Deployment Limitations. The Separation of Forces Agreement negotiated by Henry Kissinger between Israel and Syria in March 1974, and three similar agreements between Israel and Egypt culminating in the final Egyptian-Israeli Peace Treaty in April 1982, are important examples of effective deployment limitations between adversaries. They provide excellent models to consider further limitations between Israel and its neighbors once peace talks begin.[8]

Israel conquered the Golan Heights region of Syria during the Six Day War in 1967, and expanded its gains slightly in the 1973 war. The 1949 armistice line, which ran along the Jordan River and the East bank of the Sea of Galilee, was termed the 'green line,' while the 1967 cease fire line was called the 'purple line.' The cease fire line established at the end of the 1973 war was slightly to the West of the purple line. In the aftermath of the 1973 war, Henry Kissinger was able to negotiate a disengagement agreement between Jerusalem and Damascus. The town of Quneitra was returned to Syria but Israel retained control of the surrounding hills. The agreement established a buffer zone to be patrolled by a 1200-man United Nations Disengagement Observer Force (UNDOF) in the narrow area between the purple line and the new Israeli boundary. Beyond the buffer zone, two restricted zones were established with limits on the numbers and types of forces each side could deploy. In the first zone each side is limited to 6000 troops, 75 tanks, and 36 cannons; in the second zone each side is allowed unlimited troops, but only 450 tanks. Elaborate verification and monitoring procedures were established including sophisticated aerial surveillance by the United States.[9] Despite continued hostility between Israel and Syria, including two major Israeli invasions of Lebanon (1976 and 1982), the Golan front has remained relatively incident-free and is a credit to the effectiveness of the 1974 agreement.

In the Egyptian-Israeli case the results have been even more positive. Having captured and returned the Sinai peninsula and Gaza Strip from Egypt once in the 1956 war, Israel kept both territories at the end of the 1967 war, making the Suez canal the effective boundary between them.

On October 6, 1973, Egypt and Syria launched the Yom Kippur War. At the time of the negotiated cease fire on October 24, 1973, Israel had extended its control to an area on the West bank of the Suez canal, while Egypt had gained two separate beachheads on the East bank. As a result of American diplomacy, the Israeli-Egyptian Separation of Forces Agreement was signed on Janurary 18, 1974, at Kilometer 101 on the Suez-Cairo road. Israel withdrew several kilometers across the canal, leaving a buffer zone patrolled by a special UN Emergency Force, while Egypt was allowed a token presence across the canal in the Sinai.

On September 4, 1975, Israel and Egypt reached a second disengagement agreement, the Interim Agreement in which Israel agreed to pull back an additional 30 kilometers into Sinai, and to evacuate both the crucial Mitla and Giddi passes, and the Abu Rodeis oilfield. An Egyptian limited-force zone was established along the East bank of the Suez Canal, and verification and monitoring of the new buffer zone and the limited deployment zones was undertaken by the UN Emergency Force and the newly-established U.S. Sinai Support Mission (USSSM).[10]

The confidence gained by both Egypt and Israel as a result of the effective implementation of these agreements contributed to the eventual breakthroughs in Israeli-Egyptian relations that culmintated in the Camp David Accords, the Peace Treaty, and Israel's final evacuation of the Sinai. Four limited-force zones were created in the Sinai and in a narrow strip in the Negev, with a new Multinational Force and Observers (MFO) to replace the UN force and the U.S. Sinai Support Mission as the key monitoring body. This arrangement remains in place today.

An additional example of successful deployment limitations sprang from Israeli concerns about Saudi air force deployments. Strong Israeli opposition to the sale of American F-15s to Saudi Arabia in 1978 led to a U.S.-Saudi understanding on the deployment of the planes in Saudi Arabia. Sixty-two aircraft were eventually sold, but the aircraft were not to be stationed near the Israeli border. Israel was primarily concerned about the construction of an airbase at Tabuk in northwest Saudi Arabia. Under pressure from Israel, the United States insisted that none of the new planes could be stationed at Tabuk.[11]

Weapons Testing Limitations. Similarly, agreements to limit or ban testing

159

of certain weapon systems might also help to build confidence. For example, an agreement by Israel not to conduct flight tests of ballistic missiles, or not to test a nuclear device would be a significant gesture to its adversaries. If this was paralleled by an Arab agreement not to test ballistic missiles, it would be a useful, reciprocal confidence-building measure. Combined with external restraints on the supply of missiles to the region, such a measure could significantly reduce the potential for offensive missile attacks. A ban on the testing of nuclear weapons would be the first step toward a nuclear-free zone in the Middle East.

Multilateral Talks on Chemical, Biological, and Nuclear Weapons. On April 16, 1990, Egyptian President Mubarak offered an initiative to declare the Middle East a region free of mass destruction weapons. His proposal, transmitted to UN Secretary General Javier Perez de Cuéllar, states that: "It is Egypt's considered opinion that chemical weapons should be dealt with in a comprehensive and global context involving all types of weapons of mass destruction, whether nuclear, chemical, or biological, in order to ensure international and regional security."[12] Mubarak's initiative called for the prohibition of all weapons of mass destruction from the Middle East, commitments from all regional states to abide by the agreement, and verification measures "to ascertain full compliance by all States of the region with the full scope of the prohibitions without exception."[13] In explaining such a proposal, Egyptian Foreign Minister Ismat Abd al-Majd argued that the Arabs cannot be expected to be "sitting ducks" and allow the Israelis to have nuclear weapons while the Arabs catch the flak for acquiring chemical weapons.[14]

Israeli officials have expressed a similar desire to rid the region of threats from unconventional weapons. Prime Minister Yitzhak Shamir stated, "[We] have been proposing to enter bilateral and direct negotiations with any Arab country on the demilitarization of this region of lethal weapons."[15] The Israelis assert, however, that this must be done in a way that maintains Israel's security and that assures direct negotiations with Arab countries and direct inspection of one another's facilities.

Other proposals include the suggestion that Israel should unilaterally open up its Dimona nuclear reactor to inspection in return for further Arab commitments not to acquire nuclear weapons. While both of these suggestions would fall short of a comprehensive agreement to establish a nuclear-free zone, they would be regarded as confidence-building measures, especially in the wake of concern about Iraq's flagrant violation of its NPT commitments.[16]

The Negotiations Phase

Territorial Compromise. Return of territory is seen as the key to an Arab-Israeli peace, particulary parts of the territory known as historic Palestine, or Eretz Israel.[17] This will also be the most difficult issue to resolve during peace negotiations. Territorial compromise will not be possible unless there are iron-clad security guarantees among the parties, analogous to those already in place between Egypt and Israel. These security guarantees must include further force separations, demilitarization, peacekeeping forces, force deployment limitations, and inspection and verification regimes. There must also be agreements between Israel and the Palestinians concerning the internal security of a new Palestinian regime and its relationship to Israeli security. Since territorial compromise is the key to a lasting Arab-Israeli peace, and since security guarantees are necessary before there can be any Israeli withdrawal from occupied territory, the linkage between these two subjects is of the ultimate importance. (The following map shows Israel, its surrounding Arab neighbors, and the occupied territories. For a detailed review of Israel's strategic geography and its linkage to the territorial compromise issue, see Appendix IV).

Territory and Security. Israel's borders with its neighbors following a peace settlement will be influenced by three basic considerations: military relations with the Arab world, the external and practical day-to-day relations with the Palestinian regime, and the internal security problem. The issue of external security raises questions about strategic relations between Israel and Syria, and between Israel and Jordan. In the former case, the key issues relate to the control of the Golan Heights and the Israeli-Lebanese border. In the latter case, the key question concerns Jordan's eastern border with Iraq and Israel's likely insistence that Jordan agree to limit Iraqi or other Arab military access to this border (a similar agreement with respect to Jordan's borders with Syria and Saudi Arabia can also be anticipated).

Israeli experience in the Gulf war suggests some additional lessons concerning the importance of territory. On the one hand, the need for early warning of a missile attack and the forward deployment of missile defenses, especially early-warning systems, strengthens the case for not relinquishing the high ground on the West Bank, in the Golan, or forward positions in the Jordan Valley. At the same time, however, the missile threat also suggests that adding a few kilometers to the West-East depth of Israel's border is not going to make much difference with the next generation of surface-to-surface missiles (SSMs), which are much more

161

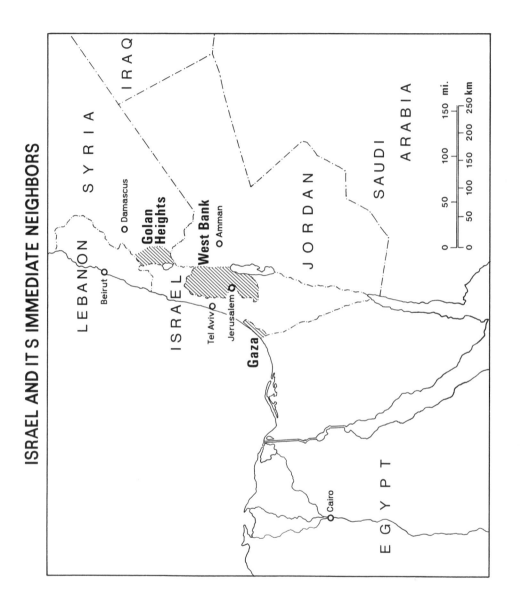

ISRAEL AND ITS IMMEDIATE NEIGHBORS

sophisticated than the Scud.

Because it sided with Iraq during the Gulf war, the Palestinian population alienated even the dovish faction in Israel that had called in the past for negotiations with the PLO and for the creation of a Palestinian State. As a result, most Israelis at this time do not believe that Palestinians and Jews can live together. This strengthens the case for more explicit physical separation. Unless Israel is willing to become even more rigid in its control over the territories, or to encourage by peaceful, or violent means the mass emigration of Palestinians, the case for Israeli-Palestinian disengagement under the format of autonomy, self rule, or even independence (with or without confederation with Jordan), becomes more persuasive.

Israeli hard-liners will continue to argue that the creation of a Palestinian State, based on the withdrawal of Israel from the West Bank and Gaza, would inevitably lead to another Arab-Israeli war.[18] They cite the proximity of the West Bank and Gaza to Israel's cities and industries, and the West Bank's strategic advantage of high ground as two reasons to retain the territories.[19] The return of the West Bank would also eliminate Israeli control of the Jordan River as an obstacle to forces attacking from the East.[20]

Such dire scenarios, while technically feasible, must be dismissed as highly unlikely. They assume that a Palestinian state will be permitted to have heavy armaments, and that its borders will be analogous to those of the pre-1967 territories. While this may be Arab wishful thinking, it is not only Israeli hardliners who would reject such an outcome. The vast majority of Israelis -- hawk and dove -- would never, under any circumstances, agree to a heavily-armed Palestinian state occupying the pre-1967 region. To dwell on such scenarios is to miss the point of the debate in Israel: what are the dangers of returning *some* of the territory to a Palestinian regime with strict limitations on its military or paramilitary capacity, together with an intrusive Israeli, UN, or international presence on the high ground of the West Bank and along the Jordan Valley? In sum, the real debate is between those supporting a plan for partial Israeli withdrawal and annexation of certain border areas, and those who believe in no exchange of territory at all.

Concerning the external security threat, many Israelis believe that the Arab states will eventually upgrade their military potential to rival Israel's both quantitatively and qualitatively, thus leaving Israel with only its territorial advantages.[21] This argument has been temporarily undercut by the defeat of Iraq in the Gulf war. However, over time, Iraq could reemerge as a threat. In the meantime, Saudi Arabia's and Egypt's inventories will likely be upgraded with sophisticated American weapons and, over the horizon, Iran and Pakistan loom as potential military adversaries. Summing up this approach, Israeli Minister of Housing and Construction Ariel Sharon, stated: "It would be unparalleled irresponsibility to ignore the danger of missiles, whether ground-to-ground or those dispatched from vessels or planes. But it would be more deadly and dangerous to ignore the fact that the chief menace is that of the ground forces, which attack and occupy."[22] Dore Gold, director of the U.S. Foreign and Defense Policy Project of the Jaffee Center for Strategic Studies, has argued "if the conventional battlefield -- and not just missile attacks alone -- still determines who won the war, then the conditions affecting the outcome of conventional war -- from topography to strategic depth are still critical for defining the security of a nation."[23]

On the other side of this equation are those who see the occupied territories as a liability rather than an asset to Israeli security. Defense analyst Ze'ev Schiff has argued that Israel should reassess the value of territory to its security. He states: "The importance of territory (in this case the West Bank) for Israel's defense cannot be dismissed, but territory does not always enhance security. Under certain conditions, like those existing in the West Bank and Gaza Strip, the risks posed by additional territory are greater than the benefits they accord."[24]

According to this argument, the best way to enhance Israeli security may now be through a land-for-peace settlement that removes some of the sources of tension in the area and creates a more stable security environment. A continued Israeli presence along the Jordan River, and early warning installations on the ridge line in the West Bank could provide the means for verifying the demilitarization of the West Bank, and assuring against surprise attack from the East. Increasingly, satellite reconnaissance can improve Israel's ability to detect hostile military action as well. For the Gaza Strip, an Israeli naval presence off the coast and army presence on land would be sufficient to deny access to hostile forces, assuming Egypt was still at peace with Israel and could patrol the region's southern border.[25] While not providing the Palestinians with complete sovereignty or providing Israel with complete security, this approach, according to its advocates, would protect both parties sufficiently and would be in the spirit of territorial compromise necessary for a peace agreement.

Walid Khalidi, a Research Fellow at the Harvard Center for International Affairs, and closely affiliated to the Palestinian National Council, lends support to some of the above arguments. He wrote in 1978 that "there is no reason why the concept of Palestinian sovereignty should not accommodate provisions designed to allay legitimate fears of neighbors on a reasonable and preferably reciprocal basis."[26] Khalidi argued further that a Palestinian state would pose little threat to Israel even if it had a small military because it would be geographically separated from most Arab states, and almost completely surrounded by Israeli territory. According to Khalidi, a future Palestinian leadership would have "few illusions about the efficacy of revolutionary armed struggle in any direct confrontation with Israel."[27]

A more pessimistic view, expressed by former deputy mayor of Jerusalem, Meron Benvenisti, has argued that successive Israeli governments have engaged in so much de facto annexation of the territories for military, political, and economic reasons that it is now unrealistic to physically separate them from Israel proper. "The process of economic integration," writes Benvenisti, "has long since been accomplished; infrastructure grids have been linked (roads, electricity, water, communication), administrative systems have been unified; social stratification has become institutionalized and political relationships have settled into well established patterns."[28] This calls into question the economic viability of an independent Palestinian state in the West Bank.[29]

Other factors complicating an Israeli withdrawal from the territories include the physical separation of the West Bank and the Gaza Strip, and the security problems presented by Israel's Arab neighbors, especially Syria, Iraq, Jordan, and Saudi Arabia. Some have proposed that Israel and its neighbors pursue a program of mutual security, based on a confederation among Israel, Jordan, and a Palestinian state. In addition to the confederation, the withdrawal of Israel from the West Bank and Gaza Strip would be accompanied by demilitarization, the right of Israel to pursue extra-territorial activities in case of agreement violations, and a reduced Israeli military presence in areas where mutual security arrangements had been negotiated. Intelligence stations could be relocated within Israel, while ground stations would need to be located in the territories; these could be manned either by American personnel or by joint Israeli, Jordanian, and Palestinian teams.[30]

In this regard, territorial adjustments to the green line for security purposes would have to take into account the Arab populations living along the line. Israel would not be able to argue successfully for new political boundaries that forced more Arab towns and villages to live under Israeli jurisdiction. However, there are a number of areas in the West Bank that offer both strategic and tactical assets, but have very low Arab densities. The entire eastern third of Samaria and Judea, for example, is almost completely devoid of Arab population.[31] At the same time, this area offers some of the best surveillance points and marshalling areas to protect against an incursion from the East across the Jordan river.

Demilitarized Zones, Peacekeeping and Verification Forces. There is now enough experience with peacekeeping forces in the Arab-Israeli conflict to say that, in conjunction with demilitarized zones, they will be essential for a new land-for-peace agreement. They not only have great symbolic value, but are instrumental in providing surveillance and verifying compliance. Although peacekeeping forces cannot prevent military confrontation, they raise the threshhold for violence and remove many sources of insecurity. In view of the success of the MFO in the Sinai and Israel's residual suspicions of the UN, it is likely that a U.S., or possibly U.S.-Soviet, military presence may be necessary to achieve further disengagements in the Golan Heights and to establish a buffer zone along the Jordan valley. Working out the details of such an operation would be complicated but, as suggested, the precedents are good.

An essential component of new peacekeeping forces will be the establishment of verification regimes and surveillance systems. Experience in the Israeli-Syrian and Israeli-Egyptian cases shows that verification and surveillance measures are effective in assuring compliance and maintenance of disengagement agreements. Verification and control measures have worked in the past because both sides saw it as in their interests to meet the demands of their agreements. These measures cannot be used to create agreements; they can only ease their acceptance and promote their implementation.

Palestinian-Israeli Security Arrangements. Israeli flexibility on the nature of the Palestinian regime to be carved out of the occupied territories will vary according to whether agreement is reached with Jordan, Syria, and other Arab countries on mutual security issues. Without a clear guarantee that its external security problem is resolved, no Israeli government is likely to accept anything more than limited autonomy for the Palestinians, with Israel controlling all external relations and retaining a military presence in key strategic regions of the occupied territories.

Concerning Israel's internal security problems, one of the most difficult questions to resolve concerns the internal security of a new Palestinian regime and how this will impact on Israel itself. There has been very little written about this topic, in part because the nature of the security regime will itself be dependent on the type of political settlement reached between Israel and the Palestinians. For example, will the new borders demarcating

Israel and Palestine be closed or open? What institutions within the Palestinian area will be given power to enforce internal security and what weapons will they be permitted to have? Will Israel have the right to liaise with the Palestine security forces, or engage in hot pursuit of terrorists? Which Palestinians will be freed from Israeli jails, and which members of extremist Palestinian diaspora groups will be permitted to return? These questions are both complicated and highly sensitive, but must be answered before a realistic appraisal of the security environment is possible.

Imagine, for instance, a situation in which Palestinian leaders acceptable to Israel have negotiated autonomy at a peace conference, but the outcome is bitterly opposed by Palestinian extremists both within the territories and within the diaspora. How does one prevent radical PLO members from returning to Palestine, or Islamic fundamentalists from launching an armed uprising? The dilemma is clear: if the terms of autonomy or statehood require the Palestinians to lower their enforcement capabilities to a small militia that poses no military threat to Israel, it may not be strong enough to cope with internal violence. Yet, the alternatives -- a strong, well-armed militia or formal arrangements to permit Israeli intervention -- are equally difficult to imagine.

The internal security problem is directly related to the type of border arrangements negotiated between the parties. There are strong arguments expressed by some Israelis and Palestinians that, ultimately, the borders between Israel and the Palestine regime must be open. In this way, Israeli access to Jewish settlements in the new Palestine region will be assured; similarly however, it will also give Palestinians the ability to move freely into Israel, raising the highly sensitive question of the Palestinian right of return to all locations in former Palestine, including Jaffa and Haifa. Open borders also make sense for use of the common infrastructure -- water, utilities, transportation -- that has been developed over the past 25 years.

Others, however, argue that open borders will not work, in part for the reasons addressed above, but also because Palestinians and Israelis do not want to live together in such close proximity. A controlled border is necessary for political, economic, and security reasons. Once a border of this type is envisaged, the question of geography and security becomes paramount. A geographical divorce between Israel and the Palestinian regime virtually guarantees that Israel will insist on major revisions to the pre-1967 borders and accept nothing less than complete control of the Jordan Valley and access to the high ground along the Judean-Samarian Hills.

167

Post-Negotiation Agreements

Nuclear, Chemical, and Biological Weapons Agreements. Once there is a peace between Israel and its neighbors, it becomes much more practical to discuss regimes to eliminate weapons of mass destruction and their means of production. No matter what happens in the multinational fora to restrict these categories of weapons, a regional agreement will hinge on former President Ronald Reagan's phrase: "trust but verify."

Trust between Israel and the Arabs will not be easy to achieve. Furthermore, since the regional conflict involving Israel has an important religious component, the potential hostility of non-Arab Muslim countries such as Iran and Pakistan cannot be ignored. For instance, it is difficult to imagine an Arab-Israeli agreement to limit nuclear weapons that ignored the nuclear capabilities of Iran and Pakistan. Yet, the political circumstances under which both of these countries might be brought into a Middle East nuclear-free zone will be subject to different considerations than those that will contribute to an Arab-Israeli peace.

Another complicating factor is that the ultimate justification for Israel's nuclear weapons program, including pressures to upgrade it and build a thermonuclear weapon, is the vast asymmetry in geography, population, and resources in favor of the Arab and Muslim countries. Thus, agreements on weapons of mass destruction cannot, in the last resort, be decoupled from efforts to put restrictions on conventional weapons, defense spending, and weapons production.

Another complication concerns verification. A regional regime that authorizes the level of intrusiveness necessary to detect covert activity in the chemical, biological, and nuclear fields will be extremely difficult to negotiate since so many parties are involved. No matter what ground rules are laid down in Geneva or in Vienna, the trust required for Israel, the Arabs, and other Muslim countries to agree to full inspection of one another's facilities assumes not just peace, but a lasting and established peace.

Conventional Force Reductions. Since conventional force reductions will be ultimately linked to limits on weapons of mass destruction, the model of force reductions currently negotiated in Europe may be of limited value as an indicator of how such reductions would be implemented in the Middle East. Clearly, there are some conventional force capabilities that will be perceived by the parties as more threatening than others. If mutually

168

acceptable equations for military balance were negotiated, so much the better. However, as noted in Chapter 2, each country in the region faces different types of threats. Deciding what is a realistic force level for Saudi Arabia vis-à-vis Israel as distinct from Saudi Arabia vis-à-vis Iran and Iraq, for example, will require complicated technical negotiations. Nevertheless, conventional arms control limitations, if paralleled by supplier agreements on weapons sales, will be essential if constraints on weapons of mass destruction are to be implemented.

Inspection of Arms Production. The Arabs will pay particular attention to the need to inspect arms production facilities in view of the very sophisticated nature of Israel's defense industry and its close cooperation with the United States. This issue will become increasingly complex in view of the fact that so many of the components of modern military forces come from dual-use technologies. Israel's future economy is dependent on a high level of technological development to utilize or employ all the skilled labor that has come from the Soviet Union. Thus, to monitor what countries like Israel are producing in the military, as distinct from non-military field, will be difficult and can only be undertaken if mutual trust and cooperation in many other areas are forthcoming.

Regional Arms Supply Agreements. If an Arab-Israeli peace exists and basic security problems have been resolved, it is realistic to discuss combined supplier and regional power agreements on arms limitations. There will be strong economic motives to hold down levels of defense spending after peace has been achieved. In the last resort, this may be the most promising development for regional cooperation between suppliers and recipients.

* * *

The above options are all feasible following a peace settlement. However, there can be no major reductions in force levels until the parties agree to them. It may be possible to design cosmetic arms control agreements immediately after a peace treaty is signed, but the serious cuts will have to wait until peace has had a chance to work.

Nevertheless, in the long run it must be in the interests of all Middle East countries to subscribe to the concept of a zone free of mass destruction weapons, and to put limits on conventional forces. The fundamental asymmetries of the Arab-Israeli conflict make it difficult to conceive of stable deterrence based on threats of mutual terror.

The Control of the Middle East Arms Race

The Persian Gulf and Arms Control

The United Nations has imposed an arms control regime on Iraq. If it is fully implemented, it will be many years before Iraq can reemerge as a major military power in the region. In the meanwhile, Iran and the GCC countries are likely to continue to build up their military capabilities. Is there any hope that confidence building measures and arms control between these parties is possible?

The key country in this regard is Iran. If the Iranian leadership were to change its highly ambivalent attitude toward the United States and the West and, in effect, rejoin the international community, a new era of cooperation might be possible. In the case of U.S.-Iranian relations, the precursor to their improvement must be the release of western hostages controlled by Iranian-backed Shiite fundamentalists in Lebanon. Once this happens, many steps could follow to bring about wider conflict resolution between Iran and the outside world. These could include the resumption of diplomatic relations and the unfreezing of Iranian assets still held in the U.S..

Under these circumstances, and in parallel to the enforcement of UN Security Council Resolution 687, it is not out of the question that Iran might be persuaded to consider joining an arms control regime for the Gulf. It is premature to speculate what items might be included, but confidence-building measures similar to those discussed above might be possible, together with voluntary restraints on advanced weapons purchases.

Ultimately, though, Iran and Iraq must reach accommodation on their own territorial disputes before there can be true conflict resolution. The territorial issue, especially Iraq's predicament over access to the Gulf, will remain even if Saddam Hussein and the current Iranian regime are replaced. Thus, like in the Arab-Israeli case, the prospects for long-term arms control regimes in the Gulf are linked to outstanding geopolitical disputes, as well as to the absence of political goodwill.

Arms Control on the Indian Subcontinent

Over the past three years, India and Pakistan have agreed to confidence-building measures in order to decrease the possibility of military confrontation. The decision to implement these measures was viewed as necessary in the face of growing tension in their relations over Kashmir and the Punjab.[32]

In January 1991, India and Pakistan ratified an agreement to refrain from attacking one another's nuclear facilities. The agreement was initially reached in 1985 by then-Indian Prime Minister Rajiv Gandhi and the late Pakistani President Zia ul-Haq, and signed on December 31, 1988, by Gandhi and then-Pakistani Prime Minister Benazir Bhutto. Under the terms of the agreement, both countries provide one another with a list of nuclear facilities, including nuclear power and research facilities, as well as uranium enrichment plants and other related facilities. These lists are to be updated annually.[33] The agreement specifically states that the countries will "refrain from undertaking, encouraging or participating indirectly or directly in any action aimed at causing the destruction or damage to any such installations or facilities in the other country."[34]

During talks in December 1990, the two countries also agreed to resume high-level weekly contacts between their respective militaries and to finalize an agreement for advanced notification of military exercises.[35]

Notes

1. A more pessimistic argument would be that arms control talks might diminish the prospects of a larger Arab-Israeli dialogue by meeting the basic demands for negotiations without compromising the various positions of the parties on matters such as recognition and territory-for-peace.

2. Helena Cobban, *The Superpowers and the Syrian-Israeli Conflict*, The Washington Papers (Washington, D.C. and New York: Center for Strategic and International Studies, and Praeger, 1991), p. 74.

3. Harvey Morris, "Explosion that Led to Ill-fated Mission," *The Independent*, March 16, 1990.

4. On a visit by the author to Egypt, Jordan, and Israel in June 1991, arms control issues were discussed at some length in each capital. Interest in steps to prevent war by miscalculation and the establishment of a hot-line was strongest in Israel, but spokesmen in all countries stressed the dangers of an unregulated arms race and the need for regional constraints. The trip was organized by the Washington Institute for Near East Policy and included meetings with senior military officials in all countries, as well as with King Hussein and Crown Prince Hassan of Jordan, and Israeli Prime Minister Shamir.

5. Other measures include: risk reduction through reports on unusual and unscheduled activities; contact developments, including visits to military facilities and the establishment of direct relations between military personnel; observation of military activities; prior notification of certain military activities; compliance and verification measures through inspections and evaluations; established communication between capitals; annual implementation assessment meetings; refraining from threats of using force while retaining the right to self-defense. See "The Vienna Document 1990 of the Vienna Negotiations on Confidence- and Security-Building Measures," November 17, 1990; and Ivo Daalder, *The CFE Treaty: An Overview and Assessment* (Washington, D.C.: The Johns Hopkins Foreign Policy Institute, 1991).

6. See Avner Cohen and Marvin Miller, "Defusing the Nuclear Middle East," *New York Times*, May 30, 1991; and "Establishment of a Nuclear-Weapon-Free Zone in the Region of the Middle East: Study on effective and verifiable measures which would facilitate the establishment of a nuclear-weapon-free zone in the Middle East," United Nations, General Assembly, Forty-fifth Session, Agenda Item 49, October 10, 1990.

7. See Moshe Ma'oz, *Asad: The Sphinx of Damascus* (New York: Weidenfeld and Nicolson, 1988), p. 138; and Avner Yaniv, *Dilemmas of Security: Politics, Strategy, and the Israeli Experience in Lebanon* (New York: Oxford University Press, 1987), pp. 60-61.

8. For details on the diplomatic efforts needed, see Chapters 18 and 23 of Henry Kissinger, *Years of Upheaval* (Boston: Little Brown & Company, 1982).

9. Itshak Lederman, *The Arab-Israeli Experience in Verification and Its Relevence to Conventional Arms Control in Europe*, Occasional Paper #2 (College Park, Maryland: University of Maryland, School of Public Affairs, 1989) p. 9.

10. 200 American technicians were located near Mitla and Giddi passes to operate electronic monitoring stations. See Lederman, ibid., p. 9.

11. William B. Quandt, *Saudi Arabia in the 1980s: Foreign Policy, Security, and Oil* (Washington, D.C.: The Brookings Institution, 1981), p. 61.

12. See letter 130/90 from Ambassador Amre Moussa, Permanent Representative, Permanent Mission of the Arab Republic of Egypt to the

United Nations, to Secretary General Javier Perez de Cuéllar, United Nations, April 16, 1990.

13. Ibid.

14. Quoted in Max Rodenbeck, "Egypt: Reasserting Its Position," *Middle East International*, April 27, 1990, p. 9.

15. See "Shamir Comments on Talks," Jerusalem Television Service, 1630 GMT, 13 April 1990, translated in *FBIS-NES*, April 16, 1990, pp. 20-21.

16. See Avner Cohen and Marvin Miller, "Nuclear Shadows in the Middle East: Prospects for Arms Control in the Wake of the Gulf Crisis," MIT Center for International Studies, December 1990.

17. The term Palestine conveys different meanings depending on whether one is referring to a geographical region, a political entity, or an historic, legally defined area. The term derives from the Philistines who occupied the southern coastal plain in the 12th century BC. They referred to this strip of land as Philistia. The Jews called this same region Eretz Israel, or the Land of Israel. Historic Palestine or Eretz Israel had different boundaries at different historic periods. The name Palestine came into vogue in Europe with the Renaissance and was used primarily by Christians, not Jews or Muslims, to describe the holy land. It was not until 1920, as part of the post-war settlement, that Britain and France set about determining the exact boundaries of the former Ottoman territory they were to administer under the League of Nations mandate. An agreement was signed in 1923, in which the French mandate of Syria and Lebanon was demarcated from the British mandate of Palestine and Mesopotamia. The original mandate for Palestine included what is now Jordan. Britain decided to divide Palestine into the principality of Transjordan and Western Palestine divided by the Jordan River. Palestine now became the mandate area West of the river. It was partitioned by the United Nations in 1947 into three components: a Jewish state, an Arab state, and an international zone, Jerusalem. The mandate formally came to an end in 1948, and during the subsequent war between the new state of Israel and the Arabs, Israel was victorious. At the time of the armistice agreements in 1949, Israel occupied more land than laid down by the UN partition resolution. See Bernard Lewis, "Palestine: On the History and Geography of a Name," *International History Review*, II, 1 January 1980.

18. Michael Widlanski, "Current Debate: How Dangerous Would a Palestinian State Be? Very Dangerous," *Tikkun*, July/August 1990, p. 62.

19. Michael Widlandski, editor, *Can Israel Survive a Palestinian State?* (Jerusalem: Institute for Advanced Strategic and Political Studies, 1985), p. 10.

20. Ibid., p. 11.

21. Ibid., p. 14.

22. Ariel Sharon, "It's Time for the Chief of General Staff to Speak Out," *Jerusalem Post International Edition*, May 11, 1991, p. 7.

23. Dore Gold, "Territory vs. Missiles: The Great Debate," *Jerusalem Post*, April 13, 1991. See also Dore Gold, "Israel and the Gulf Crisis: Changing Security Requirements on the Eastern Front," *Policy Focus*, Washington Institute for Near East Policy, December 1990.

24. Ze'ev Schiff, "Israel After the War," *Foreign Affairs*, Vol. 70, No. 2, Spring 1991, p. 29.

25. Ephraim Sneh, "Current Debate: How Dangerous Would a Palestinian State Be? We Can Live With It," *Tikkun*, July/August 1990, p. 65.

26. Walid Khalidi, "Thinking the Unthinkable: A Sovereign Palestinian State," *Foreign Affairs*, July, 1978, Vol. 56, No. 4, p. 701.

27. Ibid., p. 713.

28. Meron Benvenisti, *1987 Report: Demographic, Economic, Legal, Social and Political Developments in the West Bank* (Jerusalem: Jerusalem Post Press, 1987), p. 70.

29. Meron Benvenisti, *The West Bank and Gaza Atlas* (Jerusalem: Jerusalem Post Press, 1988), p. 43.

30. Ze'ev Schiff, *Security for Peace: Israel's Minimal Security Requirements in Negotiations with the Palestinians* (Washington, D.C.: Washington Institute For Near East Policy, 1989), pp. 51-58. For a comprehensive overview of the various territorial options see *The West Bank and Gaza: Israeli Options for Peace* (Tel Aviv: Jaffee Center for Strategic Studies, 1989).

31. See Saul Cohen, *Israel's Defensible Borders* (Tel Aviv: Jaffee Center for Strategic Studies, 1983), p. 35.

32. For a comprehensive review of possible Indo-Pakistani arms control agreements, see Stephen Philip Cohen, editor, *Nuclear Proliferation in South Asia: The Prospects for Arms Control* (Boulder, Colorado: Westview Press, 1990).

33. See Leonard S. Spector with Jaqueline R. Smith, *Nuclear Ambitions* (Boulder, Colorado: Westview Press, 1990), p. 77.

34. "Pakistan and India Sign Pact," *Washington Post*, January 1, 1989.

35. Steve Coll, "India, Pakistan Agree on Treaty," *Washington Post*, December 21, 1990.

CHAPTER NINE

A Realistic Arms
Control Policy

The Gulf war has shown why, in the long run, accommodation, mutual acceptance, and some degree of arms control are necessary to prevent the next war from becoming a virtual Armageddon. Indeed, the goal of establishing arms control regimes in the Middle East is essential as long as such initiatives complement efforts toward a stable security environment and progress toward conflict resolution. This might seem obvious, but in the aftermath of the Gulf war unrealistic expectations were raised about ending the Middle East arms race. While this is an admirable objective, the political environment requires a selective approach to arms control in light of the history of regional conflict, the complexities of the subject, and the realities of U.S. Middle East policy.

Despite these and other constraining factors -- including continued economic motives to sell arms -- new efforts to come to grips with the problem must be welcomed. The Paris meeting in July 1991 of the world's five major arms suppliers to discuss arms restraint and more openness with regard to one another's behavior represents progress. The Bush Administration's May 1991 arms control initiative, the constructive role of key congressional committees, and the changed attitudes of the governments of three of the four other suppliers explain this effort. In parallel, the growing interest in arms control in some regional countries, notably Egypt and Israel, reflects a desire to learn more about issues which, until recently, were a virtual monopoly of the superpowers and the Europeans.

Similarly, increased dialogue between private groups from the outside and the region is to be encouraged, provided that such contacts do not become a vehicle for the industrial powers to preach an arms control ideology to the regional players. The most useful role for outside groups is to facilitate talks among those regional players who have a limited, or non-existent legacy of dialogue, and to provide guidance on the more technical lessons of the superpower and European arms control experiences that may have relevance for the Middle East.

In terms of U.S. policy objectives, a multitrack arms control approach to the Middle East should be pursued that covers the gamut from unilateral restraint on arms supplies to support for multilateral regimes such as a future chemical weapons convention. These options, together with selected examples of previous, existing, or future arms control and confidence-building initiatives are shown in the following matrix. The matrix indicates that the arms control agenda is neither barren, nor limited in scope, but that there have been active regional arms control policies for many years.

However, most would agree that much more can be done. In this regard, current U.S. arms control objectives require better articulation. Although the United States approach to Middle East arms control -- including the May 1991 Bush initiative -- is by and large sensible and pragmatic, it continues to be faulted for inconsistency, obfuscation, and occasional hypocrisy. The administration and the Congress share responsibility for these shortfalls. The most persistent criticisms concern the seeming illogic of a policy that calls for arms control while simultaneously allowing for continued sales of advanced weapons to friends in the region, and maintaning silence in both branches of government concerning Israel's nuclear program.

With regard to the first criticism, as long as the United States continues to have strategic interests in the Middle East, particularly access to oil, and is committed to the security of Israel and several key Arab countries, American military power, whether in the form of a direct or distant presence or military assistance and sales to allies, will be a key ingredient of U.S. policy. The only way to reduce the military component of American policy would be to change the policy priorities. There is no indication that either the administration or a majority in Congress seeks such a change. For this reason, arms sales and military assistance will continue, no matter how controversial they seem. Furthermore, as long as Washington is intent on pursuing a regional peace process through diplomacy, the security needs of all parties will be essential factors of any settlement.

While it is hoped that arms reductions will parallel a peace process, transitional arrangements will require continued U.S. military guarantees and military assistance. This does not mean an open-ended commitment to meet all the requests for advanced conventional munitions from U.S. friends in the region. New combat aircraft and tank sales, in particular, should be carefully scrutinized; exotic systems such as Stealth fighters, cruise missiles, and the U.S. army's advanced tactical missile system (ATACMs) should not be transferred under any foreseeable circumstance. This applies especially to the Gulf Cooperation Council (GCC) countries. While they have genuine security problems, their legitimate defense needs

Matrix of Arms Control Arrangements
in the Middle East and South Asia

		FORMAL	INFORMAL
MULTILATERAL	External powers only	• London Nuclear Suppliers Club (E)	• MTCR (E) • Australia Group (E) • NEACC (Defunct)
	Regional powers only	• Notification of missile tests (P) • Warhead/weapon ceilings (P)	• Arab-Israeli understanding on missile deployments and uses of air power (P)
	External and regional powers	• NPT (E) • Biological Weapons Convention (E) • Geneva Protocol (E) • Chemical Weapons Convention (under negotiation) • Egyptian-Israeli Sinai Agreements (MFO) (E) • Syrian-Israeli Golan Disengagement (E)	
BILATERAL	External powers only		• U.S.-Soviet understanding on missile deployments (P) • U.S.-PRC understanding on missile sales (P)
	Regional powers only	• Indo-Pak. joint military commission (E) • Indo-Pak. no attack agreement (E) • Indo-Pak. chemical weapons treaty (P)	• Syrian-Israeli "red lines" in Lebanon (E)
	External and regional powers	• U.S.-individual country end-use agreements (E)	• U.S.-Saudi understanding on F-15 deployments (E)
UNILATERAL	External powers	• National laws on nuclear proliferation and munitions control (E) • Pending U.S. legislation on CBW and missiles (P)	• Supplier restraint on arms sales (U.S., U.S.S.R., and Europe) (E)
	Regional powers		• Israel, India, Pak. restraint on nuclear testing (E)
		(E) = existing (P) = potential	

must be carefully defined. Inevitably, politics and prestige cut into such calculations; if the U.S. wants far-reaching access agreements with the GCC, it must take into account the political, as well as military environment, as not all arms purchase can be justified on purely military grounds. This is not unusual; very few military establishments, including those in NATO, can justify all their procurement on the basis of exacting military cost-benefit analysis. However, putting ceilings on the number of advanced weapons sold and adjusting the delivery schedule to a realistic time frame seems a sensible compromise in the absence of regional tranquility.

Concerning the dilemma of Israel's nuclear weapons, a clearer statement of policy is necessary. The Bush Administration began its term of office with a widely publicized, but narrowly focused, and deliberately exclusive emphasis on the need for chemical weapons arms control. The regional impact was immediate and predictable: in unison the Arab states linked chemical weapons to Israel's nuclear weapons, thereby drawing attention to a subject that both the administration and the Congress have been unwilling to discuss. In this context, witness U.S. Secretary of Defense Richard Cheney's response in June 1991 when asked in Cairo what he thought about Israel's nuclear weapons: "I don't know that Israel has any nuclear capability. They have certainly never announced it."[1] This answer did little to increase confidence that the United States had a comprehensive and coherent arms control policy.

To be credible, U.S. arms control policy must be more open about nuclear weapons in the region since they are far and away the most dangerous items in the arms race. While Israel has good reasons for developing its nuclear weapons program, and has shown responsibility in not flaunting it, its existence has been a catalyst for other Middle East states to seek their own nuclear capability, particularly Iraq. But, as argued in Chapter 8, until there has been a long period of peace in the Middle East, Israel is unlikely to negotiate away its nuclear force. In these circumstances, the best way to address the Israeli nuclear weapons program is to engage in a more open discussion of its existence and seek ways to limit its further growth, without, at this time, calling for its elimination. Pushing Israel too hard on nuclear weapons while demanding that it be more flexible on giving up land for peace would be counterproductive. But to say nothing about this program, or engage in empty semantics, is equally counterproductive. If Washington expects the Arab states to participate in arms control talks, Israel's nuclear program cannot be open-ended. To be able to counter their own domestic criticism, and to address other arms control issues such as a chemical weapons ban and a freeze on surface-to-surface missiles, the Arab states must be able to show that a sincere effort is underway to limit Israel's nuclear program. This will have little impact on radical Muslim states uninterested in peace with Israel or arms control, but it will make it much easier to isolate them if Israel is a party to talks on weapons restrictions.[2]

To give greater credibility to overall U.S. policy, the best way to achieve arms limitations is to develop a sound security structure for the region and to orchestrate political negotiations between the regional antagonists. Assuring Iraq's compliance with UN Security Council Resolution 687, and brokering a serious Arab-Israeli peace process are the two keys to regional stability and arms control. Other welcome events would include the reentry of Iran into the international community, resolving Iraq's border problems, and a resolution of the outstanding conflicts between India and Pakistan. If these occurred, concern about Israel's nuclear weapons, Arab chemical weapons, Saudi defense spending, Iraqi and Iranian rearmament, and the subcontinent's nuclear and missile programs, would be partially dispelled.

This is not to detract from initiatives for arms restraint, especially unilateral restrictions on the transfer of advanced conventional munitions and multinational agreements on weapons of mass destruction and surface-to-surface missiles. Rather, it is meant to highlight the political reality for U.S. policy in the Middle East: namely, that it would be inappropriate at this time for the United States to seek even-handed arms supply policies. While U.S. policy should be more consistent and open, it must also be discriminatory and lean most heavily on the prevention of arms acquisitions by its regional adversaries. The primary focus of restraint efforts in the Middle East should be to target specific countries that have pursued anti-American policies and have supported terrorist groups. The U.S. must also be prepared to limit arms to friends if they provide support to governments engaged in violent acts against western interests. Equally, Washington should be wary of multilateral arms control efforts that are more likely to penalize friends than adversaries.

As for seeking an agreed policy between the administration and Congress on regional arms control, this is neither likely nor particularly healthy. Legislative tactics by the Congress have an important impact on the nature and direction of American policy on technology proliferation. Congress can pass laws and, equally important, can threaten to pass laws. In the former case, Congress can literally dictate action to the administration. In the latter case, it can often influence how the administration negotiates with foreign governments. Most legislation on foreign technology transfers, especially military transfers, contains sufficient latitude to allow the president to override specific constraints of the law if U.S. national security interests so warrant, and provided the president can demonstrate why exceptions should be made. In general, the process encourages caution before such measures are proposed or approved. Congress' role in determining U.S. policy is a useful counterbalance to the enthusiasm frequently displayed by the executive branch for particular clients.[3]

As for near-term priorities, the effective enforcement of the provisions of Resolution 687 is essential. Until there is incontrovertible evidence that Iraq's most dangerous military capabilities have been eliminated, it will be difficult to urge restraint on others in the region. The second priority must be to work for a suppliers' agreement to freeze further sales of surface-to-surface missiles to the region and to tighten export controls on technology and components that can be used in the manufacture of nuclear, chemical, and biological weapons. A third objective must be to facilitate a dialogue between Israel and its neighbors on confidence-building measures. These should include: discussions about eventual weapons-free zones; methods to reduce the risks of war by miscalculation; terrorism; verification; restricted deployment zones; and peacekeeping procedures in the event that there are breakthroughs in peace negotiations. Until there has been progress in these three priority areas, it would be unwise to attempt more far-reaching schemes to freeze, or stop, transfers of all other major weapons systems to the region. Proposals for more inclusive arms moratoria might undermine opportunities to control the further spread of nuclear and chemical weapons and missiles.

Ultimately, the preferred route to an arms control regime is for the suppliers themselves to monitor their own policies and to work with regional countries to establish guidelines about their minimum security requirements. If the suppliers attempt to dictate the legitimate security needs of each regional country, and to adjust arms supplies accordingly, they will be rebuffed. In contrast, if the key regional actors can be convinced of the advantages in restricting their own arms procurement, it will be much easier to gain a consensus among the supplier nations to agree to some moratoria on certain classes of technology.

This conclusion may seem unsatisfactory to those who are impatient to see more rapid progress on arms control. But Middle East conflicts defy quick solutions. Nevertheless, considering the fact that many of the key players are still technically in a state of war with one another, it is encouraging that a majority now appear to be in favor of a non-violent solution to regional problems. If this ultimately leads to peace negotiations, a new era will have began in which arms control will play a key role. If peace remains elusive, traditional means of national security will prevail.

182

Notes

1. Transcript of Secretary Cheney's Press Conference, Cairo, Egypt, June 1, 1991, Office of the Secretary of Defense, Washington, D.C.

2. See James Leonard, "Steps Toward a Middle East Free of Nuclear Weapons," *Arms Control Today*, April 1991.

3. Sometimes, the division between the legislative and the executive branches is not so clear. Within the labyrinths of the bureaucracy, coalitions between congressional committees on the one hand, and agencies in the executive branch on the other, can work to limit or override administrative policies. For example, in the mid-1970s the Office of the Secretary of Defense and the Senate Foreign Relations Subcommittee on Foreign Assistance worked together to curb U.S. arms sales to Iran that were being feverishly pursued by the White House, the Secretary of State, and the U.S. armed services. See Robert Mantel and Geoffrey Kemp, *U.S. Military Sales to Iran*, Staff Report to the Subcommittee on Foreign Assistance, United States Senate (Washington, D.C.: United States Government Printing Office, 1976).

Selected Rockets and SSMs in the Middle East and South Asia

Selected Rockets and SSMs in the Middle East and South Asia
(Operational and Under Development)

COUNTRY	Missile System	Producer	Range in Km	Payload in Kg
Afghanistan	Scud-B	USSR	300	1000
Egypt	Scud-B	USSR	300	1000
	FROG-7	USSR	70	450
	SAKR-80	Egypt	80	200
	Mod. Scud-B	N. Korea	305	1000
India	Agni*	India	2500	1000
	Prithvi*	India	250	1000
Iran	Mod. Scud-B	N. Korea	305	1000
	Iran-130	Iran	200	?
	Oghab	Iran	40	?
Iraq	Scud-B	USSR	300	1000
	FROG-7	USSR	70	450
	Al-Hussayn	Iraq	640	135-350
	Al-Abbas	Iraq	900	135-350
	Tammouz-I*	Iraq	2000?	?
Israel	Lance	U.S.	110	225
	Jericho-I	Israel-France	640	450-680
	Jericho-II	Israel	1450	454
	Jericho-IIB*	Israel	2400	?
	MAR-350	Israel	90	335
Kuwait	FROG-7	USSR	70	450
Libya	Scud-B	USSR	300	1000
	FROG-7	USSR	70	450
Pakistan	Hatf-I*	Pakistan	80	500
	Hatf-II*	Pakistan	300	500
S. Arabia	CSS-II	China	2700	2000
Syria	Scud-B	USSR	300	1000
	FROG-7	USSR	70	450
	SS-21	USSR	120	450
	Mod. Scud-B	N. Korea	305	1000
Yemen	Scud-B	USSR	300	1000
	FROG-7	USSR	70	450
	SS-21	USSR	120	450

*Under development

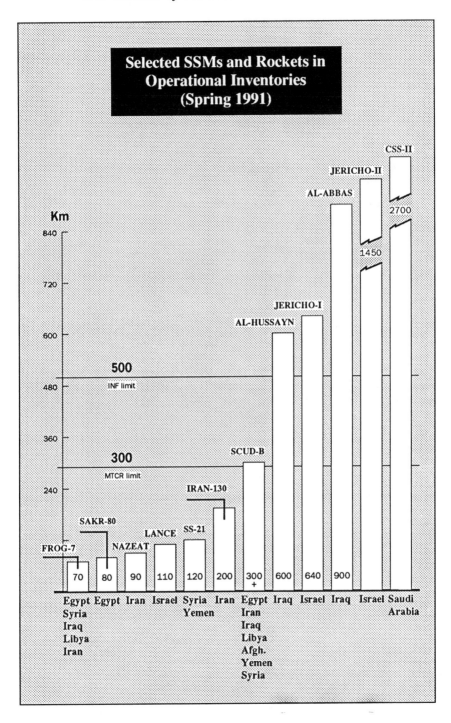

Selected SSMs and Rockets in Operational Inventories (Spring 1991)

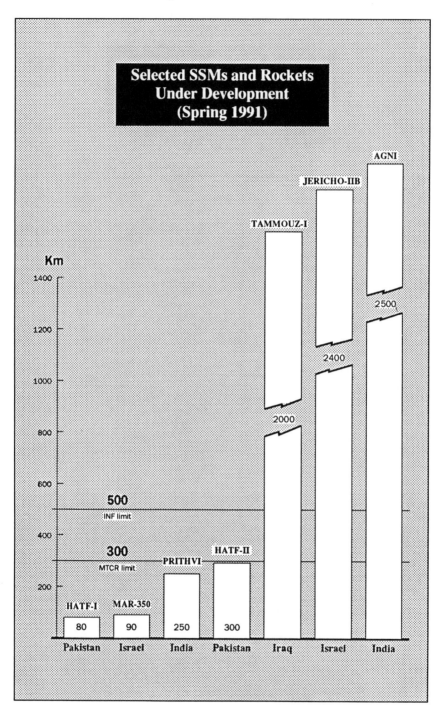

Selected SSMs and Rockets
Under Development
(Spring 1991)

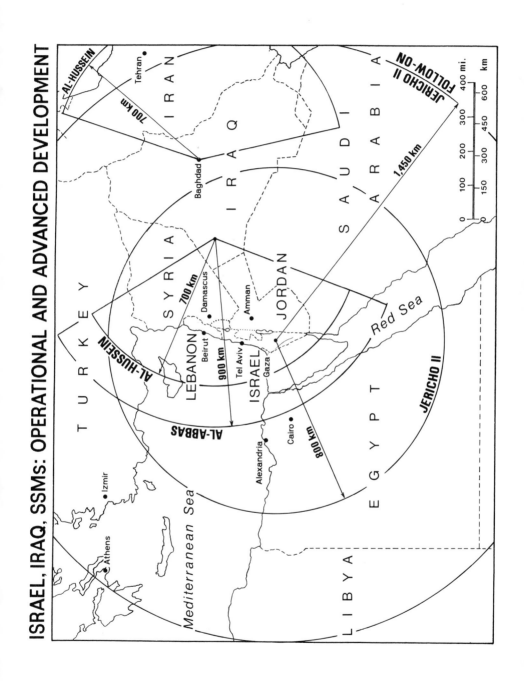

ISRAEL, IRAQ, SSMs: OPERATIONAL AND ADVANCED DEVELOPMENT

MISSILES AND CONFLICT ON THE INDIAN SUBCONTINENT

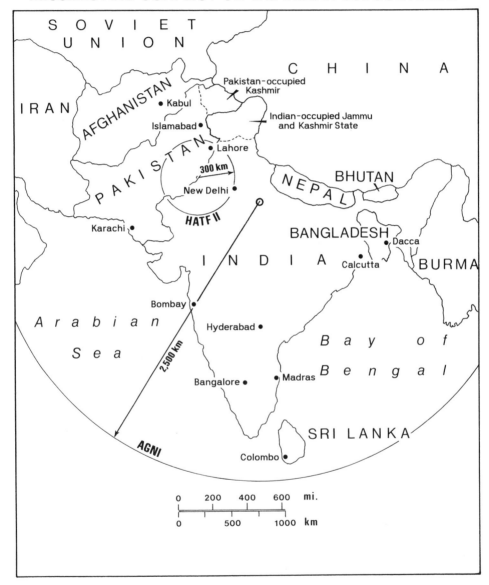

SSMs in Combat:
A Brief History

The most significant event in the development of long-range projectiles was the appearance of the powered missile, a self-propelled projectile that carries its own motor, impacting greater forward velocity and enabling it to reach targets far removed from the battlefield. The first rocket-powered missile dates back to the sixteenth century, when the Swedish used cannon-launched rocket spears.[1]

Modern day missile technology became operational during World War II with the German V-1 and V-2 systems. The V-1 was a cruise missile and the V-2 a ballistic missile. A cruise missile is an unmanned aircraft that uses an air-breathing engine during flight. A ballistic missile is an unmanned, rocket-powered weapon that is powered during launch and then follows a curved trajectory down to its target.[2]

The V-1 could reach a target up to 225 km and traveled at an average height of 280 meters with a speed of 900 km/hr.[3] During the main phase of the German V-1 offensive from June to September 1944, some 9017 V-1 missiles were launched from Pas de Calais, France; 2340 of them reached the London Civil Defense Region (LCDR) causing 20,000 casualties.[4] After September 1944, 1475 V-1s were launched against London; only 79 of them reached their target.[5]

The V-1 was a flying bomb, the precursor of today's cruise missile. During the war, the British developed a number of defensive mechanisms to fend off V-1 attacks. Anti-V-1 measures ranged from intercept missions by combat aircraft to the deployment of anti-aircraft guns and balloon barrages. Approximately 3463 V-1s were destroyed (38 percent of all those launched) by active and passive defenses en route to their targets.[6]

The development of the V-2 (A-4 was the German designation) posed a greater threat. The V-2, which could carry a 1000 kg warhead of conventional high explosives over a 320 km range, was the first guided ballistic missile. A ballistic missile does not rely on aerodynamic surfaces to produce lift. Instead, it is propelled out of the earth's atmosphere by its initial thrust, and then follows a ballistic trajectory to its target once thrust is terminated.[7] The German V-2 traveled at 1.6 km per second and attained a maximum altitude of 96 to 113 km, making its detection by defensive systems extremely difficult. Moreover, because it traveled faster than the speed of sound, there was no warning of its approach. The hit/launch ratio for V-2s was, therefore, much greater than that of the V-1. From September 8 to 18, 1944, 27 out of 35 V-2s reached the LCDR.[8] From September 1944 to March 1945, a total of 1403 V-2s were launched against London, with 517 reaching their targets, resulting in some 9000 casualties. During the same time period, approximately 2600 V-2s were fired against the port city of Antwerp, Belgium, a major allied resupply center.[9]

From the late 1960s and throughout the 1970s, the Soviet Union and the United States supplied ballistic missiles to at least ten countries.[10] SSMs were used in the 1973 Arab-Israeli war, the Iran-Iraq war, the Afghan conflict, and the Gulf war. During the early stages of the 1973 war, both Syria and Egypt launched some 40-50 of their Soviet-made FROG-7 rockets against targets in the Sinai desert and northern Israel. The rockets had little military impact and caused few casualties.[11]

More significant was the use of SSMs in the eight-year war between Iran and Iraq. Iran began using its Scud-B missiles against Iraq in March 1985.[12] Between 1985 and the beginning of 1988, Iran launched 35-40 Scuds against Iraq with many of them reaching Iraq's major population center of Baghdad. Faced with the lack of a retaliatory capability, Iraq succeeded in extending the range of its own Soviet-supplied Scud-B missiles. By reducing the size of the warhead compartment by 200-300 kg to leave more room for the missile propellant, Iraq developed the 600-700 km range Al-Hussayn missile and the 900 km Al-Abbas.

Between February and April 1988, both Iran and Iraq continued to target one another's population centers in what has now been called the War of the Cities. According to one report, Iraq fired SSMs at least 150 times, usually in groups of three, for a total of about 450 rockets and missiles, against Tehran and other cities. Iran fired about 60 missiles during this same period.[13] Iraq further broadened the scope of the conflict when, in early March, it began to target the Iranian holy city of Qom in an attempt to force Iran to accept a UN-brokered cease-fire.[14]

Surface-to-surface missiles (SSMs) have been used extensively in Afghanistan since the withdrawal of Soviet troops in February 1989. The Afghan army has been generously supplied with Soviet Scud-B missiles; in fact, more of them were used in Afghanistan in 1988 than in the War of the Cities between Iran and Iraq.[15] In November 1988, the Afghan army began firing Scud-Bs on mujaheddin bases around the eastern province of Nangarhar as a reprisal for the rebels' use of multiple rocket launch systems (MRLS) against civilians.[16] The siege of Jalalabad by the mujaheddin, which forced them to use more conventional tactics, saw an increase in the effectiveness of SSM systems used by the Afghan army. Over 400 Scud-B missiles were fired against mujaheddin troop concentrations around the city of Jalalabad during the siege, contributing, in part, to the defeat of the rebel offensive.[17] In the ten months following the withdrawal of Soviet troops in February 1989, between 900 to 1000 Scuds were fired by the Afghan army.[18] There have also been numerous reports of Scud missiles being fired against guerrilla bases in Pakistan, with one missile falling as close as 30 km northeast of Islamabad.[19] In March and April 1991, the Soviet-supported Afghan army repeatedly fired Scuds at Afghan resistance forces in the city of Khost, 30 kilometers from Pakistan. Reports have placed the death toll from Scud attacks in Afghanistan at over 300 already in 1991.[20]

In the Persian Gulf war Iraq launched 93 modified Scuds, 40 aimed at population centers in Israel and 53 at strategic and civilian sites in Saudi Arabia and other Gulf States.[21] While the inaccuracy and small warheads of these missiles rendered them militarily insignificant, they had significant disruptive and terror effects. All of the Iraqi missiles used in the Gulf war were armed with conventional warheads.

Notes

1. *Weapons* (New York: St. Martin's Press, 1980), p. 240.

2. W. Seth Carus, *Ballistic Missiles in the Third World: Threat and Response*, The Washington Papers (Washington, D.C.: Center for Strategic and International Studies, 1990), p. 2.

3. The V-1 used a pulse jet engine developed in France in 1910. See, *Weapons*, p. 243.

4. Basil Collier, *The Second World War: A Military History* (New York: William Morrow & Co. Inc., 1967), p. 402.

5. Ibid., p. 433.

6. Ibid., p. 432.

7. *The Official Dictionary of Military Terms* (San Francisco: Hemisphere Publishing Corporation, 1988), p. 46.

8. See Collier, *The Second World War: A Military History*, p. 432.

9. See *Weapons*, p. 253; and Collier, pp. 431-432.

10. See Carus, *Ballistic Missiles in the Third World: Threat and Response*, p. 3.

11. Aharon Levran, "Threats Facing Israel from Surface-to-Surface Missiles," *IDF Journal*, Winter 1990, p. 37.

12. Robert D. Shuey, et al., *Missile Proliferation: Survey of Emerging Missile Forces* (Washington, D.C.: Congressional Research Service, 1988), p. 48.

13. Aharon Levran, "Threats Facing Israel from Surface-to-Surface Missiles," p. 39-40. Estimate of the number of missiles fired by Iraq during the Iran-Iraq war between February and April 1988 by the Strategic Studies Institute, U.S. Army War College is 120 missiles. See Stephen C. Pelletiere, Douglas V. Johnson II, and Leif R. Rosenberger, *Iraqi Power and U.S. Security* (Carlisle Barracks, Pennsylvania.: Strategic Studies Institute, U.S. Army War College, 1990), p. 23.

14. Charles P. Wallace, "Iraq, in First Such Attack, Fires Missile at Iranian Holy City of Qom," *Washington Post*, March 3 1990.

15. Barnett R. Rubin, "End the Cold War in Afghanistan," *Washington Post*, November 29, 1989.

16. "Army Begins Firing Soviet Made Missiles," Hong Kong, Agence France Presse, 1350 GMT, 3 November 1988, in *FBIS-NES*, November 4, 1988, p. 47.

17. "The Ox Won't Budge," *The Middle East*, August 1989, p. 22.

18. See Martin Fletcher, "Soviet Crew 'Firing Missiles at Rebels' in Afghanistan," *The Times*, (London) 10 December 1989; and "Diplomats Note Major Soviet Arms Shipment," Hong Kong, Agence France Presse, 1119 GMT, 9 January 1990, in *FBIS-NES*, January 9, 1990, p. 53.

19. See "Afghans Fire 'Scud,'" *Jane's Defence Weekly*, 20 January 1989, p. 99. See also, "Kabul Forces Fire Scud Missile at Peshawar Area," Islamabad Domestic Service, 1500 GMT, 7 April 1989, translated in *FBIS-NES*, April 20, 1989, p. 56; and "Protest Lodged Over Afghan Scud Missile Firing," Islamabad Domestic Service, 1500 GMT, 6 June 1989, translated in *FBIS-NES*, June 7, 1989, p. 68.

20. See "Khost Lost," *Economist*, April 6, 1991, pp. 34-35; "Say Scuds Kill 10," Hong Kong, Agence France Presse, 1049 GMT, 2 April 1991, in *FBIS-NES*, April 2, 1991, p. 33; and "Kabul Said Using Scuds, Napalm," Hong Kong, Agence France Presse, 0919 GMT, 24 March 1991, in *FBIS-NES*, March 25, 1991, p. 52.

21. Department of Defense Fact Sheet, June 7, 1991.

Long-Range Artillery

Rocket Artillery

Long-range artillery rockets, unguided free-fall systems that follow a ballistic trajectory, are rarely given much attention in studies on proliferation. However, developments in this technology are beginning to blur the operational distinction between short-range ballistic missiles and free-fall rockets.[1] Countries in the Middle East and South Asia have modified existing systems to develop rockets with ranges and payloads equal to much more expensive surface-to-surface missiles (SSMs). Some examples of long-range artillery rockets in production or under development include Egypt's Sakr 80 with an 80 kilometer range, Iran's 40 kilometer Oghab, and Israel's 90 kilometer MAR-350.

Rockets have both strategic and tactical utility; for example, Iran fired Oghab and Nazeat rockets against Iraqi cities to counter Iraqi attacks with Scud-B SSMs. Unlike current generation SSMs, multiple rocket launchers, the usual delivery system, are highly mobile and can fire in large numbers over a very short time period. Saturation bombardment of population centers with artillery is now possible. In the context of the Arab-Israeli conflict, Jerusalem, Tel Aviv, Haifa, Amman, and Damascus all lie within 60 kilometers of the Israel-Syrian-Jordanian borders, easily within the range of modern multiple launch rocket systems (MLRS).

Rockets and long-range artillery can serve as an inexpensive delivery system for chemical weapons, and some states are developing warheads for this purpose.[2] Artillery rockets can also serve as a first step toward an indigenous missile program, and their less-complicated technology can be acquired without violating the provisions of the Missile Technology Control Regime (MTCR). Therefore, they hold great attraction for those states that currently lack the ability to produce missiles. Generally considered battlefield weapons, artillery rockets are widely sold throughout the region by external suppliers. Examples of these weapons are Brazil's Astros systems, the Soviet Union's BM series, and China's Type 63.

The U.S. ATACMS

The development of the U.S. Army Tactical Missile System (ATACMS), which became operational with the army at the beginning of 1991 and was used briefly in the Gulf war, could revolutionize the future of short-range missiles. The ATACMS is an important weapon for several reasons. It has a range up to 150 kilometers, is said to have a CEP of 100 meters -- three times more accurate than the Lance -- and its flight path angle can be altered during flight. Hence, it carries the designation 'semi-ballistic.' The ATACMS also carries a cluster munition warhead with a payload 70 percent larger than that of the Lance.[3] Because its area of coverage is larger than its CEP, the ATACMS is almost guaranteed to hit its target point.[4]

In addition, the ATACMS, while sophisticated, is also relatively inexpensive, with an approximate cost of $418,000 per unit.[5] Both Turkey and Saudi Arabia, among other states, have expressed interest in the system. Any state in the Middle East or South Asia able to obtain technology similar to that used in the ATACMS would have a formidable new weapon system.

The ATACMS system appeared in combat for the first time in the Gulf war. The army reported that it had sent 105 missiles to the region. Thirty missiles were supposedly fired against SAM sites, Scud positions, howitzer and rocket batteries, bridges, and logistic sites, allegedly destroying or rendering inoperable all of their targets.[6]

The Iraqi Supergun and its Ancestors

On March 22, 1990, Dr. Gerald Bull, a Canadian-born rocket scientist, was assassinated in Brussels. Bull had helped Iraq develop long-range artillery for use during its war with Iran, and that he also aided Iraq in the development of a 2000 km missile test-fired in December 1989. His Belgian-based company, Space Research Corp (SRC), also was coordinating the production, purchase, and assembly for Iraq of a 131 foot long artillery piece. The so-called 'supergun' would have been able to fire high explosives as well as unconventional munitions at ranges of approximately 1600 km, and could possibly place small satellites into orbit.[7] One of Israel's top military correspondents has said that Bull first offered his supergun to Israel in 1983, possibly earlier, but feasibility tests led the Israelis to believe that the project would not work.[8]

Further proof of the murky relationship between the rocket scientist

198

and Iraq came 21 days after his death. On April 12, 1990, British officials impounded a shipment of steel pipes bound for Iraq which, according to British defense experts, were to be assembled into a gun of unheard of proportions.[9] On April 20, 1990, the Greek Government announced that it had halted a truck bound for Iraq carrying 29.5 tons of cargo, including a 5.5 meter tube with a bore of 81 centimeters.[10] Other parts of the intended Iraqi supergun were later seized in Spain and Italy.

Both the Iraqi Government and Sheffield Forgemasters -- the British company involved -- have claimed that the pipe confiscated on April 12 was for use in a petrochemical plant.[11] A total of 52 steel pipe pieces had been produced by Sheffield Forgemasters for Iraq under the specifications of Space Research Corp, with 44 of them already having reached their destination. The steel tubes seized in England were to be used to build a gun 40 meters long with a bore of 99 centimeters. This supergun would then be used to send warheads hundred of kilometers or to launch rockets into space.[12] Sheffield's CEO said that any attempt to build a supergun would result in the destruction of the weapon upon firing.[13]

In an age when high technology weapons dominate the hearts and minds of arms controllers, and in an area where missile proliferation and unconventional weapons are constantly referred to as the principal threats to peace and stability, the development of a supergun seems misplaced. Defense experts initially failed to see any logic in Iraq's effort to acquire such an artillery piece, and they dismissed Bull as an eccentric. A more careful analysis, however, offers a different interpretation.

Bull's supergun idea was based on the High Altitude Research Project (HARP) which he undertook during the early 1960s for the United States and Canadian governments.[14] HARP explored the possibilities of launching satellites into orbit by means other than rockets. Bull built three HARP guns; one of them, an impressive 52.5 meters long, was able to send a 272 kg rocket-boosted artillery shell some 1850 km away.[15] In spite of its impressive initial success, the HARP project was abandoned as the U.S. decided to use conventional rocketry as the means for space exploration.

Attempts at constructing long-range artillery pieces are not new. In 1918, the Germans used a 120 km range gun to shell Paris, and during WWII they built an 80 cm caliber gun with a 47 km range which could fire a 4800 kg HE projectile.[16] These long-range guns were actually breech-loading mortars.[17]

As part of its super-weapons program, Germany also tried to develop a long-range gun, known as the V-3, to fire across the channel into

London. The V-3 was designed to boost a finned shell through a long gun barrel with a series of explosive charges. In August 1943, Hitler approved the construction of a site at Mimoyecques near Calais which would house the facility for the V-3. By September 1943, the Germans had a 20 mm prototype of the gun that performed well during early trials.[18] The actual V-3 would have been a multi-chambered gun of 15 cm caliber with a barrel of 150 meters. The theory behind the gun was that an initial propellant would be loaded in with a shell, and additional propellants would be loaded into side chambers. As the shell passed through the chambers, the additional propellants would fire, increasing the boost to the shell as it left the muzzle. A velocity of 1524 m/sec was predicted with a range of 280 km.[19]

Conclusion

Long-range artillery over short distances can offer a less expensive alternative to strategic bombers or missiles. Moreover, as technological developments in rocket-driven artillery shells continue, the barrier between long-range artillery and short-range tactical missiles is eroding.

Middle Eastern countries have long placed a priority on the acquisition and development of long-range artillery. In spite of the glamour of other weapons systems, it is still infantry and artillery that both take and hold ground. Moreover, in a region where distances are short and where the main population and military centers lie within close range of the enemy, rocket-propelled artillery can be a decisive weapon.

Notes

1. See W. Seth Carus, "Trends and Implications of Missile Proliferation," paper prepared for the International Studies Association, April 13, 1990, pp. 8-9.

2. Ibid., p. 7.

3. See Charles Rabb, "ATACMS Adds Long-Range Punch," *Defense Electronics*, August 1986, p. 70.

4. See Carus, "Trends and Implications of Missile Proliferation," p. 23.

5. Ted Nicholas and Rita Rossi, *Weapon System Costs 1989*, 9th edition, Data Search Associates, in Carus, "Trends and Implications of Missile Proliferation," p. 23.

6. "Army Weapons System Performance in Southwest Asia," U.S. Army fact sheet, March 13, 1991.

7. "Fog Shrouds Death of a Weapons Genius," *Wall Street Journal*, April 23, 1990.

8. Mike Wallace, "Who Killed Gerald Bull?" 60 Minutes, CBS News, September 16, 1990.

9. "Britain Seizes Tubes Going to Iraq," *New York Times*, April 13, 1990.

10. "Greece Seizes a Truck Carrying Arms to Iraq," *New York Times*, April 21, 1990.

11. Ibid.

12. "Britain is Convinced Its Customs Halted Giant Gun for Iraq," *New York Times*, April 19, 1990.

13. "Britain Seizes Tube Going to Iraq."

14. For a detailed history of the HARP project and Germany's World War I program, see Gerald V. Bull and Charles H. Murphy, *Paris Kanonen -- the Paris Guns (Wilhelmgeschütze) and Project HARP* (Herford and Bonn: Verlag E.S. Mittler & Sohn, GmbH, 1988).

15. "Aiming for a Long Reach," *The Middle East*, March 1990, p. 17.

16. "Iraq: Heir to Harp Project?" *Jane's Defence Weekly*, 28 April 1990, p. 770.

17. The difference between a gun, mortar, and howitzer, the three main artillery designations, lies in the path followed by the projectile fired to its target. Guns fire direct, fast hits; mortar shells follow a high parabola; howitzers combine these two paths, firing large shells in an indirect trajectory. See *Weapons*, (New York: St. Martin's Press, 1980), p. 164.

18. See David Irving, *The Mare's Nest* (London: William Kimber and Co. Ltd, 1964), p. 213-14. See also John Keegan, editor, *The Rand McNally Encyclopedia of World War II* (United States: Rand McNally & Company, 1977), p. 116.

19. See Keegan, ibid., p. 116

Israel's Strategic Geography

Computerized Three-Dimensional Maps

Since understanding the geography is the key to understanding the land-for-peace debate and its impact on arms control, the Carnegie Endowment project has utilized new computer imaging techniques to produce three-dimensional maps of Israel. These 3-D maps show very clearly how geographical features influence the strategic perceptions of adversaries. The computer data-base allows the mapped area to be viewed from different azimuths -- looking West from Jordan, or southwest from Syria, for example -- and to zoom in on specific geographical features -- such as the West Bank plateau, or the Golan Heights.

The current data-base for Israel includes topographical features, cities, towns, main roads, and boundaries including the 1949 armistice lines (the 'green line'). Eventually data on the water systems, airfields, villages, alternative security zones (the Allon and Sharon Plans, for example), and alternative Palestinian regimes will be included. With more elaborate data, it should be possible to indicate not only the strategic dimensions of the problem, but some of the sociological, environmental, and economic aspects as well.

The six maps shown on the following pages represent the project's first efforts in this field. Each map shows how different geographical features of Israel and the occupied territories influence the debate about land for peace. The maps demonstrate vividly the importance of the topography of historic Palestine for both offensive and defensive military operations.[1] They show not only Israel's vulnerability if it relinquishes territory, but also the strategic advantages Israel acquires vis-à-vis Syria and Jordan by holding on to the Golan Heights and West Bank.[2]

The Geography of Armageddon

It is appropriate to begin, literally, with Armageddon. On October 11, 1989, Mohammed Bassem Adel, a pilot in the Syrian air force, broke away from his squadron and flew his Soviet supplied MiG-23 into Israeli

MAP 1

Central and Northern Israel and Occupied Territories

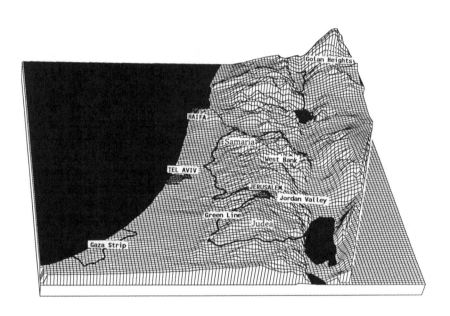

Shows the importance of the West Bank and Golan Heights for both offensive and defensive operations.

MAP 2

Central and Northern Israel
and West Bank

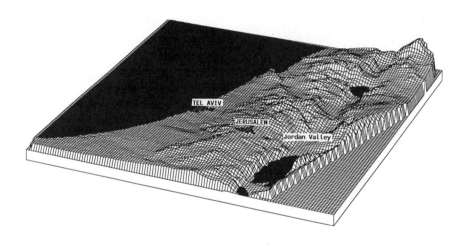

An overview of all of Northern Israel. This view shows the importance
of the Jordan Valley and the hills on either side to any force
contemplating an invasion of Israel or Jordan.

MAP 3

The Strategic Importance of Megiddo

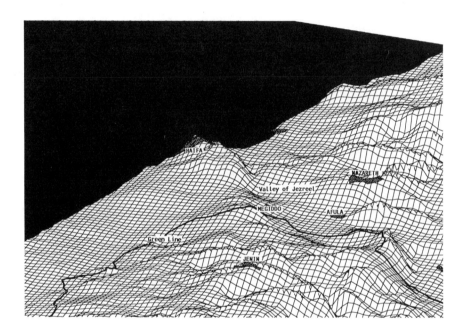

A westerly view along the Carmelite range to Haifa. In the lower
center is the Arab town of Jenin which is within the West Bank. The
map shows the strategic location of Megiddo near the "green line" in
Israel proper just below the crest of the Carmelite range. It also shows
the dominance of Nazareth over the Southern Galilee foothills and the
Valley of Jezreel.

MAP 4

Haifa from the Mediterranean

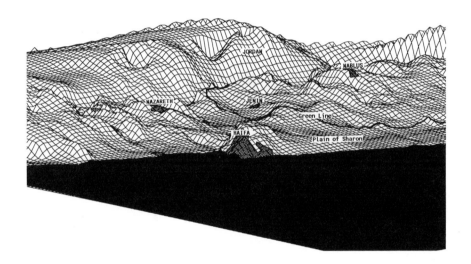

A view looking East to Haifa in the Carmelite range. The map shows
how the "green line" hugs Samarian foothills as it comes up from
the Plain of Sharon

MAP 5

Jordan Valley Looking South

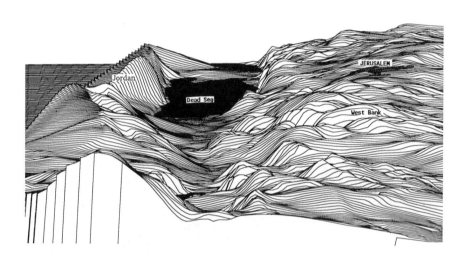

Shows the importance of control of the Jordan Valley and the access
roads to the West Bank for an invading or defending force.

MAP 6

Jordan Valley and Golan Heights

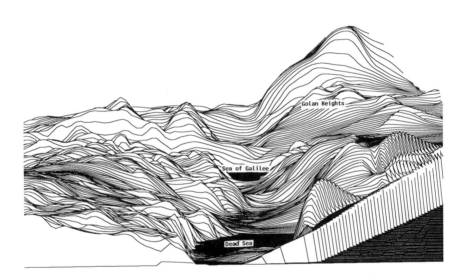

Shows the importance of the Jordan Valley and Golan Heights.

airspace. Within minutes, he landed unharmed and alone at the small civilian airfield of Megiddo and asked for asylum.[3] Only a few miles away from Meggido is the largest and probably most important military air base in Israel, Ramat David. Ramat David houses F-16 fighters and is on instant alert 24 hours a day for both conventional and chemical weapons attack. The MiG-23 was not intercepted by the IDF and caused much consternation within the Israeli defense establishment.

Megiddo is located on the northern face of the Carmel Hills, which run from Samaria to the coast at Haifa. It overlooks the Valley of Jezreel -- sometimes called the Plain of Esdraelon -- a flat, highly fertile stretch of land running from the Jordan Valley to the coast (see map 3). Historically, Megiddo was the strategic crossroad controlling the access routes South to Egypt, North to the cities and ports of what is now Lebanon, and the route to Damascus and on to Mesopotamia, now Iraq. The famous Via Maris stretched from Egypt along the Sinai, through Gaza to what is now Hadera, North of Tel Aviv. There, the road branched inland through the Musmus Pass in the Wadi Arah to Megiddo. Numerous armies fought their way both North and South through this pass. Some of the greatest battles involving Egyptians, Babylonians, Israelites, Canaanites, and others -- including some of the famous battles described in the Bible -- were fought in and around Megiddo. Whatever force controlled Megiddo could deploy mobile forces, including chariots, to block the passes or intercept armies approaching from the North or East.

Megiddo's importance in antiquity has carried through to modern times. In September 1918, General Allenby defeated the Turkish armies in a decisive battle at Megiddo in his drive North from Egypt. He then was able to liberate all of Palestine and march on Damascus. In contemporary strategy, if Arab armies succeeded in breaking through Israeli fortifications on the Golan Heights, or along the Jordan Valley, they would have to be stopped somewhere in the Valley of Jezreel to prevent them from reaching the Mediterranean North of Haifa and bisecting the country. In such circumstances, the area around Megiddo could likely be the site of another decisive battle.

The Lay of the Land. The Judean and Samarian mountain ranges, much of which is today known as the West Bank, provided sanctuary for the ancient Hebrews who occupied the highlands (see map 1). Zerah the Ethiopian, and Sennacherib the Assyrian, tried to conquer the highlands and were defeated by the natural barriers; Egypt avoided attacking them altogether.[4] Roman emperors Vespasian, Titus, and Hadrian succeeded in conquering the highlands, but Vespasian and Titus were careful to occupy all of the surrounding plains before undertaking the conquest, while Hadrian's victory was one of the bloodiest in Roman history. After he had taken Gaza, Napoleon Bonaparte refused even to attempt to conquer Jerusalem, which straddles the highlands.

The coastal plains, on the other hand, were extremely vulnerable to military conquest. Since they were endowed with large areas of arable land, they were more densely populated than were the mountains. They served as an excellent source of revenue from tolls and taxes paid by those taking goods through the region, and the harbors in the Gaza Strip and Bay of Haifa contributed to the region's growth. The cities located along the plains were vulnerable to both land and naval attacks. The Philistines and the Sakkala invaded Palestine from the sea.[5]

The West Bank. The West Bank is comprised of two ancient regions, Judea in the South and Samaria in the North (see map 2). Bordering on the Jordan River, the West Bank area is about 130 km long and an average of 40 km wide. It comprises 5500 square km, and includes the Judean mountains, the Samarian ridge, and the Jordan Valley.[6] The Jordan Valley between the Sea of Galilee and the Dead Sea is a part of a larger rift extending from northern Syria to the South African frontier.[7]

The mountain ranges are steepest toward the Jordan River on the East. From Hebron to the mountains of Mohab in Jordan, the height falls from 914 meters to 396 meters below sea level, a drop of 1310 meters in 58 km.[8] This steep climb, even with modern communications and road systems, remains the most important single constraint on the movement of armies East or West. Whoever holds the mountains holds the advantage of initiating military operations on the plains in the West.[9]

The Golan Heights. Like the Judean mountains and Samarian ridge of the West Bank, the Golan Heights overlook a flat, narrow section of Israel that contains the northern settlements. Between 1965 and 1967, before Israel captured the Golan Heights in the 1967 War, Syrian forces shelled Israeli border settlements from the Heights, some 600 meters above Israel's northeast frontier.[10] Under Israeli control, the Golan Heights now provide a vantage point from which to survey Syria. Damascus is only 40 km from the current Israeli front line, and there are no natural obstacles between the frontier and the Syrian capital. Thus, from a Syrian perspective, Israel's continued military occupation of the Golan poses an unacceptable danger.

Gaza Strip. The Gaza Strip covers an area of 363 square km in southwest Palestine, stretching 40 km along the coast South of Tel Aviv, and contains no natural fortifications.[11] Because of its location on the Via Maris, this strip of land has fallen to numerous invaders. It has been under Israeli military administration since its capture in the 1967 War.

The strategic importance of this land comes from its access to the sea and its border with Egypt along the Sinai. In addition, the population of Gaza, primarily Palestinian refugees, is extremely hostile to Israel and for years has been a center for rebellion and terrorism. The Palestinian uprising began as a riot in Gaza in early December 1987, and quickly spread to the West Bank and Jerusalem.

Israel's Current Borders. The creation of the State of Israel by the partition of Palestine was recognized by the United Nations in 1948, but the Arab states refused to accept the partition plan. In the war that followed, Israel repelled a joint Arab invasion force and when a cease fire was negotiated, occupied additional Arab land. The cease fire boundaries became the de facto frontiers between Israel and its neighbors when separate armistice agreements were signed between Israel and Egypt, Lebanon, Syria, and Transjordan in 1949. The armistice agreement with Lebanon remains in effect, while those with Syria, Jordan, and Egypt were breached during the 1967 War. As a result of that war, Israel captured and occupied the Sinai, Gaza, the West Bank, East Jerusalem, and the Golan Heights. Israel's only formal border, the boundary along the Sinai, was determined by Egypt and Israel in their 1982 peace settlement. Israel's borders with Lebanon, Syria, and Jordan, and within the area of Palestine are all de facto boundaries, the legal determination of which must be part of a future Arab-Israeli peace process.[12]

The basis for a territorial settlement between Israel and its Arab neighbors is contained in United Nations Security Council Resolution 242, signed November 22, 1967, and later reaffirmed in UN Security Council Resolution 338. Resolution 242 calls for: "(i)Withdrawal of Israeli armed forces from territories occupied in the recent conflict; (ii)Termination of all claims or states of belligerency and respect for, and acknowledgement of, the sovereignty, territorial integrity and political independence of every State in the area and their right to live in peace within secure and recognized boundaries free from threats or acts of force." The Resolution further affirms "the necessity: (a)For guaranteeing freedom of navigation through international waterways in the area; (b)For achieving a just settlement of the refugee problem; (c)For guaranteeing the territorial inviolability and political independence of every State in the area, through measures including the establishment of demilitarized zones."[13]

Both Palestinians and Israelis, as well as third parties involved in the

Palestinian-Israeli peace process have different interpretations of the meaning of Resolution 242. These interpretations hinge on specific language in the text. The key words are "territories" and "secure and recognized borders." The Arab states and the Palestinians interpret this resolution to mean that Israel should return all lands captured in the Six Day War and return to its pre-1967 borders. Israel focuses on the concept of "secure and recognized borders." According to the Israeli view, the notion of land-for-peace embodied in this resolution did not equate a simple return of all territory with the establishment of peace. Israelis believe that the creation of secure borders would require alterations in the pre-1967 boundary lines.

On the issue of Palestinian rights, Resolution 242 refers only to settling the refugee problem. In the Israeli view, then, land-for-peace means some Arab land for peace with those Arab states that existed at the time of the resolution. Angered at the absence of any specific reference to the Palestinian people, or to a Palestinian state, the Palestinians have insisted that Resolution 242 nevertheless implies the creation of a Palestinian state in exchange for peace with Israel.

All Israeli governments since 1967 have insisted that any return of the territories captured in 1967 would have to include adjustments to the pre-1967 boundaries, no matter what other concessions the Arabs are prepared to make in exchange for formal peace and an end to belligerency. In other words, the 'green line' -- the area separating Judea and Samaria from the rest of Israel would have to be changed. The green line (green is the color used to denote the border on Israeli maps), is not a planned boundary or border, nor does it follow natural topographical features. It is the collection of cease fire lines between the armies of the Arab countries and the Israelis fighting in 1948-49. These cease fire lines, collectively called the green line, divided 65 Arab villages and the city of Jerusalem.[14]

The areas of the West Bank enclosed by the green line are especially important in the context of the Arab-Israeli security debate (see map 1). These areas almost bisect Israel, creating an extremely narrow strip, down to 15 km at some points, along Israel's central coastal region. The West Bank geographically dominates Israel. As one Israeli strategist stated, "the regions of Judea and Samaria can be described as the mountainous backbone of the area known in Hebrew as Eretz-Israel."[15]

For most of the period after the 1967 War, the green line lost its relevance as a functional boundary. While Israel never formally annexed the West Bank, it was seen as an integral part of a larger Israel. There was an effort to reduce the significance of the green line in the Israeli psyche, demonstrated by the absence of this boundary on most Israeli maps. However since the outbreak of the Intifada in December 1987, this line has reemerged as a functioning boundary; during the major surges in the uprising, the IDF has used the green line as a boundary to cordon off the Palestinians and to keep them from entering the rest of Israel.

Water and Population Issues

The Problem of Water

In addition to security concerns, arguments can be expected between Israelis and Palestinians over access to water sources, and the need for population and industrial growth space. Israel's water concerns focus on three areas, and in each case compete with Arab water concerns. First, Israel seeks to assure its access to the system of headwaters, rivers, and tributaries in the Golan Heights. According to one analyst: "Future territorial adjustments that will help secure Israel's water supply require that Israeli sovereignty be exercised over the Banias-Har Dove-Hermon Shoulder headwaters region, the Golan slopes east of the Upper Jordan, and the Golan Heights that overlook Yam Kineret and the Lower Yarmuk and its tributary."[16] Israel has long-standing disputes with Syria over access to these areas as well as over fishing rights in the Sea of Galilee. Second, prior to the 1967 War, Israeli access to the Dead Sea was restricted to the southern half of its western shores. Israeli control over the entire western bank of the Dead Sea affords it greater access to mineral extraction and recreational opportunities.[17] Third, Israel needs to assure its access to the water tables lying under the Judean foothills East of the green line, which supplies the coastal plain. To ensure Israeli access to this water would involve shifting the political boundary a few kilometers to the East of the green line, incorporating an area that currently houses a substantial Arab population.[18]

On the Arab side of the water issue, Israeli water policies have prevented, or retarded Palestinian agricultural development.[19] Gaza has only one aquifer which is already highly contaminated and will be unusable by the year 2000, while towns in the West Bank have been prevented from digging new wells by the Israeli authorities.[20] Jordan is concerned with Israeli plans to build a canal linking the Mediterranean and Dead Seas (the Dead-Med Canal). The Jordanians predict that the subsequent rise in the level of the Dead Sea would prevent, or at least inhibit the extraction of phosphates and other chemicals, would prevent the reclamation of the Wadi Araba for agricultural use, and would pollute much of the Jordan Valley's fresh water supply.[21]

To the North, the Israeli diversions of the Litani and Yarmuk Rivers also affect Lebanese, Syrian, and Jordanian water supplies. Lebanon, unlike its neighbors, has an ample water supply fed by sufficient amounts of precipitation. If properly managed, the water system in Lebanon could exceed the country's demands and be shared with its neighbors. Political turmoil, however, has led to a breakdown in Lebanon's existing water system. Arabs have long believed that one of Israel's objectives in its 1982 campaign in Lebanon was to gain access to the Litani River, which flows through the Israeli occupied security zone in Southern Lebanon.[22]

Both Jordan and Syria face grave water shortages. The Syrian capital of Damascus is without water most nights and loses about 30 percent of its water supply due to a leaky pipe system. Syrian and Jordanian officials have planned to build a $350 million 'unity dam' on the Yarmuk, to be funded by the World Bank. Israel, which receives three percent of its national water supply from the Yarmuk, will not approve the construction of the dam unless it can be assured of its continued access to Yarmuk waters. The World Bank cannot extend financial support for international water projects unless all riparians consent. While such a project would greatly benefit Israel, Jordan, and Syria, mistrust and political haggling have prevented agreement.[23]

Due to the seriousness of regional water problems, and the inability of any one party to deal with them independently, water issues must be treated in the Arab-Israeli and Palestinian-Israeli peace processes as part of the land-for-peace debate. The only hope for finding a just solution is through cooperative agreements between Israel, the West Bank and Gaza, Jordan, Syria, and Lebanon. Failure to adequately address this problem will undoubtedly lead to increased tensions and possible military confrontation in the future.[24]

Population Growth

Concerning the issue of population growth, Israeli policy-makers have long recognized the need to assure substantial room for the growth of Jewish population and industrial centers. The mass immigration of Soviet and Ethiopian Jews highlights this issue. Around Tel Aviv, the natural growth of the metropolitan area is already putting pressure on the green line; the natural direction of the city's growth is across the boundary into the Samarian foothills. Modest shifts in the pre-1967 borders would be able to ensure substantial areas for Israel's continued growth, would bring many Israeli settlements now in the West Bank into Israel proper, and would allow for the unification of once divided Arab villages. However, in the absence of a peace process, de facto annexation of increasing areas of the West Bank only serves to further inflame passions on the Arab side, while convincing Arabs that the Israeli government has no intention of ever giving back the territories.

Nevertheless, if a compromise is deemed politically expedient, it is possible to imagine a new set of boundaries that goes some way to accommodate the various needs of the aggrieved parties. Israel could withdraw from significant areas of the West Bank and the Golan Heights without seriously compromising its defense strategy, provided that adequate safeguards were established, such as a third party buffer force to assure Israel, Syria, and Jordan that they were each protected against possible attack.

The Egyptian-Israeli peace treaty is a model for future agreements between Israel and its Arab neighbors, including the Palestinians.[25] The infrastructure of future Arab-Israeli peace agreements must be sufficiently durable and credible to withstand the periodic shocks that are bound to effect new compromises between adversaries. The Egyptian-Israeli arrangements have proved sufficiently stable. This relationship was able to withstand Israel's war in Lebanon, Egypt's active help of Iraq during the Iran-Iraq war, the Intifada and PLO relations with Egypt, numerous border incidents between the two countries that have sometimes resulted in loss of life, and unilateral weapons developments by both sides that might otherwise have caused serious concern about military intentions.

Notes

1. In order to enhance the three-dimensional perspective, some deliberate distortion of height is entered into the program (usually 5 to 20 percent). This exaggerates the hills and valleys without significantly altering the horizontal relationship between high and low ground.

2. The technical work for these maps was undertaken by Professor Poh Chin Lai of The Ohio State University, Department of Geodetic Science and Surveying. Professor Poh Chin Lai is pioneering a new technique for improving the ability to digitize data and present it in a more visually graphic form: the "Picture-Oriented Geographic Information Management System." The primary goal of a geographic information system (GIS) is to

provide rapid access to organized, comprehensible, and up-to-date information.

3. The fact that the pilot landed at Megiddo was ironic; it is one of the most famous historic sites in Israel. For thousands of years it was a key strategic city in the Middle East. According to the New Testament, the final battle between good and evil will take place at Armageddon, a bastardized version of the Hebrew Har Megiddon, which means the Hill of Megiddo.

4. Mordechai Gichon, "The West Bank: The Geostrategic and Historical Aspects," historical supplement to Aryeh Shalev, *The West Bank Line of Defense* (New York: Praeger, 1985), pp. 180-81.

5. Ibid., pp. 186-88.

6. Michael Widlanski, editor, *Can Israel Survive A Palestinian State?* (Jerusalem: Institute for Advanced Strategic and Political Studies, 1990), p. 10-11.

7. Ibid. See also Shalev, *The West Bank Line of Defense*, pp. 9-12.

8. Yohanan Aharoni and Michael Avi-Yonah, *The MacMillan Bible Atlas* (New York: The MacMillan Company, 1968), p. 7.

9. Shalev, p. 11.

10. Richard F. Nyrop, editor, *Syria: A Country Study* (Washington, D.C.: United States Government Printing Office, 1979), p. 196.

11. Mark A. Heller, *A Palestinian State: The Implications for Israel* (Cambridge, Mass.: Harvard University Press, 1983), pp. 17-18.

12. Israel's border with Lebanon is a legacy of the Sykes-Picot agreement, through which France and Britain divided up the Middle East following WWI. The northern border of Palestine, which was to be under British control, was drawn such that the French-ruled greater Syria would retain control of the Litani and Yarmuk rivers. Following its War of Independence, Israel signed an armistice with Lebanon on March 23, 1949, which recognized the Palestine-Lebanon border as the cease fire line. On March 16, 1978, Israel launched Operation Litani as a reprisal for a Palestinian terrorist attack against Israeli citizens. As a result, a buffer zone was created in Southern Lebanon in which a United Nations interim

force -- UNIFIL -- of 3000 men was placed to prevent further terrorist infiltration into Israel. A second security zone was established by Israeli forces and was patrolled by the Israeli supported Christian South Lebanon Army (SLA). In 1985, following its 1982 invasion of Lebanon, Israeli forces began patrolling the security zone again and support for the South Lebanon Army was increased. The UNIFIL forces continue to patrol their buffer zone.

13. United Nations Security Council Resolution 242 Concerning Principles for a Just and Lasting Peace in the Middle East, November 22, 1967, UN Document S/RES/242, reprinted in John Norton Moore, editor, *The Arab-Israeli Conflict Readings and Documents* (Princeton: Princeton University Press, 1977), pp. 1083-84. See also UN Security Council Resolution 338 Concerning the October War, October 22, 1973, UN Document S/RES/338, reprinted in ibid.

14. Saul Cohen, *Israel's Defensible Borders* (Tel Aviv: Jaffee Center for Strategic Studies, 1983), p. 12.

15. Shalev, p. 10.

16. See Cohen, *Israel's Defensible Borders*, p. 28.

17. Ibid., p. 29.

18. Ibid., p. 30.

19. Joyce Starr, "Water Wars," *Foreign Policy*, No. 82, Spring 1991, p. 27.

20. Ibid., p. 25.

21. John K. Cooley, "The War Over Water," *Foreign Policy*, No. 54, Spring 1984, p. 5.

22. Fida Nasrallah, "Middle Eastern Waters: The Hydraulic Imperative," *Middle East International*, April 27, 1990, pp. 16-17.

23. Douglas Davis, "Water Shortages Could Lead to War," *Jerusalem Post International Edition*, June 9, 1990, p. 9.

24. Ze'ev Schiff, *Security for Peace: Israel's Minimal Security Requirements in Negotiations with the Palestinians* (Washington, D.C.: Washington Institute for Near East Policy, 1989), p. 22.

25. For more on the making of the Egyptian-Israeli peace see William B. Quandt, *Camp David: Peacemaking and Politics* (Washington, D.C.: The Brookings Institution, 1986,).

Index

Italy, 53, 79, 80

Jericho missiles, 78
Jordan
air force, 142
Arab-Israeli conflict and, 20, 22, 25
arms control and, 139
defense and security, 2, 16, 31-33, 109-110
Europe and, 32, 52
Gulf war and, 31-32, 63-64
Islamic fundamentalism in, 32
Israel and, 110
military capability, 32-33
security interests, 2
Syria and, 110
U.S. and, 32
water issues and, 215
West Bank, 32-33

Kashmir (and Jammu), 42, 54, 102, 170
1990 crisis, 113
Kelley, John, 37
Kennedy, John F.,
policy toward the Arab-Israeli conflict, 4
Khalidi, Walid, 164-165
Khomeini, Ayatollah, 34
and Iranian nuclear program, 73
Kissinger, Henry, 4n.6, 158
Kitchener, Herbert, 121
Korramshahr, 38
Kozyrev, Andrey, 7, 58
Kurds, 6, 49
Iraqi chemical bombing of, 34, 75
post-Gulf war crisis, 11
Kuwait. *See also* Gulf Cooperation Council
air force, 142
Gulf war and, 6, 63
security threats, 16, 19

Lampedusa, Libyan bombing of, 53

'Land-for-peace', 166, 213
Lavi jet program, 83
Lebanon
Europe and, 52
occupation of, 31
water issues and, 215
Libya, 35
air force, 83
arms sales to, 10
biological weapons program, 76
chemical weapons, 2, 6, 59, 76
missile program, 144
nuclear program, 73-74
terrorism and, 50
Litani River, 25, 215
London Club (of nuclear suppliers), 134-135
Long-range artillery, 197-200
comparison to missiles, 197
history of, 199-200

McCloy, John J., 4
Megiddo (Armageddon), 210
MFO. *See* Multinational Force and Observers
Middle East
arms control, 124-128
arms race
economic constraints on arms purchases, 62-65
historical roots, 9
origins of, 15-16, 119-122
possibility of arms control, 9-10
regional conflicts and, 19
chemical weapons, 102
indigenous conventional arms production, 86-88
nuclear weapons, 102
regional balance of power, 88, 101
regional conflicts, 20
regional water management, 3

227

Perez de Cuéllar, Javier, 160
Permissive action links (PALs), 145
Persian Gulf war. *See* Gulf war
PLO. *See* Palestinian Liberation Organization
Plutonium, 1, 74
'Poison pills', 145, 146
Poland, 60
Portugal, 53
Pressler Amendment, 74n.14
Punjab, 170
'Purple line', 158

Qadaffi, Muammar, 53
    Libyan chemical weapons program and, 76
    nuclear programs in Middle East, 73-74
    regional ambitions, 16
Qatar, 85
    See also GCC
Qian Qichen, 8
Quneitra, 158

Rabta chemical weapons facility, 59, 76
Raytheon, 107n.8
Reagan, Ronald, 168
    address to the UN (September 1988), 6
    chemical weapons control initiatives, 5-6
    Israel and, 27
    U.S. military build-up under, 55
'Red lines', 152, 157-158
Rocket systems, 2

Saad-16 complex, 80
Sabha, chemical weapons plant, 59
Sadat, Anwar, 152
Saladin, 26
Salman Pak biological weapons research facility, 77
Samarra facility. *See* Muthanna State Establishment
Saudi Arabia
    arms transfers from, 62

defense and security, 2, 16, 19, 83, 85, 142
defense industry, 87
    GCC cooperation on arms production, 87
    Gulf war and, 63, 87
    Iran and, 81
    Iraq and, 81
    Israel and, 81
    missile program, 80-81, 144
    U.S. arms transfers, 11, 159
Schiff, Ze'ev, 164
Scud missiles, 8, 78, 192
    arms control and, 144
    attacks against Israel, 22, 26, 106, 107
    Iraqi missile program and, 79, 80
Sharon, Ariel, 25, 164
Shatt al-Arab, 37-38, 127
Sheffield Forgemasters, 199
Shevardnadze, Eduard, 6
Simla agreement, 42
Sinai peninsula, 124, 152
Singapore, 82, 83
Six Day War (1967). *See* 1967 War
South Africa, 137, 139
South Korea, 137, 139
Space Research Corp, 198, 199
Spain, 53
Strategic Defense Initiative, 85
Sudan, 3
    conflicts with Egypt, 16
    British-Egyptian occupation, 121
Suez Canal, 63
Sundarji, Krishnaswami, 113n.24
Supergun (Iraq), 198-199. *See also* High Altitude Research Project
Surface-to-air missiles (SAMs), 84-86
Surface-to-surface missiles (SSMs), 6
    arms control and, 142-144
    China and, 62

9069

DATE DUE

OCT 0 7 1995		
JAN 0 5 2005		
MAR 1 0 2005		
MAR 0 8 2005		
GAYLORD		PRINTED IN U.S.A.